CLAWS
AND PURRS

PETER NEVILLE

CLAWS
AND PURRS

SIDGWICK & JACKSON
LONDON

First published in Great Britain in 1992 by Sidgwick & Jackson
Limited, a division of Pan Macmillan Publishers Limited, Cavaye
Place, London SW10 9PG.

ISBN 0 283 06123 5

Typeset by The Bessant Neville Partnership,
Tisbury, Salisbury, Wiltshire SP3 6LZ

Printed and bound in Great Britain by
Billing and Sons Ltd, Worcester

For Claire and Sinead,
and in loving memory of my mum, Pauline.

Contents

SECTION TWO
An Evolutionary Licence to Kill

SECTION THREE
A Wild Pet

SECTION FOUR
Feral Cats: A Life Still on the Wild Side

SECTION FIVE
Cat the Pet

Acknowledgements

With many thanks to my lovely wife Claire for all her love and support, and to my delightful new baby daughter Sinead for not yelling too much during the production of this book! Thanks to Helen at Sidgwick and Jackson for her firm but fair editing and encouragement, and to Clare, in my own office, for her humour and enthusiastic skill. My family and Claire's, and all our friends deserve a medal for putting up with me when I'm writing, and the continuous valuable input and searching feline questions of Bullet, Bean and Flirty Bottom must be recognised. Thanks also to Professor Eric Harley and his colleagues, not only for their outstanding discoveries, but also for their kind permission to cite their work in advance of its publication. I would also express my gratitude to my friends and clients who have generously allowed themselves to be mentioned in the pages that follow. And finally my heartfelt thanks to cats everywhere, whatever their lifestyle; they are a lesson to us all at how to survive and enjoy life to the full.

Introduction
Cats – a time to reassess

'A dog is a dog, a bird is a bird, but a cat is a person'
Mugsy Peabody

Cats are fast becoming our most popular larger pet. They're clean, friendly and undemanding in a world that has less and less time for close relationships or commitments. Yet with so little to put in, we need ever more friendship, relaxation and affection from something in our lives. Cats fit the bill better than any other of our traditional pets and, sometimes, can even offer us more than our own kind. With cats we feel better, safe from the ravages of our day-to-day lives and the often unreasonable demands of human relationships at work, play and even at home.

Cats are almost too perfect a pet for modern lifestyles. There are virtually no demands and no problems in owning them and we all sing our pet's praises as the clean, economical, quiet companion. But there is one drawback. It's a problem conveniently almost totally confined to the outdoor life of our pet cats, unless you also happen to keep a budgie or a caged mouse. Ask any loving owner what they dislike most about their cat, and they will usually say that it's the hunter in him: that trail of death around the garden every nesting season, and the little furry and feathered bodies brought stealthily, or sometimes proudly, into the kitchen. Or it's the dumping of little cadavers on the mat, dead but discarded, and wastefully not even eaten by the top predator of the garden.

1

We usually feed cats more than adequately, give them the best love and care that money can buy, and rush them to the vet whenever they are sick so, surely, there should be no need for them to hunt to survive and wreak such devastation on all those poor mice and birds. But they do, and we simply sigh and pop another little body into the bin, knowing that there is practically nothing we can do to mute the killer in our pets. And later, when the sense of outrage has died away, we'll respond as ever to the affectionate rubbing and demand for a cuddle by the fire and stroke and pet them for hours. And they'll purr and stretch and go back to sleep, knowing that they've got us exactly where they want us and that they have, as ever, avoided compromising their evolution or embarrassing their ancestors.

For those who particularly enjoy the uncompromising character of our cats – despite the carnage – there's no doubt that they are exceptionally good value. A tiger in the living-room with all its hunting skills intact and the undeniable appeal of a perpetual, playful kitten and social friend is all rolled into one. But why is that hunter so unmodified by our efforts at domestication? Why, when one of the primary aims of domestication is to reduce the level of aggression in the beast, be he a farm animal to produce food for us, or a pet that we want to cuddle, control and live with safely? Allowing themselves to be petted and handled by us is clearly part of the success of pet cats, yet the aggression of the predator unequivocally remains within them.

To make dogs, we have mollified and modified the wolf, and, though our pet dogs in all their forms remain genetically eighty to eighty-five per cent wolf, the rest has been tamed to a large extent. We have manipulated the genes that code for canine appearance, size, shape and hair type and colour enormously but have also generally taken the wolf out of the character of dogs. That is unless we've gone back and deliberately enhanced aspects such as territorial defence capability in German Shepherd Dogs or hunting skills in spaniels or modified the hunting ability of collies into herding skills.

Contrastingly, the cat has remained largely resistant to our efforts to breed new forms. There are only about a hundred recognised breeds and most are colour variants of a type, such as the Red, Lilac and Seal Point Siamese cats. While there are short, long, crinkle-cut and no-haired cats, most are roughly the same size and there certainly isn't the variation in size and weight as exemplified by the difference between a Chihuahua and a Great Dane, despite all our efforts at controlled breeding. Irrespective of breed and appearance, the cat's inherent desire and ability to hunt remains intact, despite our selection of beautiful forms or colours or our more recent efforts to breed pet cats specifically for docility and good temperament. And we haven't been able to go back and select a particular type or breed of cat for any specific function as we have with dogs, nor make any strain a better rodent controller through artificial selection. Natural selection for hunting and lifestyle in the wild has already done the job and produced the perfect feline model. It seems that we simply can't hope to improve on, or undo, thirteen million years of development when it's achieved such a level of perfection. Yet somewhere along the way, cats must also have made a singularly important mutation to be able to live in such close association with man and become such a successful pet. It was the one that makes them friendly towards us when, for the amount and type of effort that we have put in over the centuries, there is no reason why they shouldn't view us as most wild animals still do, that is as a dangerous threat and an enemy.

More than simply understanding that cats are less directable or controllable than dogs, we largely choose to tolerate the pet cat's predatory killing habits, presumably because of the benefits they offer when warm and curled up on our laps. Perhaps we intuitively accept that predatory aggression is a very specific form of aggression and one clearly evolved to enable a predator to feed itself and survive. Cats are rarely aggressive under any other circumstances, except perhaps for a little territorial yowling directed at the rival next door. Best of all, they are hardly ever aggressive towards us except in a controlled form in play or if they are ill. So, while we can understandably get very worried about the level and control of even 'natural' forms of aggression – such as territory guarding – in dogs, we have had to accept it in cats. They've got away with it because this predator thankfully views us as a surrogate mother and a friend and not an item of prey!

The following chapters take a closer look at this marvellous dual feline character and its place in our hearts and why the cat is enjoying an ever increasing popularity at little or no cost to itself, and certainly at none to its genes. We'll look afresh at feline design and its evolution and the cat's association with man. We'll compare the pet cat with some of its wild relations and feral counterparts and, as the *Claws* part of the title suggests, at its hunting abilities and just why the cat is probably the most highly specialised and successful mammalian predator the world has ever seen. We'll look too at the *Purrs*, the irresistibly affectionate side of the cat that lies behind its popularity and the reason why this fascinating friendly mammal is set to become the most highly undomesticated pet the world has ever seen.

SECTION ONE

A Shrink's Cats

'We cannot, without becoming cats, perfectly understand the cat's mind'
St George Mivart

Two years ago, I started my book-writing career by asking *Do Cats Need Shrinks?*, in a book that looked at the behaviour problems that cats can present to us as pets and how to treat them. It only seems fitting now to allow the cat's riposte and ask 'Does a Shrink Need Cats?' As the answer is obviously short and affirmative, and wouldn't take up a whole page, let alone a book, I'd like to explore what I have been able to learn from those cats I have been lucky enough to know and enjoy, and indulge myself a little with a look at their personalities. After all, the best studied animals from a biologist's point of view are those that he or she lives with.

1
Lessons learned

Lesson 1. Lulu – When the going gets tough, the cat moves on

'We're all motivated by the same urges. Cats have the courage to live by them' Jim Davis (American cartoonist)

My first memorable experience with a cat was as a four-year-old with a tabby and white cat called Lulu who could have put me off for life! Lulu was a slightly spiteful little cat who didn't like small boys mauling her around. Unfortunately, inflicting a few scratches didn't deter my interest in her so, like so many cats unhappy with home, she decamped from our house in Twickenham, near London, and moved in with a child-free family a few hundred yards away. Too young to feel upset, for weeks I asked my parents why Lulu had left home. They didn't have the heart to tell me that it was probably my fault. Understanding Lulu's decision to clear off, however, doesn't help with the several calls I now get every month from distressed owners who have no horrid four-year-olds and have lavished every care and affection on the cat, only to find that she's moved out and taken up residence elsewhere, sometimes with clearly less doting owners and in less comfortable surroundings. There is little more hurtful to owners than to find that their cat, who, for a while has convinced them that they are surrogate mothers and has purred and crooned at them, has for some reason decided to leave them for another mother and another den. There may be obvious causes when the defection is seen

6

from the human point of view, such as the disruption caused by redecorating, or having a disliked friend or relative to stay, or the presence of a new dog or tough stray tom cat in the gardens around the home. But often nothing appears to have changed and the fickle cat seems to have left for no reason at all. If we could really communicate with the cat, we'd probably find it had good reason, but I'm sure in many cases it's simply that love in human terms from the original owner was not what that cat wanted . . . too much disturbance simply to be cuddled, wrong type of physical affection, or perhaps the cat wasn't able to initiate the contact even though it received plenty when the owner wanted to pet it. Perhaps after a chance encounter with the owners of the house down the road, the cat found that they suited his requirements for being mothered better and moved in. Perhaps he was left alone when he wanted and could turn them on at will when he wanted fussing, or perhaps they gave him food that he preferred even to the most expensive steak that his first owners used to save up for.

The lesson learned from Lulu, apart from making sure that my baby daughter has lots of contact with my cats but is never left alone to maul them around, was that the relationship we all enjoy with all our cats is highly individual. And that because the cat has evolved so that each one has its own preferences and desires and expects them to be fulfilled just as much as we try to fulfil our own demands of the relationship. Sometimes, we can do our cat a disservice by thinking only in human terms about what we think cats like and forget that our own cat is always going to differ from the average or our mind's eye view. If we not only 'think cat' but also think 'our cat', then perhaps there will be fewer Lulus moving home.

Lesson 2. Thumper – Enjoying the family pet cat and coping with the loss of a friend

'With the qualities of cleanliness, affection, patience, dignity and courage that cats have, I ask you, would we be capable of becoming cats?'   Fernand Mery

I have only one enchanting black and white dog-eared photo of Lulu, being happily wheeled down the garden in a wheelbarrow, but then I didn't know her for long. I have a few more of the real cat of my childhood, a fine long-haired ginger and white tom called Thumper after his less than delicate feline descent of the stairs as a kitten. He was one of a litter bred by the man who installed our central heating. By then I was seven and old enough to understand that the cat wasn't to be mauled and pursued relentlessly.

Thumper was a gentle lion who lived to be seventeen, always firmly in charge of the dogs but never overtly aggressive to anyone. He loved being handled, as do most long-haired cats and dogs for whom daily grooming is a feature of life in the human den. Introduced to the brush and comb early, they soon tolerate it, learn that putting up a fuss can lead to discomfort and so come to enjoy the experience for the most part, except perhaps in certain delicate little places. Indeed, because of the close bonds that are built up during mutual grooming by social animals such as monkeys, humans and dogs, and the similarity of this type of touch to maternal grooming, brushing the cat frequently can cause him to remain or become much more sociable with his owners. Mutual washing and licking is clearly also an important part of the enjoyment and maintenance of relations between friendly adult cats.

It is interesting from the animal behaviour therapist's point of view that I cannot ever recall seeing a case of despotic aggression by a long-haired cat towards its owners or their visitors, yet I have seen several such referrals involving short-haired and usually Oriental cats. Even these cases are few and far between and unreliable for drawing precise conclusions as to whether necessary early handling for grooming affects later docility. But it is certainly true that neither myself nor my colleagues encounter many cases of dominance in long-haired dogs because they get used to such attention as puppies and throughout their adolescence and, for their own good, are usually never allowed to resist. Such handling can be viewed as a dominant insult and the owner's insistence at having the right to do it helps convince the dog of his place beneath the owner in the family pecking order. Contrast the normally placid, happily subordinate long-haired German Shepherd Dog that I usually encounter with the many cases of the ungroomed shorter haired version who starts to view himself as high ranking in the family and presents dominance problems by seeking to direct the owners around the den and growling at or biting them when later they expect to handle or touch him in sensitive places. The message is, whether you own a long-haired cat or dog and *have* to groom it, or whether you own a short-coated pet which doesn't need so much attention to his coat, brush and comb him daily anyway from the day you first get him. In social terms it'll make you both feel better and produce a more docile friendly pet, providing you're careful with those sensitive bits!

Aside from being a gentle soul with his human family, Thumper was a vigorous defender of his patch, sometimes at the cost of a few clumps of ginger and white hair left on the lawns. We never saw his victims, but always knew their colour from the fur he extracted in return! He had no feline friends that we knew of and perhaps fitted the bill of the typical territorial hunter – a solitary cat outdoors who was docile and affectionate indoors. He was a pretty good hunter and I'm sure taught me at an early age that nature was as much about death as life. Thumper did what came naturally when he killed birds and brought them home and I remember while still very young simply picking up their little bodies from where Thumper had left them and giving them a decent burial without a tear. On the other hand, I also remember bursting into tears when my brother shot a sparrow with his air rifle and still crying as I buried it. Thumper couldn't help his murder, my big brother could and I didn't speak to him for weeks.

Thumper also taught me about the playfulness of cats. He seemed to understand that his people were his playmates and in all his long life he never once played with his claws exposed, only ever pawed and mouthed our hands and never bit hard once. I'm sure it had something to do with all that grooming my mother gave him from the day he arrived in a cardboard box.

There can surely be no doubt that growing up with a pet is good for children and I really do pity those who are deprived of the experience by unknowledgeable or over-protective or overly health-conscious parents. While I had been too young to learn from Lulu, Thumper taught me about the need to handle all other creatures and, by extension, people, considerately and gently. He taught me about the tooth and claw of nature and about the peace and serenity of old age. As he grew older, he was less active, slept a lot but was always ready to be friendly when he was up and about. By the time he got old and frail, I had already been to university and gone on to work in faraway places. But even as an old boy, he was always there when I went home to see my parents and gave me a croaky welcome and presented a dignity in old age that seemed at peace with his inability to rush around playing and hunting. He accepted the limitations his

9

old body placed on him and I hope taught me about how to accept old age myself when it really starts to gain momentum on me!

I wasn't there when, like so many cats when they realise that it's time to move on, he walked arthritically into the garden and lay down under the hedge to die. I'm glad I wasn't there, not because of cowardice but because I think that cats deliberately move out of the warm comfortable home where it might be nice to drift away and want to be alone, independent in the final act and not make a fuss for their human friends. Maybe they move away as some form of ancestral behaviour designed to distract the attention of predators or scavengers from the den, or maybe by moving away they feel it will take those imaginary scavengers longer to locate them and give them more chance of dying in peace. As it was, Thumper was missed by my mother that July morning and, realising that he'd been lying under the hedge dying for some time, she saved him from further discomfort by asking the local vet to ease his passage onwards. In death, Thumper taught me how to grieve. I'd never lost a member of my family or a close friend until Thumper died. In reflecting on the pleasure of his life and his companionship, going through the self-analysis and recrimination of my lack of contact with him in his final years and being away when he died and then crying for his loss, Thumper's death taught me about the process of grieving and made it a little easier for when human bereavements came later in life.

Although, as we shall see in Lesson 3, I was lucky enough to be studying and working with cats from the age of twenty-two, I didn't share my life and home with another cat for a few years after Thumper died, mainly because I was travelling a lot and never really had a settled home for a while. But as soon as I was in reasonably settled digs in St Albans, Hertfordshire, I convinced my flatmates that even with a couple of budgies, a home wasn't home without a cat. Grudgingly they agreed. Like so many people in search of a kitten I responded to an advert in the local newsagents of 'home wanted for kittens'.

Lesson 3. Nimrod and Wandsworth – Accepting that my home wasn't the best for my cats

'Cats know how to obtain food without labor, shelter without confinement and love without penalties'   W.L. George

I collected Nimrod, as she was called, from a large impressive house where she had clearly wanted for nothing. She was a beautiful lightish coloured seven-week-old brown tabby and was extremely friendly and playful. She stalked my housemates' soft toy bears relentlessly and certainly did grievous bodily harm to the dog of the house, my Snoopy toy, a present from a long-gone girlfriend. But I almost immediately sensed that something was not right. Poor Nimrod had no one to play with all day with the three of us out at work.

My work by this time chiefly involved studying feral cats in London's Regent's Park and working with a feral colony in Wandsworth in south-west London. And, like Paddington bear, that was how Nimrod's friend got his name. Wandsworth was a beautiful silver tabby feral kitten but when I caught him, he was more of a playground for fleas, lice and ear mites than a kitten. And, unused to being handled, he wasn't about to curl up readily on my lap and be petted in the same way as he used to enjoy being fussed by his mother! For a few days, residing in a cage in the isolation of a spare bedroom to protect him, Wandsworth hissed and spat at anyone who came near, especially if, like me, they had to get hold of him to treat him for the nasty parasitic pets he had brought with him. But with tender loving care and frequent handling and feeding Wandsworth soon became a friendly little soul. Clean and flea-free, he was allowed to roam around the house and soon struck up a great friendship with Nimrod. Like so many kittens born feral, Wandsworth's street-urchin background made no difference to the way he ultimately responded to me and to the other people he met, and one would never have known that he and Nimrod had come from such vastly different backgrounds. They were both meticulous in their personal hygiene and use of the litter tray, and made a complete transfer to using the outdoors once their vaccinations had been completed and the local vet gave them the all-clear to go out.

It's funny sometimes how certain things repeat themselves, but nowadays whenever I recommend to a client who owns a cat that has suffered a breakdown in house training that they should use fine litter, sand or a sand-and-garden- soil mixture in their cat's litter tray because fine-grain material is more attractive to cats than many coarser grain or pellet commercial litters, I think of Nimrod and Wandsworth. They were known as 'those bloody cats' by one of our neighbours in St Albans. He never learned their names and was, or at least pretended to be, a real ailurophobe . . . that most hated of

11

people, a cat hater. Of course he was fighting a losing battle because Kath, his wife, and their two kids loved Nimrod and Wandsworth to come calling and fed, fussed and played with them. Alas, the day came when David started building an extension to his house and a huge pile of sand was duly delivered outside his front door. Nimrod and Wandsworth, and for that matter every other cat for a ten-mile radius, ceased using the garden to defecate in and came to David's sand pile instead. There was a feline 'cable' in every shovelful and David would spend his evenings plotting various dire fates for all the cats in the neighbourhood.

The cat's attraction for using sand as a toilet is perfectly understandable given that pet cats originated from a small desert-dwelling ancestor in north Africa and therefore developed a preference for burying their droppings in sand. They make do happily with soil or cat litter but, given the choice, a sand-pit is irresistible and, likewise, they can often be persuaded to start using a litter tray again if it is filled with sand or fine-grain material. Of course, David failed in his efforts to dissuade my cats from dropping in on his sand pile but this gave him an added spur to build his extension as fast as possible! And in any case, the cats would always have the last word, for though David removed most of the 'cables' before he mixed his cement, some will have got through to weaken the mix and make fault lines in the brickwork of his extension. One day it will collapse and there will be hordes of cats to watch it go!

Someone was mindful of David's frustration, however, and bought him an inflatable grinning cat with a heavy base. This was placed around the house for David to kick and relieve the tension. Propelled by a hefty boot, it would somersault around the room and then pop upright again, grinning as ever. If only it was really 'those bloody cats'! Kath, David and family are incidentally still our very good friends and even David has been seen sneaking a cuddle with our present cats whenever they come to stay. Age, and a lack of soiled sand-pits, seems to have calmed one obsessive cat hater at least . . . so maybe there's hope for the rest.

Nimrod and Wandsworth played endlessly in the St Albans suburbs and gave us all hours of fun, though the day I came home to find Nimrod sitting proudly on the budgies' perch was one beyond even the ordinary mayhem of living with two young kittens. The cage was firmly locked in a safe room thereafter but the day did come when I forgot to close the door, and, to my eternal shame, 'those bloody cats' got in and did for one of the budgies. And that taught me never to take chances with the ruthless predatory nature of the cat and always make sure that the budgies and tame rats that I kept later were always totally safe from their natural enemies. It also taught me that while a cat may largely ignore even such fancied morsels as caged birds and rats, and even in some cases show no inclination to make a grab for a pet mouse running over it because they know each other, you should never trust a smiling cat. You never know when he'll change his mind! Only last year in the UK there was a marvellous television advertisement for British Gas which showed a contented pet Bulldog lying by a gas fire. He was then joined by a languid heat-seeking cat who duly curled up next to him. So far so good, my dogs certainly recognise my cats as members of their pack and don't chase them even though they send all other cats darting up the nearest tree. And then the white mouse entered the comfort zone of the British Gas advert. The cat turned, sniffed and licked his little twitching nose and all three settled down to an evening's laze in the warmth. What a successful advert . . . until you saw the out-takes. Our friendly cat, happy to settle next to the dog, certainly sniffed the mouse and then made a definite attempt to give him a quick nape bite and eat him! A large restraining hand entered the frame to deter the cat from following his natural instincts and saved the mouse while, no doubt, the owner of the cat uttered the immortal words that I and so many vets hear on a regular basis from the owners of our patients: 'Oh, I am sorry. He's never done that before!' After an undisclosed number of takes, the advertising company finally got the sequence that British Gas wanted . . . with a little cutting and editing. This advert was followed by others promoting the use of electricity which used an animated toy dog and cat with Liverpudlian accents lying by the fire with not a mouse in sight . . . clearly safer for all concerned!

After a happy couple of years at St Albans, the time came to move to France and the prospect of taking Wandsworth and Nimrod with me in the Land Rover. Well, why not? Everything else, including my Canadian-Greek girlfriend Marie, was going! So I arranged for the cats to have all their anti-rabies vaccinations in an extraordinarily complex process caused by the fact that the anti-rabies vaccine is only available from vets in the UK by special licence from the Ministry of Agriculture. It's all part of anti-rabies control measures that dogs and cats aren't routinely vaccinated against the disease in the UK, despite the fact that totally safe virus vaccines are available throughout the world. The logic behind maintaining a whole nation of pets with no resistance at all to rabies if it ever did manage to re-enter the UK (an increasingly likely prospect with rabies being detected now at the gates of Paris in the fox population and because of the increased traffic flow of people once the Channel Tunnel is completed) is that public awareness would drop if our pets were protected and the risk of illegal importation would be higher. It sounds like a crazy logic to me, after all, if or when rabies does enter the UK, it is far more likely to spread rapidly through an unprotected, unvaccinated cat and dog population than through one made at least partially resistant by vaccination, even if feral cats, stray dogs and susceptible wildlife species would be harder to protect.

Anyway, Wandsworth and Nimrod were duly vaccinated and prepared for their cross-channel ferry journey. But with true French style, I received a phone call the day before I was due to sail from the appropriately named Professor Coq of the veterinary school in Nantes where we were bound, to say that my appointment was now in jeopardy due to changes just announced by the Department of Immigration! It was too late for me to turn back, I'd left my job, my house, got all my affairs in order and packed the Land Rover. Hastily I decided to turn to my old friend Blake, whose real name is Steve, for help. I stayed at his house back in good old Twickenham, cats and all for a couple of days while, like so many Englishmen have done, I tried to unravel the vagaries of French governmental processes. In the end, I went, but unsure of the future, I left the cats behind with Blake who, like so many people before him, found that fate had made him into a cat owner. We stayed in France for just a few weeks, ending up, as I had expected, with no post with Professor Coq, but staying a while to get ourselves together in Normandy with two friends whom I had met in Athens the year before. Peter and Gary were and are cat mad. I met them in the National Gardens of Athens where they were feeding the feral, stray and abandoned cats every day. I had gone there, with Blake and an old veterinary friend, Dave Cuffe, on behalf of the Hellenic Animal Welfare Society, to instigate a humane neutering programme to control the numbers and problems posed by the cats . Peter and Gary were performers . . . singing, dancing, acting and piano- playing their way around the world, though they live in Normandy in northern France. When I met them they were based in Athens for a season and we all worked happily together on the cat project.

14

Gary is American and Peter Scottish, so why live in Normandy? Because of the cats of course! Peter and Gary, who now work on board cruise ships and perform around the world on a continuous basis, have a habit of taking in strays and caring for them secretly on board until they get home. Last time I saw them, they had a truly international collection with a cat from Japan, one from Mombasa in Kenya, one from Morocco, one from Athens and one from Paris! And because they never wanted to put their cats into quarantine for six months as they would have to do if they wanted to live in the UK, they chose to live in northern France, just a few miles from the cross-channel ferry port at Cherbourg so that they could get to London to see their agent if they needed to. When they were working, the cats all went off to enjoy the luxurious home and grounds of a very wealthy friend nearer to Paris. As far I could ascertain, she was the only person that Peter and Gary could ever trust with their cats and who would understand that when their ship came in, it usually meant that there was another cat, rescued from some far-flung exotic place to be integrated into the group. Peter and Gary really brought home to me just how dedicated owners can be and just how far some will go to adapt their lives to suit their cats. I learned then, long before I went into practice, never to take lightly the bond that so many owners, and not just true ailurophiles like Peter and Gary, have with their cats and just how much they value and love their pets.

After a cat-filled six weeks playing the piano bars of northern France with Peter and Gary, Marie and I returned home briefly to tie up a few loose ends, visit Blake and see how Nimrod and Wandsworth were doing. They were okay, but Blake, who was never a cat person in truth, was even less of one by then. Wandsworth had shown his unease about his new home and all the recent upheavals and the departure of his owner by doing something that is probably the least tolerated behavioural problem I get to treat in my clients' cats these days. Blake went out one night and returned with his girlfriend, now wife and mother of his two sons, to find that dear but upset Wandsworth had left a smelly pile in the middle of his duvet! For sure, neither of their sons was conceived that night!

Wandsworth and the innocent, but nonetheless feline, Nimrod were thereafter banned from the Blake household unless directly supervised and who was I, having left 'those bloody cats' with him in the first place, to waffle on about them needing sympathy for being upset and how a secure predictable routine would help Wandsworth settle down! As it turned out, Wandsworth and Nimrod took the hint and, like Lulu in my childhood, moved in with a very kind lady called Sue just a few doors down. She loved them dearly, fed them and bought them toys and treats. Working from home as she did, she provided Wandsworth with exactly the frequent loving contact that neither his original owner nor his temporary landlord could provide. He must have been happy because he didn't leave distress flares on the bed ever again!

I went to see the cats later to collect them and take them with me wherever I was bound. After all, their anti-rabies vaccinations were still effective if I went overseas, but when I saw how happy they and Sue were with each other, I didn't have the heart to uproot them yet again. I made the heart-wrenching decision to give the cats to Sue 'officially' and for good. She had thought that they had taken her over anyway, so who could now say that they owned these cats when they so obviously owned her. Another lesson learned. I wasn't the best possible owner for my own cats, and neither are some other people, including some of my clients. But it hurts to admit it and even after you have, it doesn't make the parting any easier. So nowadays, if I do feel it would be for the best for a cat to be rehomed because its behaviour problems are unresolvable reflections of its inability to enjoy life with its owners, I tackle the subject very carefully indeed and never rush the process. Owners definitely need lots of help at that stage, and they may only start to feel better some time later when the new owner reports that the cat has settled in very well and is no longer spraying the whole house or defecating on the bed or whatever. But for Blake, temporary cat owner, his joy at their departure was more immediate. It began as soon as the door closed for the last time behind them and he knew that his forthcoming marriage was not to be delayed or blighted by that 'bloody Neville's cats!'.

Lesson 4. Nitwit, Tripod and Hitler – A Greek trilogy

'Come worthy Greek . . . possess these shores with me'
In *Ulysses and the Sea* by Samuel David

Nitwit – A Greek tragedy

So it was on to Greece, a five-day haul by Land Rover and a three-month project on behalf of the UK-based Greek Animal Welfare Fund turning round a desperate animal welfare centre run by a local so-called animal protection society in Thessalonika. Three months became nine and of course, there were many cats whose lives became entangled with ours. The first was a delightful skinny tabby stray called 'Nitwit' or, as one of the well-meaning local German supporters of the society called him, 'Nitvit'. He lived around the shelter but would come in at feeding time. He would jump gleefully into the puppy compound and elbow his way to the food bowls through anything up to thirty jostling puppies. He took no notice whatsoever of the odd one who tried to chase him or growl at him across the food bowl, he simply carried on eating. Puppies being puppies of course, they invariably wanted to play with anything novel in the pen and a cat's tail was a great invitation for a good game of tug-of-war! Nitwit simply pulled his tail out of the way and got back to the job in hand. We never brought him into the pens in the shelter, indeed I tried to avoid penning any cats unless they were genuinely unwanted pets and were likely to get a good home. We tried to have the strays and feral cats neutered and put back where they'd come from rather than have them end their days languishing, albeit fed and healthy, in a cage but with no prospect of becoming a pet.

Sadly, the policy of allowing Nitwit to run free around the shelter and organise his own relations with all the dogs and puppies was probably the wrong one. Though he was first class at keeping dogs in order and extremely friendly with everyone who called, like so many cats, he was fatally useless at dealing with cars. Few cars indeed passed the shelter on the dirt road; perhaps if there had been more traffic he would have learned to avoid them as many streetwise city cats do. The rural cat and those in relatively traffic-free areas may never come to appreciate the dangers that come so fast down the roads they sunbathe and dustroll on. We arrived to open the shelter early one fine Greek spring morning, but this time Nitwit wasn't there to welcome us with his tail high and his skinny little legs scampering to jump on to the Land Rover bonnet to rub the wing mirror and make sure that our first job of the day was to fuss over him. We knew immediately that we had lost a friend and there just a few yards down the rough road on the verge lay a lifeless Nitwit, struck dead by a rare passing car. Even the puppies seemed quieter that day as we all mourned the loss of Nitwit, for whom one car was one too many.

Many people argue that, as so many cats end their days under the wheels of a car, they should be kept permanently indoors and protected, especially in the city or near busy roads. I think it all rather depends on the cat in question. If he's never known the free life then I suppose it's a case of 'what you've never had, you won't miss' and providing the cat has plenty of human and feline company and get lots of attention and opportunity to play, he can arguably lead a happy enough life. But I still treat plenty of indoor cats that have never been outdoors but who, on reaching that exploratory adolescent phase of development, pace and cry or scream to be allowed to tread over the threshold where everyone else goes and from where all those interesting smells seem to emanate. Some get frantic in their desires and if their energies can't be directed on to toys or a new feline friend then I usually advise people to take the risk and let them out or rehome them to somewhere where they can go out more safely. Most do surprisingly well; perhaps the more developed the exploratory instinct, the more equipped the cat is to deal with challenges and dangers. Perhaps curiosity doesn't always kill the cat. It may be an essential requirement of being fit to survive.

For a cat like Nitwit, who was brought up in the streets and largely fended for himself until he discovered free handouts in the puppy pen, being penned would be equivalent to a stretch in prison. Any cat which has known the fulfilment of territory patrols, hunting and lying in the sun should surely never be then kept permanently indoors. Even with all the best food, care and play in the world, the cat would suffer enormous frustration at being prevented from doing what comes naturally. And though we wondered, after Nitwit had been killed, whether we should have been more protective of him, frankly it never occurred to us beforehand even to think of caging him up. For Nitwit, used to the outdoor life from kittenhood, it was much better to have had a short happy life than a long boring unhappy one, and the same reasoning has been applied to my pet cats ever since.

Tripod – A tale of feline fortitude

Tripod was luckier than Nitwit. He survived his first main contretemps with a car. He was even luckier considering that he lived in Greece – where compassion for animals does not feature high on the list of national characteristics – to have another driver stop and pick him up. The nice man brought him to the shelter and wouldn't leave until we'd agreed not to put the cat to sleep. His compassion didn't stretch as far as leaving us money to pay for the treatment that this scruffy black and white street cat was clearly in need of, but the man was a ray of hope after all the cruelty and neglect cases we'd had to deal with over the previous weeks. My instinct was still to put this cat to sleep immediately. His left foreleg was not only crushed, but a large broken bone protruded through his skin and he bore all the injuries of a direct hit. I guessed that he would also be suffering from internal injuries and with money and time both at a premium it seemed illogical to go to all the trouble of treating the cat and then never be able to find him a home afterwards. No one wants cats as pets in Greece, except the north Europeans and Americans on work contracts, and those that were wanted by Greek people were mainly the snob-value ones we never had, like Persians, Siamese or beautiful long-haired tortoise-shells. But a promise is a promise, and so we agreed to do what we could for this poor cat. I gave him a shot of antibiotic and sedative to make him a little more comfortable and we took him along to the veterinary surgery in town that evening.

Panos, the society's vet, was a delightfully plump and cheerful chap who liked his food and his fags, despite being able to discourse at length in appalling English about the physiological dangers of obesity and smoking. He is quite one of the best people I've ever got to know through a lifetime of working around animals. Panos and his gentle wife, Milly, were two of the few genuinely pleasant people I was to meet and keep contact with after our spell in Greece. Unlike many Greek vets, Panos chose his profession because he loved animals and not because he didn't get the grades to be a human doctor, dentist or, as the really clever ones there normally become, an engineer. In fact he was extremely bright except at English, but then my Greek never reached any dizzy heights, even after nine months, so who was I to moan? Now six years on, I can really only remember enough to impress in Greek restaurants! Panos could have studied engineering if he'd wanted to. 'But if you make a road better, it doesn't lick you afterwards to say thank you,' he said, and that's why his surgery in the middle of Thessalonika was so popular with everyone in town.

Panos ran a pointed finger across his neck when he saw the cat we had brought him. 'Why you bother with thees?' he moaned, but still smiling, which is quite difficult to achieve when you think about it! I explained the circumstances while Panos examined the strangely friendly cat, who had started to purr, despite his injuries. 'I cannot save hees leg,' announced Panos, 'so if you want, I will cut it off. I have never done thees amputation surgery, so it ees good practice, innit?' Then he laughed and said 'and no crazee owner to worry for crying in

19

my new surgery eef he . . .' He ran a pointed finger across his neck again and went to scrub up. We were there for a long evening and with great gory skill, Panos removed the cat's leg and stitched him up. The scars were enormous, the table was a red mess and there, macabre in the middle of all the swabs and blood, was the amputated leg. We'd already realised that this cat was destined to come home with us to get the post-operative care he needed but Panos wasn't finished yet. 'One more leettle cut while we have him asleeep' and, if losing a leg wasn't enough, with the unkindest cut of all, Panos removed the the two bits at the back end as well. Our tom cat would be less smelly if ever he could stand still enough again to spray on three legs. The cat was now a pet and so had to have a name. We called him Tripod. Well, what else do you call a three-legged anything?!

Tripod made a remarkable recovery in our traditional little house by the sea in the lovely fishing village of Nea Micanonia, though our Greek neighbours, who had already adopted the 'smile and make allowances for the mad English' approach towards us, really couldn't understand why anyone should be nursing a three-legged cat! I had made up my mind to give him a month and then take a close look at his quality of life. I needn't have worried. Cats are, after all, highly adaptable. Though he was understandably weak for a couple of days, after six he had become very friendly and used to struggle and stumble to greet us when we returned home from the shelter. After two weeks he had all but mastered the art of walking on three legs and he even made his first wobbly jump on to a chair. Getting around the house was clearly not going to be a problem, but how would Tripod cope if he was allowed back outdoors? We pondered that question again as to whether Tripod, as a cat used to the free life, should be kept indoors even on such blatant medical grounds and the fact that he probably wouldn't be able to defend himself against the tough strays which abounded around the village. We let him out to sit in the sun in our little courtyard one Sunday morning and he seemed relaxed and pleased to be breathing fresh air again.

The second time he went out, he disappeared in a flash up the vine that grew around our back door and sat on the roof. Not only walking but now running and climbing on three legs! We decided that Tripod was certainly not going to be happy cooped up indoors for the rest of his life and that henceforth he would be free to come and go as he pleased. An hour later, as a token of his appreciation, Tripod brought home a dead grey bird and deposited it on the kitchen table!

Tripod illustrated just how resilient cats can be and just how well they can respond to the right sort of care and overcome enormous difficulties. From a cat's point of view, losing a leg only represents a twenty-five per cent loss, whereas for a human, life gets more difficult with a leg-loss worth fifty per cent. But even with a weapon gone, Tripod's hunting ability certainly didn't seem to have been curtailed by his loss. Whether he could actually have hunted and scavenged enough to live on is perhaps doubtful, but such harsh living was now a thing of his past. He got fed by us of course, but even the locals had taken his bravery to their hearts and he used to cadge extra meals in all the cafes that opened out on to the village square just a few yards from our home. Indeed, as time went by, he spent more and more time on the cafe patios in the sun exchanging stories about his war wounds with the old men of the village. He got quite fat, which only made the effort of walking home after a hard day's lounging all the more difficult. But the day he tackled the concrete steps down to the beach was the day we said goodbye to Tripod. Not because he couldn't get back up– he did come and see all his old friends when the fancy took him – and not because anything dire befell him down on the beach. In fact, Tripod found his true role there and by the jetty where the fishing boats came in. He'd sit, like some feline Long John Silver, waiting for his favourite food of fresh fish off the boats in the early morning and evening. During the day, he was a cool beach bum, cadging food from the tourists at the beach restaurants in true Greek stray-cat style. With an injury like that, he always got fed more than the other cats and to the best of my knowledge, he's still there, impressing them all with tales of his fortitude against all odds!

Hitler – Appearances can be misleading!

For a while, Tripod shared our home with a cat who was perfectly ordinary. He was friendly and clean and no trouble at all. His misfortune was to be a cat brought to the shelter as an unwanted pet, but no one ever wanted to take him home afterwards. After a few weeks, I decided that his friendly disposition had won and he was to come with me. Probably the reason no one except an English cat nut with a bizarre sense of humour would want him was that he looked like Hitler, which was the name I gave him! He was white in colour except for a black tail and uncanny black splodges on his face. There was a large angled black patch across his forehead and between his ears looking just like Hitler's hairstyle, but most bizarre of all, he had

21

a neat little black moustache that extended from beneath one nostril across to the other. There was absolutely no mistaking his appearance, yet he was quite the friendliest sweet-natured little soul and bore none of the megalomania and danger of the man he so resembled. Even the old men in the square, many of whom had suffered badly at the hands of the German occupying army in the Second World War, had to laugh when Hitler sauntered round. One toothless old boy even used to spring to his feet, click his heels and give the Nazi straight-arm salute, accompanied by a throaty Greek accented *'Heil'* to a very bemused cat! The only element of Hitlerite character in the cat was that, hard on the three heels of Tripod, he also used to invade the cafés on table mugging exercises. When we finally left Greece for good in 1985, we gave Hitler to the café owner with the toothless old customer, in the safe knowledge that, because of his remarkable looks, Hitler would always be good for business and well cared for.

Lesson 5. Campbell – A consideration of domestication

'No tame animal has lost less of its native dignity or maintained more of its ancient reserve. The domestic cat might rebel tomorrow'
William Conway (Archbishop of Armagh)

The old Land Rover was still with me, but by the end of 1985, Marie and I had parted and Claire, my wife to be, and I had met at a symposium in London about the use of dolphins to help autistic children! We went for a weekend's break with friends who owned a delightfully picturesque hotel between Oban and Fort William, on whom we inflicted our three madcap dogs. Cath and Evan didn't mind a bit, in fact they looked forward to our coming. Our paths had first crossed the previous year when they used to have two large beautiful Bullmastiffs called Isla and Cassie. Their vet had referred them to me as clients but unfortunately I had felt it unlikely that the fights that used to occur occasionally between the dogs could be safely resolved and so Claire took on Cassie and brought her back to London. This left Isla to be spoiled utterly by the gentle-natured Evan (though he liked to think of himself as a tough-dealing businessman) and Cath's wonderful cooking. But, they missed their other daughter and so there were always great celebrations when Cassie came to stay, even though the old animosity towards Isla remained and they were always carefully kept apart.

So, it was a friends and doggie holiday, we thought, but as we drove through magnificent Glencoe the day after the first snows had dusted the upper peaks, cats were to join the party again. There, tumbling across the road, damp and bedraggled, were two little kittens, perhaps cruelly thrown out by some passing motorist. When I went to take a closer look, it seemed that these were no ordinary pet kittens, they didn't have a cleanish, recently abandoned feel to them, their thick tabby fur was grubby down to the skin and immediately I thought of Scottish Wild Cats. I wondered whether simply to put them back in the heather and hope that their mother wasn't far away, but then that would be to condemn them if, in fact, they had been unwanted castaways with no mother for miles. With hindsight, I shouldn't perhaps have allowed my protective emotions to run so high, but as I stood in the pouring rain with two cold hungry squeaking kittens in my hands, there really was no option but to take them in. And anyway, I'd handled the kittens and my scent might make their mother abandon them if I did put them back. Claire sighed as I got back in the car, it was a portent of things to come, for ever since she's had to put up with a houseful of various beasts and always a 'just more than we ought to have to be convenient' number of pet cats and dogs!

We dried and fed the four- to five-week-old kittens back at the hotel and though they seemed a little spitty even at that age, I assumed that they were probably feral or perhaps Scottish Wild Cat hybrids and would calm down with frequent attention. Conversation ran and ran that night in the hotel bar, first about Scottish Wild Cats, and local gamekeepers described how rarely seen they were. One local chap had apparently raised a few kittens in his time until they reverted to a wild nature and wouldn't acknowledge him any more. But then, the same chap had also raised one or two very assertive and unmanageable black cats, which though they looked like pets were as wild as any Wild Cat and were probably hybrids. That led as inevitably as the beer flowed to tales of local sightings of large black cats, escaped pumas and unidentified beasts, which always seem to be caught fleetingly in the headlights as they cross the roads in front of people's cars at night and usually shortly after closing time at the bar!

Next day we drove back to London, feeding the kittens periodically and trying to keep three sweaty dog noses out of their cardboard box. We named them Campbell and MacDonald after the battling Glencoe clans but, sadly, MacDonald, like his clan, was suffering. He never really kept a hold on life and died a few days after we got home. But by then I had contacted the Nature Conservancy Council in Edinburgh with my tale and they advised me to put MacDonald's little body in the freezer for subsequent analysis and to get a blood sample from Campbell to see whether he had any maternally derived antibodies as this would give some sort of clue as to whether he had come from a pet background. The call introduced us to Dr Nigel Easterbee, who was working on a major Scottish Wild Cat population survey and study. Nigel became a good friend, pitching up to stay with us whenever he came to London for meetings. He was an enormous font of information on all cats and especially interested in Campbell as perhaps a first opportunity to study a live Wild Cat kitten. Nigel was a great traveller too and postcards from all sorts of places used to arrive from time to time. It was desperately sad when in December 1990 our friend Nigel tragically lost his life on a stretch of road in Scotland that he drove on almost daily when he was back at the NCC. I remember how, even as a professional scientist, Nigel understood my urgent desire to have Campbell vaccinated against the usual feline diseases as quickly as possible, even though this would deny him the opportunity to study Campbell's blood profile and disease resistance other than from the single blood sample a veterinary friend had taken from him. He knew that Campbell's survival was more important, whatever he was, than the process of scientific study, and it was that compassion in a world where some scientists think only of their research or their career and forget that they are dealing with living creatures that I know Nigel will always be remembered for.

As it turned out, that sample only confirmed that Campbell could be a Scottish Wild Cat, but could not be identified as such for certain. Indeed Nigel and other experts such as Terry Moore of the Cat Survival Trust in Hertfordshire all felt that Campbell was a first-generation hybrid, a cross between a Scottish Wild Cat and a feral, stray or pet cat, who just happened to bear the coat colour and most of the characteristics of the Wild Cat. More of real Wild Cats and the threats they face from the pet, feral and stray cat populations later, but as life continued with Campbell, it was clear that here was no ordinary little fluffy kitten. He played and even purred in our arms

24

from time to time. He also growled a deep growl when he was unhappy or frustrated, a growl I have never heard from even the most unmanageable, agitated feral cat. The dogs, including the 130-pound Cassie, all kept well out of Campbell's way, though to my knowledge he never actually swiped any of them as a kitten.

He grew into a magnificent looking thick-coated tabby cat with a real banded brush of a tail but, at four months of age, it was clear that he was not to be caged in my flat in Surrey for much longer. He would pace up and down by the door and along the window sills first growling then yowling, and though he could be pacified with a stroke or a game, his tolerance of being approached and handled was falling with every day. Already I had learnt not to surprise him and always approached after first catching his eye and then moving slowly towards him. His games became rougher and more painful as he bit and scratched readily, and more than one dog's tail bore the dental impression of a Campbell in hunting-and-killing mode. He still enjoyed a cuddle and purred loudly, but the times this happened became increasingly dictated by his demand, and not mine. Family and friends used to phone first before calling round so that Campbell could be put elsewhere as no one really felt safe with him around. Then he started to protect his food with his head held menacingly above the bowl, growling and with malevolent intent written all over his face for those who might think of coming near. And he was growing up too. As well as being large and impressive, his testes had descended and I knew it was decision time. If he were a pet of five or six months of age it would be time to castrate him and obviously it was well past the time when he should be let out. There was no question that he would cope and survive well outdoors, the question was whether it was right to give him his freedom but try to maintain him as a pet, castrated as the price of the compromise, or to hand him to a zoo or the Cat Survival Trust, or even to take him back up to Scotland and release him. None of these options was entirely satisfactory, though had we been able to tell exactly what he was, Wild Cat, pet strain or hybrid, this could have forced the decision one way or the other. As it was, he certainly wasn't behaving like any other kitten or nurtured young cat I have ever known and looked to be growing wilder in temperament every day, just like the young wild rabbits and squirrels I had raised as a child. They were totally manageable and friendly until adolescence and that fundamental drive to leave the pseudo-maternal nest set in. Then it was just a matter of time and I felt the same about Campbell.

I took the 'let it roll' option and, while choosing not to have him castrated in case he was the real thing and accepting that this would only hasten his wild development, I started to allow him outdoors. He loved it and even learned to use a cat flap in a matter of minutes. The dogs loved his absence even more! He would go off on hunting excursions of a few hours and, for several weeks, he brought his many victims back to the garden or into the kitchen to eat. He would still come in for bowls of cat food and for a while was always friendly and sought a cuddle when he did turn up. Indeed, for a couple of weeks I thought that letting him have his freedom had acted as a valve for his wildness and that he would still be my pet cat, albeit with a greater instinct for self-determination. Should I now have him castrated? How could I, as one who had spent so much time instigating neutering schemes around the world to control feral cat populations, and as a strong supporter of neutering pets to prevent unwanted births, allow my own cat to roam with all his genetic potential intact?

Campbell must have known what was being contemplated for him, for in a matter of days he had stopped coming home except on very rare occasions and always at night. He then stopped coming into the house at all and would only come to me in the garden if I stood very still for several minutes and called him gently. It became an honour just to see his magnificent form, the type of excitement you get when you spot a rarely seen wild animal such as a badger, rather than sadness at being unable to get near a pet. I knew that Campbell had saved me from having to make any decision about his future; he had made his own and was living the wild life in the woods and fields around my Surrey home. Over the next year or so, I saw him maybe half a dozen times, once crossing the road at night and picked out in my headlights, though I wasn't going to start any rumours about strange wild cats roaming the county. The last time I saw him was in late 1986, by which time he really was a magnificent looking animal and obviously surviving very well by fending for himself. Whatever Wild Cat component there was in his make-up was serving him more than adequately and providing him with enough wits to survive in semi-urban Surrey even though there may not have been enough Wild Cat genes to make life bearable in the harsher climate of highland Scotland. I was proud of him in a paternal sort of way, and admired his refusal to sell his soul for a regular place by the fire and a frequently refilled food bowl. Though many would rightly criticise me for letting him have his freedom, or not putting him in a zoo for further analysis, and letting him go uncastrated into a world where he may meet fertile females and maybe father unwanted kittens, I felt his genes deserved their opportunity to get stuck into life and fight for their survival. Was Campbell a true Scottish Wild Cat? Physically, developmentally and behaviourally he can't have been far away from it, but in the scientific world of taxonomic definition, Nigel Easterbee and his colleagues were still developing the genetic analysis techniques that might have told us the answer. However, when Nigel died, Campbell was already an adult free-living cat and not going to give up his tissue samples or blood easily for anyone!

But if I had at least saved and reared Campbell and allowed him to go his own way, what Campbell did for me was to set me thinking far more academically about the nature of the cat and to question seriously the suggestion that our modern-day pet cats contain any element at all of the Scottish sub-species of *Felis sylvestris*, the Scottish Wild Cat, or his cousins in the forests of Europe. Good luck to you wherever you are, Campbell, and thanks for letting me touch the true uncompromised cat in you.

Lesson 6. Scribble – Understanding the special relationship between man and cat

'Whatever you say to them, they always purr'   Lewis Carroll

From the wild side of the feline world to the highly cultured friendly nature of the first Siamese cat I ever kept, and what a character Scribble turned out to be. I already had Bullet, a black and white ex-feral cat, and we decided to get Scribble as a friend for him. He would agree that Scribble was a cat among cats and a cat among people. She was one of those remarkable cats with such a huge personality that everyone loved her. She was polite, affectionate and impeccably behaved according to the circumstances. She never annoyed the three dogs she shared her life with, they were her friends, and though she was head and shoulders above Bullet in the brains stakes, she always had time and patience for him even to the point of allowing him to be macho and tough with her when he felt the need.

It was once a little unkindly said of me that as builders' houses are always in a state of disrepair and doctors' children are always falling ill, the fact that I owned three mad dogs was only to be expected! So when the time came actually to choose a new cat instead of having one adopt us, or finding a stray or a semi-wild cat in Scotland or being landed with someone else's disaster area (always my excuse for the dogs' unruly antics!), we were determined to get it right. I had always wanted a Siamese cat for their wonderful sharp character, sensitivity, precision of design and yes, even that amazing voice. Claire was only midway overcoming her allergy to cats since she'd moved in with me a few months earlier with Cassie. But she'd desensitised herself a lot with frequent short contact with Bullet and had stopped the mid-sneeze-and-scratch exclamations of 'that cat's got to go'. Last in, first out I used to reply with no sympathy at all and here we were, about to get a Siamese cat. I pacified her with the fact that because of their thinner single coat, Siamese were less likely to cause allergic reactions anyway, so things wouldn't get any worse. I had a chat with Bullet and he meowed gently when I mentioned the prospect of getting him a nice Oriental girlfriend to look after him and wash behind his ears. No macho strutting tom competing over status and warm spots in our house with little Bullet, a girl it had to be!

With breed and sex decided and with the approval of girlfriend and existing cat, we set off to the National Cat Show at Earls Court in London to have a look and meet a few breeders. Not inclined to give two hoots about show victories or rosettes, we set about chatting our way along the benches of Siamese with a view to meeting a family person who happened to breed Siamese cats rather than someone for whom cats and winning prizes were the be-all and end-all of life. Having found many nice people, we went to have a closer look at all the different types of Siamese – Lilac, Chocolate, Seal and Tabby Points as they are known because of the colour of various parts, but most noticeably the ears and tail. It was the delicate brown of the Chocolate Point Siamese that we fell for and also for one particular breeder, Brenda Mason. She had the added attraction of having a litter of kittens nearly ready for sale and with a few choccies already identifiable in among them.

We went to visit Brenda shortly afterwards to select our kitten. We walked straight into a mad house! There was redecorating being done in the front hallway, there was a clatter of kids rushing through with their friends, there was a flurry of cats and kittens in all directions and a large friendly black standard Poodle trying to keep nimbly out of harm's way. In the living room we were faced with a line of ducks and chickens which were outdoors in the garden but pecking at the louvre windows for attention. This was the place for a kitten to be brought up in. For years I'd been saying to would-be kitten owners on radio phone-in shows and in magazines that the best place to get a kitten from was as active a house as they could find. Cats born into mayhem grow up thinking that mayhem is normal and will always be well-equipped to take anything that they encounter in a new home in their stride.

Cattery bred cats may benefit from the ultimate in hygiene and protection from illness but when it comes to being able to cope with challenges and novelty, they start at a disadvantage compared with those brought up in a mad house and are far more likely to be nervous or incompetent at dealing with everyday events and become my patients later in life. Fortunately, most kittens are adaptable, self-initiating in terms of play and exploration and don't necessarily suffer from an apparently emotionally deprived development. Sadly, the problems I treat in many dogs have arisen purely and simply because as puppies they weren't able to experience sufficient contact with other dogs or people or a broad enough range of novel objects and situations to explore. There was no danger of emotional lack of opportunity in Brenda Mason's house and attracted by a particularly friendly kitten we settled on 'Scribble' and left Brenda in her asylum to await the day when the wee thing could come and join our social herd.

As soon as our extremely well-socialised kitten's course of vaccinations had been completed, Brenda phoned to say that we could collect Scribble. Two hours later we arrived back at the asylum complete with stout carrying basket and warm blankets. Brenda was excellent. No simply writing a cheque and walking straight out with a kitten in the basket in one hand and a pedigree certificate in the other hand. 'Sit!' she said. 'This is what she eats, this is a list of what she likes and what she'll need as she grows up and this is how she is and what she's used to. This is her medical insurance, this is her pedigree and, if you want to show her, please do, and let me know how you get on.'

'No chance of a show career for this one,' I said as I wrote out a cheque feeling like I was paying for someone's child, 'though she may be making a few media appearances.' And she did, much to Brenda's delight. Off we went with the tiny kitten curled up asleep, not in the dark warm nest we had created for her in that stout carrying basket, but wrapped up and purring loudly on Claire's lap. No homesickness there, and not much regard paid to allergies either!

Once home, it was time to follow some of my own advice with introductions to those three mad dogs and the more benign but nonetheless territorial Bullet. A spare bedroom had been prepared with a large secure mesh pen, normally used to house and protect two of the dotty dogs in the car. In it was the most comfortable draught-proof bed, some safe soft dangly toys with no dangerous detachable bits, a litter tray containing the same type of litter that Scribble had been raised on and, as far from the tray as possible, food and water bowls. Proximity of food to litter trays is a major cause of the development of house- training problems in cats . . . it's logical, after all, how many people want to eat near the loo? Cats will eat their food but then choose another loo, like under someone's bed or behind the sofa!

Scribble went straight into her protective pen and slept like a log for three hours. The pen was to be her safe haven, a den for undisturbed sleep and, later, a way of managing her introductions safely to the dogs and Bullet. For the first couple of days of course we went in to see her all the time, frequently handling and playing with her and generally getting to know each other. When we were with her we allowed her to run around the room, having first removed anything that might be dangerous like flimsy curtains or curious fireplace openings with chimneys above! After a couple of days she was allowed free run of the room but always chose to sleep in her safe den. There really is no better way to introduce a new kitten or puppy to the home than by using an indoor pen, especially if the fragile little creature needs protection or time out to rest from the attentions of eager young children or other pets.

Scribble was clearly a very confident and precocious character and got to know us very quickly indeed, so it was soon time to show Bullet his new companion and make sure we'd made the right match for him from the dating agency. We took him in to see Scribble who, after a mad half hour of dashing around, was sleeping in her pen. Bullet, only famous for his laid-back approach to life, and never his brains, looked confused, sniffed and then settled down to stare at Scribble through the bars of the pen. Normally quite territorial in the surrounding gardens, Bullet remained calm, but jumped back in amazement when Scribble, realising she had an admirer, shot out of bed and rubbed her face and body outrageously against the bars to say hello, as only an appallingly flirtatious Siamese can do. Bullet didn't know quite what to do, so he hissed once as a token gesture, looked around to make sure no one was watching and then stretched a nose forward to touch Scribble's and sighed as if he knew his cover was blown already. Later the same day, Scribble was allowed out to meet her man and they immediately chased and played, during which time Scribble made it clear that she was in charge of the whole relationship. Bullet, like many a male lucky enough to have such a delightfully strong character as a girlfriend, was happy to sit back and let Scribble make all the decisions – in fact it was quite a weight off his mind! He let her do as she wished, from biting his tail gently to eating his food, and by the second night they were curled up asleep together.

It had all been so different from the traumas that I frequently get to treat of trying to forge relations between two cats who haven't got on from the start and, unprotected by a pen, have become involved in serious scuffles. But now it was time to meet those slobbering mutts with a combined weight of more than 200 pounds. Cassie, then Colonel, the Greek Dobermann, and Bandit, the Large Munsterlander who is generously and leniently described as a hyperactive, highly vocal, cat-chasing (except Bullet) maniac, were brought in one at a time on leads to meet the kitten, now safely back in her pen. Cass looked at her a moment, looked at us and went back to doing what she has always done best – nothing – but always very sweet-natured about it! Scribble looked at Cass, took stock of the ugliest creature she'd ever seen (Cassie's other name is Blugly, short for bloody ugly!) and then rubbed furiously against the bars and said hello. Cass yawned and sloped off to the region of the food bowl, where all of life's useful events occur. Colonel, another brain-free but very sweet and playful dog, just thought he was going out for a walk because someone had put his lead on. As he had spent his life carefully avoiding cats since an altercation with a tough street cat in Greece where he came from, we knew he wouldn't pester the new arrival. Scribble got up, rubbed against the bars and said hello anyway, but Colonel the clot didn't even notice, so she went back to bed.

Bandit, on the other hand, always too bright and too tough for his own good (moral: always get a stupid dog, never a clever one if you want a nice pet), charged into the room, always having known that

31

there was something in there because his highly developed nose had told him so. Strangling himself on the lead, he lunged forward and banged his nose on the pen. With a flurry of whimpering, yipping and wagging tail, he stalked, pointed with his nose and stared at the kitten, looking round every few seconds to tell us what he had found and awaiting instructions as to what to do next. Scribble stayed in bed. Bandit settled down after a few moments, nose pressed against the bars of the pen, snorting and dribbling. Scribble got up, stretched and slid towards him, rubbed furiously against her side of the bars and said her customary 'hello'. Bandit had met his unflappable match. While we had prevented possible disaster with Scribble well protected in the pen when introducing him for his first few encounters, she had gained the upper hand hand already and Bandit's efforts to chase her had failed. Henceforth he was to hang up his membership of the clever-gun-dog club and was reduced simply to searching for her around the room and then staring at her, pausing only to look over her shoulder at us to make sure that we'd seen how clever he'd been at locating her, cornering and freezing with a stare a sleeping fourteen-week-old kitten! Scribble, used to the Poodle she'd been brought up with, knew exactly how to deal with dogs and took control of them more with every day.

Onwards now to introducing Scribble to the rest of the house, one room at a time. The pen was moved around to establish her right of access in each room and get her smell incorporated into the communal smell shared by all of the other pets and their two human keepers. First entries to new rooms were always carefully supervised and, once she seemed settled, the introductions with the dogs and Bullet were repeated. Ordinarily I advise owners in similar circumstances to proceed very slowly, taking two or three weeks to get their kitten used to having free run before leaving the pen door permanently open and even longer before all the pets are allowed to run free around the house together, even when supervised. With Scribble, it was all over and done with and her pen was put back in the car after four days. By the evening of the fourth day her invasion and integration were complete and she was able to play with or cuddle up to Bullet wherever he was, stare Cassie off her large warm bean bag bed and totally ignore the demented Bandit. The mad gun-dog now developed a new tactic. Waiting motionless while she fell asleep on an armchair, he would then sneak quietly up and, with his head held as still as a statue two inches over her, try to drown her by dribbling on her for hours on end. He never sought to chase her or harm her and over the next few weeks the novelty of her presence did wear off, but for the time being she would wake up, wash down and then wait until he was asleep to take her revenge by jumping on his head to get to the floor! If he hadn't resigned already, poor Bandit would certainly have been drummed out of the gun-dog club for allowing that to happen! Madam had arrived indoors and soon she spread her persona to the garden, making friends with all of Bullet's cat friends and even his hated rivals. She would simply ignore their arched backed threats, walk up as bold as brass to touch noses and then rub her body along theirs . . . as only an appallingly flirtatious Siamese can do!

Placid with everyone, confident wherever she went, Scribble was always in control and would almost purr on command. With the launch of my first book, *Do Cats Need Shrinks?*, Scribble and I toured the country together, staying in the best hotels when we were due to promote the book on television, to the delight and adoration of the hotel staff. She crooned on all channels and became famous for being totally relaxed and unflustered in the studio. She was even asked to close her legs and point her bottom and rude bits away from the camera on Sky television because the interviewer Frank Bough felt that she would be overexciting all the randy toms watching in the alleyways of Europe! She received mail from far and wide and yet took it all, wherever she was, totally in her stride. And if good breeding, frequent early handling, lots of early socialisation with cats, dogs and kids and careful introductions in her new home made any difference to her then I was proud to have helped. But somehow I think she was always going to be queen anyway.

Why she wandered down to the railway that terrible April afternoon we'll never know. She'd never been there before and always stayed in and around our garden, playing or resting in the sun on fine days but preferring to stick close by the fire on cooler days. The last time I cuddled her, I was on the phone to someone when she reached up with her front paws on my shoulders as she always did, purring and pressing her warm body against my chest to invite a good all-down-the back stroke. It was a long call but she stayed with me and then dropped down and sauntered out of the door. She didn't come back that evening and we fretted and worried all night. We left the doors open for her to come in but somehow we knew that she had gone. At five o'clock in the morning after a sleepless night I got up to check on my worst fears and walk the railway tracks to look for her. There she

33

was, cold and dead, her precious confident life ended. I fetched a box and laid her inside. Claire had also got up and had come down to join the search. She met me coming back to the house and together we sobbed for the loss of our dearest of friends. We showed her little body to Bullet and the dogs and for several days, like us, they seemed miserable and unwilling to play. I buried Scribble next to the dog's pen where she liked to sit and planted a white rose over her. Many people might say that she should have been kept as a permanently indoor pet but there was just no way that her massive character could have been so confined. She loved the outdoors and though she was to die there and her life was so short, she enjoyed a very happy life while she was with us. Despite the pain of losing Scribble I would still never deny a cat access to the outdoors if it wanted to go and, if conditions were just too dangerous, then I wouldn't keep a cat at all.

We still miss her, even though it's more than a year since she died and even now we often come downstairs expecting to see her coming up to meet us yelling at the top of her voice, as she used to do. After a while we plucked up the courage to tell Brenda that one of her babies had gone, and we all cried again. We went back to get another Siamese cat from her; to try again, knowing full well that there never would be a second Scribble. The house just felt so empty without even the sight or cry of a Siamese, so we waited until Brenda had a litter ready and went to select another. The Lilac Point kittens before us were delightful, so delightful that we went overboard and decided to take two sisters. Bean and Flirty Bottom (so named for being even more blatant in her bottom-raising flirtatious greetings than Scribble) duly arrived back home, now in the beautiful countryside of Wiltshire in south-west England. They were put through the same introductory processes to integrate them as Scribble was. Bandit was the same as before, only desperately confused over which kitten to keep his eye on or dribble over if they slept separately. Fortunately the two girls are usually curled up in each others' arms, often with Bullet intertwined in there somewhere too.

We wondered what Scribble would have said if she'd met our two new Siamese kittens and whether she would forgive us for sometimes calling one or other by her name by mistake or out of habit if they did something similar. In a strange way, she gave us her answer. The rose we had placed over her grave was not due to flower until the following year, but, just a couple of days after Flirty Bottom and Bean arrived, two white roses budded and flowered as if Scribble was welcoming them and giving her own special seal of approval.

Scribble was a cat in a million, but in her electric short life and her devastating death she also taught us both just how deep a relationship can develop between anyone and their pets and how impossible it is to avoid the emotional involvement that shatters you when the bond comes to such a violent and unecessary end. Loving your cat or your dog is an inevitable result of sharing your life together, and being torn to bits when he or she dies and breaks the ties is impossible to avoid, no matter how many pets you keep in your life and how many times it happens. Only the emotionless or stupid could save themselves from the heartache, but then they would miss out on the pure pleasure of sharing some of their life with a cat like Scribble. We try to remember her life rather than her death and though I can look happily at photos of her and remember the good times, I've still not been able to bring myself to watch any videos of her many television appearances.

Lesson 7. Bullet, Bean and Flirty Bottom – The current incumbents

'There are no ordinary cats'   Colette

Bullet is a rather different cat altogether compared with his Siamese housemates. No nurtured formal upbringing for him and no price attached either. Bullet was a street urchin, born to a feral mother on a cold and grey London morn in the rough ground behind the buildings of a Polytechnic in south London. A few feral cats were eking out a living there on the wild side, a living made all the easier by virtue of the Polytechnic's caretaker's wife giving them at least one good meal per day along with any leftovers from the plates of the family, her dog and her own two cats. It was ironic that her kindness, supplemented by other bits and pieces provided by the cleaning staff, probably enabled the small colony to survive and made it possible for queens like Bullet's mum to have at least a chance of raising a few kittens per year. Ironic because it was her husband who called me one morning to see whether I would go and trap the colony and get their numbers under control! He was blissfully unaware of his wife's involvement . . . and as soon as I went to see them she ushered me aside and made me promise not to let on in return for some co-operation with the

35

trapping! We duly trapped and neutered the healthy adult cats in the colony and returned them to their site using the system described in Chapter 15, reducing the numbers a little by homing a couple of the tamer adults and all the healthy kittens. Everyone was happy afterwards, especially the caretaker's wife, whose secret has remained intact for over five years until now!

One of the kittens I trapped was a skinny undernourished little spitter whose mother was a tiny little waif herself. Mum went back to life on the tiles suitably sterilised and spared the burden of any further reproductive drain on her resources, but the kitten was one that no one seemed to want. I phoned all my feral contacts but when you're spitty and mainly black, there just aren't the potential homes available compared with the queues for ginger or tortoiseshell kittens, including grubby feral ones, not even if you've got a pretty white bib and white socks. So, as befalls anyone who gets involved with cat rescue work, this kitten ended up at my home in a pen and subjected to an intensive handling programme to tame him down and give him a better chance of finding a new home. He seemed to be taming nicely after a week or so and so I let him out into the room. Whoosh! He shot behind the sofa and resisted all attempts at recapture for a week. If he was sighted, he was always belting across the room at top speed, hence he was named Bullet. Bullet, like so many supposedly temporary feline lodgers, stayed and, finding no other home for him and after having got hold of him again and completed the taming process, he was duly vaccinated and castrated as the price of his future comfortable lifestyle.

How glad I am that Bullet never was sent away to another home for he really is a remarkable character. Not hugely endowed with the brains or sensitivity of his higher born Oriental cousins, he is nonetheless an extremely sweet-natured cat. Whether as a result of being born to a small mother or undernourishment in his early kittenhood or a slice of both, Bullet has remained quite small for an adult tom. He has a huge heart, as shown by his relaxed acceptance of Scribble, Bean and Flirty Bottom and all the strays and feral cats who have passed through my hands on their way to new homes. He shows great friendliness to, not to say accomplished mastery of, the four dogs he has had to share his home with and always greets our friends with a tail up and a purr, if he can be bothered to get up, that is. He is a cat who loves affection and is particularly adept at catching you on the chin with the friendly head butt and cheek to cheek wipe!

However, as much as he is the ideal affectionate pet that brings out all those nurturing feelings in everyone who meets him as well as in Claire and me, Bullet is also a perfect example of the uncompromised predator. Enhanced perhaps by having to fend for himself early in life and being taught the rudiments of hunting and killing small prey by his feral mother, Bullet has turned into a great black hunter, permanently dressed for dinner with his white bib! Though extremely gentle with anyone who handles him and always ready to purr and drool over them, Bullet is the scourge of all small living things in the garden and surrounding countryside. Like any other much loved pet, he is fed lashings of the best of cat food and all sorts of tasty titbits on top, but as usual, this does nothing to curb his serial-killer instincts which began almost from the first day that he was allowed back into the outside world that he had come from.

The sparrows of Surrey were no match for Bullet and despite living around lots of cats, they seemed totally unprepared for this London-derived model. Massacring up to half a dozen a day, Bullet soon moved on to pretty songbirds, then rodents and even the odd young rabbit from the fields opposite. But the prize of note from the first two years of his life spent in the hunting plains of Surrey was the cock pheasant he brought home in the dead of one spring night. I was awoken at three o'clock in the morning to the sound of an irregular clackclacking at the back door. Bullet usually brings his prey back to the garden and occasionally into the kitchen to share with his girls since we've moved to Wiltshire and Bean and Flirty Bottom have moved in to share his den.

The girls, despite running free outside, have yet to claim their first trophy even after well over a year of observing and following the masterly Bullet. Their hunting skills are still limited to the fine art of stalking and pouncing on flies, with even light bemused moths proving something of an excessive challenge, despite the cats' agile and athletic frames and well-toned musculature. They are unfortunately at something of a disadvantage due to their single thin coats causing them to feel the cold rather easily. Indeed, like Scribble, their winter or 'indoor' season seems to last from the end of September to the beginning of the following August in the all too summerless climate of England! And when finally we get our summer of two hot days in succession, it's usually too bright for their sensitive little eyes and though they go out to enjoy the warmth, they keep their eyes at a fine squint or completely shut, so totally missing any chances for stalking the birds cooling off at the edge of the duck pond! Perhaps their day will come yet when the predator in them will surface above the very kittenish and much-loved pet sides of their characters.

In the door of our Wiltshire home we have yet to install a cat flap, but we did have one in Surrey and this was what was making the clacking noise. With his bottom dangling inside and all four feet perched on the lip of the flap frame, Bullet was desperately trying to haul in his pheasant with a series of strong tugs. Each one sent the flap up and then down with a crash and it fell to me to pull the poor dead thing through lengthways for him instead of the sideways approach he was failing with! He gladly gave it up and I plucked it the next day and fed it to him, shared out with all the other beasts of the house. My good friend Russell Jones went on to draw a wonderful cartoon of Bullet sat outside the back door having placed a hugely antlered dead moose on the doorstep, with me looking over his kill and yelling indoors 'Now look what the little bastard has brought home!'

But a single pheasant in the over-exploited hunting grounds of Surrey was nothing compared to his achievements, if that is the word, in Wiltshire. On page 40 is a list of every species he has killed. It's a staggering account, though by no means atypical, as we shall see in the next chapter when we look closer at the hunting capabilities of the small wild cats and later at the domestic cat when it is a nurtured pet, or living rough as a stray or as an urban, rural or remote tropical island feral predator. As for Bullet, well, his hunting exploits are the distasteful price of being allowed to share the pleasant affectionate side of his character and we certainly go off him a bit when he kills such sweet little birds as robins, wrens, blue tits or nicer 'small and furries' such as pygmy shrews and dormice. However, he does earn himself some points for killing rats, especially when they're almost as big as he is and it demands no small amount of courage to take them on. Even a biologist like me finds it hard to rake up much sympathy for a dead rat, slaughtered unnecessarily at the instinctive whim of a well-fed pet cat, but I do wish he'd go and eat them away from the front door mat, and that he wouldn't eat the heads first and leave half-gutted rat corpses for me to step on in the morning when I let the dogs out!

What I hope this rather self-indulgent run through the story of the cats who have shared my life so far has shown is the enormous variety of feline characters, survival tactics, hunting abilities and degrees of self-reliance. Whether semi-wild or genuinely so, feral, exstray, house-raised moggy or pampered pedigree, the legacy of the cat's ancestry enables it to survive and take what it needs from life without the compromises of reduced choice, unless they themselves choose to reduce it. That high level of adaptability and refusal to compromise over the secret to survival, and the ability to locate and consume the next meal, will ensure that the cat will be on the planet for as long as any species. The contrasting ability to inspire protection, love, mutual friendship and the need to care and nurture in man, the most aggressive animal that the earth has ever produced, is just another facet of the success of their evolution. To learn more about the cat, we should look to the cat's ancestors and wild pedigree, at what Mother Nature produced in the cat before we introduced our emotions and demands and then study the results of our involvement, and this I will do in the ensuing chapters.

Stop Press (November 12, 1991) Bean has at last discovered her hunting skills and in the last day has brought in a live shrew, released in the bedroom but eventually captured and returned safely to the garden, and a common mouse, alas dead on arrival! Flirty Bottom, though a little bemused by her sister's change of heart, has been encouraged by her to share in the play with the corpse.

Bullet's Hit List

Mammals (thirteen species)
Brown rat
Grey squirrel
European mole
Rabbit
Common bat (pipistrelle)
Long-eared bat
Bank vole
Field vole
Common shrew
Pygmy shrew
Woodmouse
House mouse
Dormouse

Reptiles and Amphibians
Slow-worm
Common frog

Insects
Various!

Birds (twenty-three species)
Pheasant
Wood pigeon
Racing pigeon
Feral pigeon
Collared dove
Jackdaw
Blackbird
Song-thrush
Starling
Pied wagtail
House martin
Swallow
Robin
House sparrow
Tree sparrow
Dunnock
Greenfinch
Goldfinch
Chaffinch
Great tit
Blue tit
Coal tit
Wren

SECTION TWO

An Evolutionary Licence to Kill

2
The perfected design for a predator

'The smallest feline is a masterpiece' Leonardo da Vinci

There are thirty-seven recognised species of cat to be found around the world, divided into 235 or so sub-species, depending on whose classification you study. The cat, in all his forms, is the most highly specialised mammalian predator on the earth, indeed the whole design of the cat is geared around his specialisation as an obligate eater of meat and the need to capture his food.

Though the thirty-seven species vary enormously in size, from the lion of the African plains to the tiny Rusty Spotted Cat of the tropical rain forest of Sri Lanka, all are remarkably similar in design and physical attributes. They occupy a huge range of habitats and though they vary a little in their approach to hunting or raising young and in their social organisation, that variation is really only a reflection of the adaptability of their perfected design. As we have already seen with Bullet, the pet cat retains all the prowess his wild ancestry has endowed him with, despite his decision to share so many habitats with or around man. So this book would not be complete without a look at the basic blueprint of the cat and just how he is so highly evolved that, even in the form of a coiffeured Persian pet, he is still a top-of-the-food-chain predator and still easily capable of stalking and killing his natural prey.

Cat sense: Prey detection
Prey detection, of course, is what has most honed our cats' senses. That and the need to relate with the world at large, with other animals

both friend and foe, and to stay alive. While all mammals basically have five well-developed senses some species are better developed in certain respects than others. As a result, it is difficult for us as human beings with usually a good sense of sight, a medium-quality sense of hearing and poor sense of smell to comprehend exactly how a cat with good sight and, by comparison, extraordinary senses of hearing and smell, relates to the same world around us. We can understand the basics because we have roughly the same inputs, and can measure artificially what a cat sees or hears, but actually experiencing the cat's world is beyond us in the same way as our speech and language is to the cat. He can understand the basics of tone and a few words such as his name perhaps, but he cannot repeat them. The cat lives in a different world in many ways, a world crammed with noises and smells that simply go unnoticed by us.

This alone may account for the 'other worldliness' quality sometimes ascribed to cats. At times they seem to be just sitting and thinking, perhaps trying to process all that information, and it is this possibly that has lead to suggestions that cats may have a sixth sense and be capable of ESP. Extra-sensory perception ... 'extra' to us would be true in some respects, but not necessarily 'extra' as meaning beyond the physical world. This in turn may also help account for the allegations by cat-haters that cats are forever suspiciously plotting and scheming. In the Middle Ages, such suspicions and lack of understanding led to the belief that cats held associations with the devil and witchcraft, suggestions that in turn led to the wholesale persecution and cruel torture of cats throughout the period. Nowadays, though lack of understanding still causes many people to be suspicious of cats or even fearful of them, their rising popularity indicates an increasing admiration and appreciation of their view of life. There is now a growing acceptance that cats and many other animals are more advanced than us in terms of their perception of the world because their senses have evolved in a different manner to our own.

Seeing

'Who can believe that there is no soul behind those luminous eyes?'
Theophile Gautier

Most cats do hunt to some extent during the day if the opportunity arises or if certain types of prey are more available at particular times of year, such as during the spring in Europe when birds are nesting and they and their fledgling offspring are more vulnerable. Smaller cats are, however, usually nocturnal hunters or crepuscular, hunting at dawn or dusk. As they detect their prey mainly by sight, cats' eyes are relatively large with respect to head size or in comparison with the eyes of a predominantly daytime hunter. The elliptical pupil (our pupils are round) of the eye is large but notably alterable to allow maximum light in at low light levels (cover your cat's face for a few seconds and see how large the dark pupil area has become. The pupils of some pet cats can open to over a centimetre in diameter) and close up to a slit at higher light intensities (watch the dark area become a slit again after you have removed your hand). The eye also has a relatively large and curved lens to focus the image into the eye, an especially important adaptation in the reduced light of crepuscular or nightime hunting. The cat, like other predators, has forward facing eyes with a good depth of field to enable it to locate rodent prey which, as one might expect, are more likely to have eyes located on the side of the face to enable them to see the cat coming from more angles! The cat's field of vision in each eye is over 200 degrees and their binocular vision overlaps by ninety-eight per cent. They have the most highly developed stereoscopic vision apart from that of primates such as ourselves. In primates and the cat, signals from each eye go to both sides of the brain because some nerves cross over to the other side. This means that two overlapping fields of vision enable two 'fixes' to be made on an object on each side of the brain and so identify its position more accurately by seeing almost in three dimensions. Two-thirds of cat optic nerves cross over compared with about half of ours and this enhanced sense has proved vital for the cat in judging distance and depth of field at speed when on the move running, leaping and climbing and when gauging his stalking of prey.

A cat's eyesight is extremely well-developed for use at low light levels, and cats can see well enough to hunt in what to us is almost total darkness, but without compromising daytime vision. Cats' eyes are believed to be about six times more sensitive than ours due partly to the *tapetum lucidum*, a reflective layer of cells behind the retina, the light sensitive layer of cells at the back of the eye. The *tapetum* reflects light that has already passed through the retina back again across the light sensitive cells and so enables the eye to detect a clearer image. This is, of course, the reason why cats' eyes and those of many other animals reflect camera flashes and at night, headlights or torch beams so brightly. The cats' eyes in the road that guide our pathways when driving at night are aptly named!

There are two types of light-sensitive cell in the retina, named after their respective shapes. Rods function mainly at low light levels and do not detect the colour of the image, while cones react to higher light intensities and are colour sensitive. Cats' retinas consist mainly of rods on a ratio of twenty-five to one with cones compared with our four to one. Although there is a concentration of cones at the centre of the cat's eye, it is thought that they use mainly black and white vision. Although experiments have shown that cats can distinguish different colours, it is believed that their cones are used more to provide a good sense of vision in daylight when the rods are less functional. Most of the cones are green sensitive with few reactive to blue but even less respond to the longer red wavelengths of light. So your cat doesn't have complete colour vision on a par with yours, but probably has enough to distinguish the different coloured cans of his favourite food and pick out the one he wants, even if it is red.

Most importantly for the hunter, there is a central concentration of nerve cells which lead to the optic nerve. This concentration increases the cat's ability to detect movement along the ground and focus on one particular object while the surrounding field of vision remains less distinct. This accounts for the paradoxical behaviour of the cat which pursues the fast rolled ball of newspaper with pinpoint accuracy only nearly to crash into the chair! It's almost as if it's the whiskers encountering the chair that tell him to take quick avoiding action, usually by leaping vertically. Because the muscles that regulate the lens are rather weak, the cat cannot focus well on objects much closer than thirty inches and comes to rely on its other senses close up to its prey. The cat's vision is at its best between six and twenty feet when stalking small fast-moving prey on the ground and, in conjunction with extraordinarily quick reflexes, accounts for its speed and accuracy at chasing and pouncing on its hapless victims before they can dart to safety. The process has doubtless developed partially as a result of the freeze adopted by many rodents which suspect danger nearby. If the cat has already pinpointed a mouse and is about to pounce and it doesn't run, it will usually be too late for that mouse, but a perfect piece of judgement for the cat. One of the reasons that cats may waggle their bottoms just before a pounce is to alter slightly their view of a static mouse and 'fool' their movement sensitive eyes into rapid alternate reassessment of the mouse's position so enabling them to pinpoint it and gauge the final strike more accurately.

Like human babies, all kittens are born with blue eyes, though this often changes as they grow up into the range of colours we see in our pets from bright orange or yellow to vivid green and the odd-eyed Persians, with one blue and one orange eye. The colour arises from the iris around the pupil and is one of the most obviously appealing features of the hunter that we prize in our pets.

Hearing

A few cats, such as the serval and caracal, with their conspicuously large ears, prefer to use predominantly their sense of hearing when hunting. The hearing abilities of all cats are extremely acute so as to be able to detect the slightest sound of some tasty morsel making its way through the undergrowth. Though the hearing of the dog is famed, that of the cat is in fact superior, as would be logical in a usually solitary predator that depends on its own wits and senses to survive rather than on the group approach of a pack. The audible range of a cat ranges from 200 hertz (Hz), about the same as ours and the dog's at lower frequencies, right up to sixty-five kilohertz (KHz) and perhaps, in some species, even as far up as one hundred KHz which is audible to bats. Our ears hear little beyond about twenty KHz and dogs hear little beyond thirty-five KHz and it is reasonable to presume that the cat's sensitivity has evolved to detect the squeaks and very high-pitch noises made by rodents when moving and communicating with one another. In what to us is largely in the realm of ultrasonics, most rodents chatter away at around twenty to fifty KHz and so are easily detected by the cat. However, such sounds are usually of low intensity and only audible over a short range so the cat often moves through its hunting ground listening in order to detect and then capture enough prey, rather than standing still for long periods and hoping they may walk past. As well as hearing across a far greater range than us, they also hear sounds which are too faint for us to detect.

Cats can not only hear over ten octaves and distinguish between notes a mere tenth of a tone apart, they can also identify the source of a sound and pick one from another when two are close together far more efficiently than either man or dog. They can also determine the source of any particular sound more accurately and gauge its distance to help them co-ordinate the stalk and pounce. This can be done because the cat's external ears can be moved independently through over 180 degrees. Over twenty muscles enable the cat to orientate each ear to best effect towards the source of the sound and pinpoint that source from its two independent detectors working in co-operation with each other. The cat also has approximately twenty-five per cent more nerve fibres in its auditory nerve than we do and is better able to process this amount of auditory information through to the brain. It is interesting to observe deaf cats compensate through having to rely on other senses of sight and smell and even develop improved sensitivity to vibration via the feet. This is perhaps a crude form of replacement hearing because airborne sounds will be muted as they pass into the ground, but the cat, even if deaf, may be highly sensitive to vibrations.

Of course the hearing ability of all cats declines with age and, as with humans and older dogs, a degree of selective deafness creeps in to requests such as 'it's time to go outside' on colder evenings! Strange, isn't it, how a cat can hear the fridge door open when fast asleep in any room of the house but just doesn't hear such a reasonable request when you're standing next to him with the door wide open! But in the wild, outright deafness of a younger free-living cat would usually cause its death through its inability to detect prey or hear the approach of danger. So it's all the more pity that some people deliberately produce congenitally deaf cats, most notably blue-eyed white cats, in pursuit of selfish human values based simply on the appearance of the cat rather than the form and function arising from its beautiful evolution, of which hearing is such a vital part.

The inner ear is also responsible for the cat's sense of balance, another highly developed and remarkable feature. Fluid in closed canals flows past sensory hairs which tell the cat, via nerves to the brain, exactly how and where he is moving and how his position relates to the ground below. That famous self-righting mechanism of falling cats is not only facilitated by a flexible skeleton but also by this highly sensitive detection system.

Touching . . . skin, hair and whiskers

The whole body surface of the cat, like ours, is sensitive to touch but the long guard hairs, which stand slightly above the rest of the coat, are particularly sensitive. Movement of the hair tells the cat that it is in contact with the environment, either obviously and in conjunction with the nerves in the skin when it brushes through a bush or, more subtly, to detect direction of the wind against it so that it may orientate itself downwind if hunting in the open. But the sense of touch is most developed through the concentration of pressure receptors in the pads of the paws. Despite the need for protection of a thick leathery skin on the pads, the forepaws, like hands and fingers are to us, have evolved to be very important information gatherers for the cat. By patting unfamiliar objects cats can learn about their size, shape, texture and whether to proceed with firmer pawing or closer investigation with other senses, such as by smelling the objects.

But touch is more than a sense of pressure on the body. It also includes detection of heat, cold and pain and, unlike the senses of sight and hearing, the sense of touch is already well-developed at birth in the cat. Different nerve endings in the skin are sensitive to the four sensations, quickly passing the information to the brain to enable it to adjust the cat's position in the world. Once again, the environment experienced by the cat varies from our own in terms of sensitivity to heat. Cats are comparatively insensitive to heat, not showing any reaction to hot things such as lying next to fires until their body temperature reaches 52 degrees centigrade (126 degrees Fahrenheit) while we feel decidedly uncomfortable at 40 degrees centigrade (104 degrees Fahrenheit). This is because cats simply have fewer and perhaps less reactive heat-sensitive nerve endings in their skin, probably because they have evolved to let their fur protect and insulate them against temperature changes. Cats are however capable of detecting temperature differences of 0.5 degrees centigrade (3.3 degrees Fahrenheit) via the uncovered detectors in the thicker nose skin. This is an adaptation that has become specialised and concentrated, like most other senses, on the face, which encounters most new environments first for the cat and needs to pass the information quickly to the brain. This local improvement in heat detection has also evolved because heat is one of the determinants of recognition and palatability of food. Cats like their food to be at about the same temperature as their tongues, about 86 degrees Fahrenheit, which explains why cats don't like food straight from the fridge and why warming his food when your cat has lost his appetite due to illness can encourage him to eat.

One of the most notable and typically feline things on a cat's face is the whiskers, which are actually large stiff hairs with lots of nerve endings at the roots. When hunting, quite possibly in reduced light, the cat moves head-first into new places and while the eyes will be especially used to detect the movement at distance of any likely prey, the whiskers detect the proximity of any object close to the face. They enable the cat to blink to avoid any small objects between him and the goal or take quick avoiding action if confronted with larger challenge. The sense of touch concentrated in the whiskers enables the cat to make instant minor corrections leaving the eyes and ears to concentrate on the main job of prey detection or co-ordination of the strike. It is also quite probable that the relatively stiff mystacial whiskers on the side of the muzzle can detect small local vibrations in air currents and low frequency sound and perhaps, like the electrical field detection system in the face of the shark, help with the precision of the final lunge towards the prey from close quarters when the view of the victim may be obscured by the cat's nose. Indeed, these whiskers are projected forwards at the moment of strike and so must presumably help detect the prey and aim the bite. Certainly, cats with broken mystacial whiskers seem less able to direct that final killing bite so accurately and while cats with broken whiskers seem able to hunt as efficiently during the day because their eyes can compensate for the loss, they are far less successful when hunting at night. Perhaps this is why mother cats sometimes bite the whiskers off their kittens as they get older and more playful. It may be to make their exploratory play bites aimed at her tail and feet a little less accurate and give her a better chance of avoiding a painful nip!

Touch sensors at the base of the teeth may also help the cat fine-tune the aim of the final killing bite between the appropriate vertebrae of the neck of his victim rodents. As well as all these nerves from the oral touch sensors being routed through the same passage to the brain, information from the eyes and sensory tactile areas is co-ordinated in adjacent areas of the brain, adding further weight to the argument for a link between sight and touch during hunting. This is further evidence that the evolution of the cat as a hunting machine is extremely highly developed internally as well as externally.

There are several other bunches of whiskers on the cat's face as well as the mystacials: the one above the eyes is called the superciliary tuft and those at the side of the face behind the cheeks are known as the genal tufts. Unusually for a carnivore the cat has no inter-ramal tufts of whiskers under the chin. But there are a few whiskers on the inside of the front legs which probably help the cat to gauge exactly where to put his feet when stalking as silently as possible in undergrowth, while the rest of his senses are directed on the prey and he cannot look to exactly where his feet will land.

Smelling

In contrast to the highly developed eyes, ears and whiskers, the cat's nose is not so well-developed for any hunting purpose. Only the serval and leopard have been observed using their sense of smell to detect their prey, though larger cats such as the cheetah which need to suffocate larger prey in order to kill it, do have wider nasal passages to enable them to draw more breath, especially after a high energy chase. In the dog there are nearly twice as many cells in the nasal epithelium (skin lining the inner nose) which are receptive to scent, as there are in the cat. The area which processes that information in the brain of the dog, which tends more to hunt by scent, is also nearly double that found in the cat. Even so, it is estimated that while humans have only nine million olfactory nerve endings in the nose, cats have over 140 million in an area of three to six square inches, if all the folds are unravelled, which is twice as large as ours. As a result of having this larger and concentrated area of scent receptors cats live in a far more exotic world of smells than we do, which helps explain why they spend so much time sniffing and concentrating on smells of special interest in and outdoors, as well as around the food bowl.

Cats almost certainly use some input of airborne scent in detecting their prey, even if they do not usually appear to follow their noses when hunting. The cat smells the air with every breath, scanning it for the scents such as prey or enemies, rival cats or noxious substances, so that other senses may then be employed to investigate further at distance. The sense of smell may be re-employed once the cat is closer to the source, thus enabling it to plan its responses. Rapid sniffing is used to investigate concentrations of smell or the scent of objects of particular interest. The cat makes the most of any scent information by not exhaling air breathed in during rapid sniffing. Instead it is retained above a shelf-like structure in the nose to have more chance of coming into contact with the sensory cells of the nasal epithelium.

The newborn kitten has a well-developed sense of smell at birth presumably to enable it to detect its mother, locate a nipple for food and orientate itself towards the safe centre of the nest. The heat receptors in the skin of the nose will also assist these early crucial motions of survival when the senses of sight and hearing have still to develop. That sense of smell may be particularly sensitive to the scent of fat and oils secreted by the mother's coat and in her milk and once detected will naturally cause the kitten to feel contented and relaxed. While the older cat seems to be able to taste protein, he 'smells' fats rather than tastes them. He can readily distinguish one type from another, perhaps building on that early sensitivity to fats that will have determined his ability to locate mum and a suitable nipple quickly. This may explain why many pet food companies seek to serve that apparently discerning palate by providing such a huge variety of different flavours based on different inputs of rabbit, kidney, beef, turkey, etc. Perhaps the development of favourite flavours in some cats occurs not so much through any perceivable difference in taste but because the cat can readily distinguish the smell of one type of animal fat from another and comes to develop preferences because good tasting fats produce feelings of contentment and relaxation, or in dietary terms, satiation. This would be borne out by the fact that while most of the sensory input of smells leads to the cerebrum, the area of the brain responsible for organising sensory information, some impulses also lead to the ill-understood limbic area. The limbic area is where emotions evolve, so the smells of certain fats and oils in particular make cats feel good and hence ensure that they are attracted to them in their food.

This may explain the wide range of individual likes and dislikes of pet cats when they are relieved from the pressure of having to kill and eat whatever is available and are given prepared food on a plate. Some seem totally attached to just one brand or even one flavour, though few cats, as we know, will starve themselves to death in the presence of something edible. Our look at the highly variable diet of wild and feral cats around the world in later chapters will confirm that your pet cat is simply doing a good job of training you only to offer him one or two preferred types of food by huffily rejecting a different flavour of the same brand! In the wild, he would eat the lot, so perhaps a little persistence is required, especially if the cat has become hooked on consuming only one exclusive but inadequate food such as liver or fish.

But while the sense of smell may become less crucial for the cat hunting to feed itself as it grows older, it plays an increasingly important role in communication. The adult cat uses its sense of smell to relate to its own kind in pursuit of mates, to recognise feline and perhaps non-feline enemies and to define his relations with us, his human companions. The development of a communal scent in the home incorporates scent elements of the cat, his owners, the family dog, other cats and the scent of inanimate objects such as carpets and paint on doors. This facilitates quick recognition of friends and identification of foes or new arrivals and many of those scents will contain those longer lasting fatty residues which are so discernible to the cat. It's one of the reasons why it's important to incorporate the scent of any new creatures, such as babies or a new cat, into the existing cat's scent perceptions of home as soon as possible. This can sometimes mean crudely running our gloved hands through the new cat's litter tray and then grooming the existing cat and vice versa so that they each carry elements of the other's scent and map it into the communal scent as they rush off to wash themselves afterwards. Understandably that can all be a bit too much for some owners who are trying to improve the recognition and acceptance of a new cat to a household when there has been a problem with an existing cat. Thankfully, brushing and stroking the essence of catnip on to both cats so that they both encounter a pleasant and acceptable smell on each other when they meet has proved equally successful for those cats which are sensitive to catnip. The sensitivity appears to be genetically determined, so where one or other cat is not sensitive, it's back to the gloves and used litter trays!

We tend to overlook just how important scent and communal scent must be to our cats, despite the fact that they spend so much time reinforcing the communal smell on their own bodies through scent-exchanging rubbing of us, the dog and the furniture. To the cat, we must sometimes appear like people who consistently fail to answer our letters, when we pay so little attention to the world of scent. It's not our fault, we just can't smell what they're on about! We usually get away with a successful scent relationship because we like to pet our cats physically and they enjoy it. Touching and mutual grooming are of course key elements in the maintenance of friendly relations between friends, feline or human, but few of us ever think of approaching our cats to exchange a smell or two! We happen to do it anyway in pursuit of a cuddle, and the cat is more relaxed and comfortable in the shared smell of our company as a result.

The importance of scent may become all too apparent when the cat decides to use super-scent applications to communicate in the home. When treating problems of cats spraying urine indoors in my practice, one of the first things I always try to do is impress on the owners just how important scent is to the cat, comparing it with the importance of sight to we ill-refined humans, who can barely distinguish between an apple and an onion unless they are stuffed up our noses. Spraying scent around can make a cat feel more at home and in dentify new or significant objects in his patch. Some cats are more bizarre than others in this respect. Probably the most unusual indoor sprayer that I have been asked to treat in recent years was Nelson (name changed for political expediency!) from south London. Nelson chose only to spray a picture of Tsar Nicholas II and Tsarina Alix hanging on the wall halfway up the stairs. To achieve this he had to go up on to the landing above and, poking his rear end through the balustrade, squirt his presumably left-wing comment at them, hitting them usually squarely on their royal faces. Quite why Nelson singled out this particular picture might be clearly political in human terms, but how to explain it from the cat's point of view is rather difficult. Perhaps it carried an age-old message from another cat in times past who sprayed it while it was on the floor. Or perhaps Nelson was just the reincarnated cat that belonged to another Tsar, Nicholas I. Vashka was a blue cat who was probably the most pampered cat of all time, allegedly having been fed on caviar poached in champagne. Perhaps in his new life as Nelson, Vashka was simply harking back to past glories and identifying his association with royalty with a bit of name dropping feline style.

It always strikes me as amusing that one of the original bases of many perfumes is a musk-like scent extract from the testes and associated glands of civets. Lord knows what scent messages highly perfumed people must be giving off to cats by the time the manufacturers have added lemon, rose and other more heady fragrances, even if the scent is supposed to help attract the attentions of a potential human mate. We may be fooled but I supect that many cats must be highly confused!

Tasting

The senses of smell and taste are closely linked. Taste-buds on the tongue are of little use in detection and capture of prey but enable the cat to detect and recognise substances which dissolve in water or saliva once they have their teeth into their victims. Taste-buds are only found at the front and side edges of the tongue and at the back, not on the rasping, backward-pointing papillae in the centre which are specialised for prey handling and grooming. While the cat's sense of taste is unusual in that most show no response to sweetness, they do respond to salt, bitter and acid tastes and are very sensitive to the taste of water which may account for the sometimes bizarre individual preferences of some cats for certain types of water, such as filthy muddy puddles rather than fresh clean but chlorinated supplies put out for them by their owners. Contrastingly few people can discern variations in taste between different clean fresh waters, and the ability is probably as frequently found as those with the refined sense of taste or 'nose' of a true wine taster. People like me who simply drink the stuff and have little understanding of their experiences when tasting the 'flowery bouquet' of a 1986 compared with the 'lavish fruity succulence' of a 1975 claret, thank the Lord that the water-sellers have restricted themselves to images of fresh mountain streams and pure spas so far. 'Neau' water has yet been described as 'an eloquent little quaff' with a price to match! I suspect that if that ever happens, we should all look to our cats to tell us which waters really are drinkable!

A cat's meat diet is high in protein which can be tasted and strongly influences palatability and thus food choices. Fats, which, as we have discussed, tend to be smelled rather than tasted, also greatly affect a cat's feeding preferences and both points are well researched by pet food company nutritionists. While nutritionists and physiologists also tell us that cats show little ability to detect or show preference for sweet-tasting food, one of my Siamese sisters, Flirty Bottom, would maim, kill and mutilate anyone who tried to stop her from pursuing her right to lick a pudding bowl clean! While the cat's taste for cream may be dictated by sensations other than sweetness, Flirty Bottom is just as persistent about jelly, blancmange, trifle and chocolate, yet her sister and the affable Bullet have no sweet tooth at all.

As we have already seen, temperature affects a cat's overall sense of taste especially in relation to the aromas given off by warm food, but the sense of taste is not markedly better in the cat than in other mammals and, unlike the other senses, shows no specific adaptation to help the cat hunt or survive. The combination of taste and smell may, however, play some role in the detection of prey and in the communication between one cat and another by scent. Like dogs and horses, cats possess a sense that is midway between smell and taste which allows them to concentrate smells in a special structure known as the vomeronasal or Jacobson's organ, found above the palate in the roof of the mouth. To direct the scent-laden air over this half-inch long organ, the cat grimaces in a bizarre-looking manner known as a 'flehmen' reaction with its neck stretched forward and its top lip curled up in a snarl. Air may be drawn in in a series of short gasps and the tongue flicks back and forth over the two small openings behind the front teeth to the vomeronasal organ to dissolve the scent and direct it in. However, the flehmen response is seen mostly in response to the detection of scent left by other cats at spray posts or on faeces, rather than in cats 'scent-tasting' the smell of prey on the wind, though receptors in this organ do connect to areas of the brain concerned with the initiation of aggression and appetite as well as sexual responses. Flehmen is mainly performed by male cats and is particularly marked when they investigate the rear end of a queen in season or encounter her urine mark. It has been found, like so many other 'male' reactions, to develop in response to the presence of testosterone, though it continues less frequently as a learned response in neutered males. The vomeronasal organ is little understood simply because we do not possess it, though non-functioning vestiges of it can be identified, but we can only guess at what the information it obtains means to the cat.

ESP or a question of touch?

'While rain depends, the pensive cat gives o'er
Her frolics and pursues her tail no more'　　　　　　Jonathan Swift

From the previous descriptions of the cat's senses, it is clear that our pet cats exist in a super-sensory world in many ways compared with ours. The anatomy and function of their eyes, nose, ears and tactile receptors are all highly specialised, very sensitive in most areas across ranges well beyond our own and have been maximised for efficiency, for example with the reflective tapetum of the eye and convoluted nasal epithelium. It's not surprising that we view our cats as sensitive creatures who seem to miss nothing that goes on around them.

　　　As we have seen, the whole body of the cat is sensitive to vibration to some degree, but it is thought that the cat's paws are especially competent in this respect. This may help explain why cats are reported to be able to predict the imminence of certain types of earthquakes. They can simply feel the pre-shock tremors, detect the sudden local fluctuations in the earth's magnetic field or sense the atmospheric changes that we miss. We can only measure such changes with complicated machinery specially built to be far more sensitive to vibration, atmospheric content and magnetic field than our own senses can ever be. Positively charged ions are released into the air prior to some earthquakes and it is highly likely that cats could detect a change in atmospheric static electricity through the reaction of their fur. Dr Ernst Kilian of Chile, who has made a thirty-year study of animals and earthquakes, believes that pre-shock tremors may follow a specific vibration pattern which the cat can discern above the usual vibrations in the ground. However, that would almost certainly require the cat to have previous experience of those vibrations and the subsequent quake to know what was coming next time. But for sure, there are well-documented incidences of entire villagefuls of cats taking to the hills, mother cats moving their kittens to safety and normally placid pets scrabbling in a panic to be let out a few hours before earthquakes have struck. In 1975 in the Chinese city of Haicheng, cats and other animals were one day noticed as behaving very oddly and a full evacuation of the city was ordered. A day later a huge earthquake struck causing massive damage. Thousands of human lives were saved as a result, but it isn't known if anyone remembered to take the seismographic cats out of the danger zone in time as well!

The ability of cats to predict weather changes is usually recorded by owners who have observed their cat's reluctance to go out when it is about to rain or taking shelter in a secluded resting place prior to a storm. Owners also report their cats taking up a relaxed snoozing position in a favoured sunspot prior to the arrival of fine weather. The weather forecaster in our cats is almost certainly due to their refined ability to detect atmospheric pressure changes through their very sensitive inner ear, the organ of balance detection that keeps cats so assuredly on their feet and helps them land on them after falls great and small. Such sensitivity may explain why cats rub and wash their ears vigorously before a storm, another type of feline behaviour often referred to as a portent for impending bad weather. The cat's highly sensitive nasal epithelium and ability to taste water will also certainly help him detect humidity and approaching changes in weather and so plan his day accordingly.

Sensitivity to vibration can also perhaps account for the cat's homing ability. One of the problems that owners frequently call me about is how to stop their cat from continually returning to their old home after they have moved. The problem is most common when the owners have only moved a short distance away from their old home and the cat, even after being kept indoors at the new home for a few days to acclimatise, continues to encounter old walkways when he is allowed to go out again. He simply follows the old routes home, even though he may have come from a different direction. While the first step in such cases is to make sure that the new owners of the old house don't encourage him by letting him in or feeding and fussing over him, many such cats are so persistent that they end up being given to the new owners as a subsequent part of the home purchase deal. Cats may be creatures of habit with regard to their bonding to territory, and while most can move happily with their owners to a new home even a short distance away, others insultingly prefer the old home, even if the new owners are downright nasty to them. Perhaps the reason for the perpetual return is beyond the cat's control. He simply has a map in his head, not only of the visual and scent aspects of his old territory but of the 'feel' under his feet. Place him anywhere on established routes and he simply follows the map to the old home.

Perhaps this 'feel' mapping sense may also account for those extraordinary cats who travel miles and miles to the old home from faraway places where there is absolutely no prospect of them ever having encountered previously used territorial walkways. This is referred to as 'Type 1' homing by David Greene in his interesting book *Incredible Cats*, published in 1984. According to Greene, the distance record for Type 1 homing was achieved by a cat called Rusty who walked 950 miles home from Boston to Chicago to be reunited with his owner. Another good effort came from a Russian cat called Murka. She was banished from her home in Moscow to Voronezh, 400 miles away, for the 'crime' of eating her owners' two canaries. Some time later, she turned up back at her Moscow home, dirty, pregnant and tatty . . . but home!

Cats navigate, it is usually thought, in Type 1 homing, using homing instincts similar to those used by homing pigeons and migrating birds and mammals, such as many species of whale. This could be regarded as an extra sense, which we lack, and so we have designed a map and compass, and more latterly satellite navigation aids, to compensate. The ability to navigate may occur in some creatures through an ability to map accurate views of sunlight and the spread of the spectrum to an internal compass which is sensitive to the earth's magnetic field. Certainly in some experiments, attaching a magnet to a cat's collar seems to disrupt his homing ability. But perhaps accurate journey making, self-orientation and mapping can also occur through a fine sense of vibration. The cat is simply extremely sensitive to vibrations and can navigate by them exclusively, or use the sense in conjunction with his sense of smell and other unidentified navigational senses to pick a route to where he wants to be, on his familiar patch.

So the old wives' tale about smearing the cat's feet with butter when you move home so that he comes back to the new home when he's let out rather than shooting straight back to the old one may have some truth in it. We used to think that it may work by giving the cat a scent trail to follow back but this never seemed quite reasonable as the cat would still be able to detect its old scent on any old pathways it encountered. Perhaps the real explanation is that the butter insulates the cat's paws and scrambles the vibration map. As the butter wears off, the cat steadily maps its new vibration routes and recognises the position of the new home. It's all fancy conjecture of course, but just goes to show how differently our cats and ourselves experience, view and find our way around the same physical world.

But what of well-documented tales such as that of Pooh who, in four months, walked 200 miles from his old home in Georgia to his owners' new home in South Carolina, never having been there in his life? How can one explain the case cited by David Greene of a kitten called Pitchou who followed his recently departed owner to the military barracks in Strasbourg, seventy-five miles away across the Vosges mountains? This is known as Type 2 homing and defies explanation according to known science, or even the development of reasonable theories, as with Type 1 homing. Could Pooh and Pitchou, and all the many other documented cases of cats finding their owners after travelling vast distances to places they'd never been to, really have been following up a scent gradient or are they just billion-to-one coincidences? That cats will follow owners for long distances and across rough terrain is not in doubt when they can see them. Many cats are happy to follow their owners out of the front gate and along dangerous roads into uncharted territory unless deterred or kept in by other members of the family. In 1950, one four-month-old kitten even followed a climbing expedition to the summit of the 14,690-foot

Matterhorn, but these incidents are no more than one might expect from some cats who are closely bonded to their owners or to people in general and perhaps see them as leading mother figures that will help protect them. It's a very different type of recognition to heading for previously departed owners with no clues to their whereabouts as far as human sensory awarenesss goes, and finding them.

Of course, it's a great temptation to ascribe supernatural powers to such a cool, enigmatic creature that seems nearly always to be so confident and self-assured, especially when the escapades of cats such as Pooh and Pitchou are reported and substantiated. But the vast, vast majority of cats would not be able to emulate Pooh's feats. So, for me, the knowledge that a cat's senses are so finely developed already means that he lives in a much more refined and extensive sensory world compared with ours, and particularly sensitive individuals may stand out in the feline world as the wine-taster's nose does in our more limited one. It's no wonder that the cat looks so at ease and in control with all that information coming in. It's also no surprise that we should sometimes feel so outclassed by the cat as to believe that he must have even greater powers of perception than those provided by his senses, and perhaps through communication with higher forms of life. A sixth sense? I think not, just five extraordinarily well-developed ones!

3
Catanatomy

'. . . and unneth is hurt when he is thrown down off an high place'
                                    Bartholemeus Anglicus (c. 1260)

Coat and skin: camouflage and protection

The beautiful fur of many cats has been one of the major reasons for
their persecution by man. Thankfully in many Western cultures the
wearing of clothes made of animal furs and skins is now definitely
regarded as socially unacceptable, and not before time. Alas, even as
close to home as Germany and Austria the wearing of fur is still
regarded as some sort of luxurious tribal status symbol. As the poster
of the animal protection group, Lynx, said: 'It takes twenty dumb
animals to make this coat, but only one to wear it', and never could this
be more true from the human dumbness point of view than when
someone tries to flaunt themselves in the coat of a large cat.

The cat's coat is designed to keep the cat warm in the cold and
cool in the heat. Different cats in different environments therefore
have varying lengths of coat and may shed a thicker winter covering
for a cooler one in summer. There may be up to 130,000 hairs per
square inch in a cat's coat but the variable length and the beautiful
array of stripes, spots and blotches to be found across the family has
arisen as a result of the need to be concealed in the natural environment
and approach prey as close as possible without being detected. It is a
highly evolved camouflage that merges each cat into its background,
be it the spots of the jaguar or margay in varied thick forest vegetation,

60

or the plainer lighter colour of the Sand Cat in the desert or of the lion in the brown grassland. Though startlingly beautiful to us when displayed on some poor specimen in the zoo, the stripes of the tiger are one of the keys to successful hunting in the tall native grassland of India. And like the tiger hunting in the long grass in the orange light of a real Indian summer evening, the jaguar's blotched coat is perfectly matched in the forests to blend him not only into the plant background but also in with the shafts and spots of light that percolate irregularly through the vegetation.

There are various theories as to how the different patterns of cats' fur have evolved and this is now of particular interest to the owners, showers and breeders of pet cats. The genes that code for colour and pattern are some of the few that man has been able to manipulate in the otherwise genetically intransigent cat. The basic coat colour of the small wild cat species around the world and of many other wild animals such as mice and rabbits is known as agouti, a brownish brindle which arises from each hair having bands of differing colours from black to brown through sandy to grey. Variations abound, from the light sandy-coloured cats of the desert to the more pronounced tabby markings of the Scottish Wild Cat. Rural feral cats are often found with agouti or tabby coats as these are favoured to help them merge into their background. Brown tabby markings actually occur because parts of the coat are devoid of the pale sections of each hair and so appear as black stripes against the brindle colour and similar striped variations in coat colour gave rise to the beautiful Silver Tabby and the darker ginger stripes against the orange fur of the Red Tabby. Uniformly coloured hairs are common in domesticated animals with different colours appearing often in blotches as in Friesian cattle.

With cats, certain urbanised moths and many other species living in dark habitats, uniformly black colouring can become established by a selection process that favours dark forms. The development of dark forms is known as melanism and in cats is caused by the selection of a normally recessive gene, so it can even occur occasionally spontaneously in animals such as lions where there is no advantage in their environment to being black. Black leopards, bobcats and servals have been recorded, but the black cat is most noticeable in urban populations of feral cats, where merging into the shadows of a concrete built-up environment is one of the keys to survival. But black cats occur also when the non-agouti colouring occurs on all hairs. However, the cat may still carry the tabby genes and sometimes, when the light falls at certain angles on the coat, the tabby pattern can be seen to beautiful effect, especially on a large black leopard or streetwise black feral tom.

Most cats have a coarse top coat comprising tough guard hairs with twenty-five times more densely packed shorter secondary hairs forming the soft undercoat. The exceptions are usually the ones without a top coat that we have engineered, such as many of the Oriental breeds of pet cat, or, in my mind, disgracefully, the near hairless varieties such as the Sphynx cat. The guard hairs are primarily to provide a sense of touch – with some waterproofing and temperature regulation function – through being erectile. The cat, of course, also erects these hairs when defensive or alarmed to give his enemies the impression that he is larger than in reality. The tail is especially pronounced at such times with its bottlebrush appearance. The undercoat acts as the main insulator and can be fluffed out in cold weather to trap a layer of warm air next to the skin.

Cats must spend a long time grooming to keep their coat layered and effective as a thermoregulator, and though this is primarily achieved with the spiky tongue combing its way through to align the fur, the hairs themselves are covered with a scaly outer layer which helps keep them interlocked.

The cat's skin is thin at about 1/64 inch on the stomach though thicker around the neck (1/12 inch) where delicate musculature and blood vessels need protection and male cats tend to grasp females with their teeth during mating. Cats have fewer sweat glands than we do in their skin, hence the increased importance of the good upkeep of the coat and the application of saliva which evaporates to cool the cat in hot weather. In man the apocrine sweat glands release sweat to cool us as required but, in the cat, they are employed mainly to produce scent and so have more of a communicatory function than a thermoregulatory one. The apocrine glands are concentrated in areas that are investigated by other cats such as at the base of the tail or, for example, under the chin, which the cat uses to mark his living area. Eccrine sweat glands which produce watery sweat are only found on a cat's footpads and release sweat when the cat is hot, or when frightened. The cat relies far more heavily on his coat, application of saliva and sensible behaviour in cool places in hot weather to keep his temperature regulated though in extremely hot conditions cats may also pant like a dog to cool off blood passing through vessels in the mouth through the evaporation of saliva. In cold weather of course, there is no greater exponent of the the the art of finding warm spots and staying in them all day than the cat!

Skeleton and movement

A glance at the skeleton of the cat or even a closer study of the live cat reveals the vital suppleness of the body and flexibilty of the skeleton. The speed of all cats in hunting is facilitated by a skeleton that allows that controlled quiet stalk with occasional sprints and then the extremely rapid, explosive final chase and pounce or grab. Working upwards from the feet, cats differ from us in that they walk on their toes and so can run fast from a standing start. The foot and ankle bones are arranged so that the cat only walks on what, in our foot, is the section in front of the ball. The cat's knee, ankle and foot cannot move sideways, a sacrifice of manoeuvrability for the benefits of rapid acceleration from a standing start, and high speed. The leverage for the push-off and run comes from the relatively long lower parts of the legs compared with the upper parts and, as only a small area of the foot touches the ground when running, there is less resistance and the leg can be brought up quickly into the next stride.

With animals built for strength rather than speed it is the upper bones of the limbs which are longer. The length of the cat's stride is increased still further by the ability to flex and extend its spine when running, a feature of particular note in the fastest animal on earth over a short distance, the cheetah. One scientist has even measured this and found that, at fifty-six kilometres per hour, the cheetah has a stride length of just under seven metres (twenty-three feet) with an astonishing eleven per cent of this due to the extension and flexing of the spine. At full speed, cats move in a series of long half-bounds propelled by the back legs and balanced and propelled a little by the front ones. All this means that while the cat can reach extremely fast speeds, the muscles tire quickly from the massive amount of energy used and so hunting occurs in short explosive bursts. Cats give up if they don't succeed in capturing their prey quickly in chase rather than trying to run it down over a sustained period.

The absence of the collar-bone means that the shoulder joints and forelimbs of the cat can extend further, though the muscles around the shoulder-blade and its shape vary depending on the cat's lifestyle. A back and forth arrangement and a longer shoulder for the cheetah allow it to hunt by running its prey down in short bursts, and a shorter stronger model is suited to the leopard, which spends much time in the trees and needs strength to haul the prey, captured on the woodland floor, into the safety of the branches above.

Cats can alter their body shape into a huge range of postures from a tight curl when sleeping to a long stretch in running or hunting. This is all due to the stretchable and flexible spine. The vertebrae are also extremely flexible in rotation to allow sharp turns and changes of direction and wrestling of larger prey by the big cats. The spine can rotate the forequarters through 180 degrees relative to the hind quarters and, in the pet, that rotational flexibility is best demonstrated by the self-righting reflex of a falling cat that always enables it to land on its feet. This is also another advantage of balance for those cats which climb.

Cats are reported frequently in modern cities as surviving enormous falls from skyscraper apartment blocks. In New York, ninety per cent of falling cats survive impacts that would certainly kill a man or child, and some are barely even injured. This is because when falling, the cat rotates its body and offers maximum wind resistance and drag on the way down, like a parachute. Even so, they still hit the deck with an enormous force, dampened by the elasticity and design of their skeleton, particularly in the feet and legs. The tail too can be twisted and stiffened to help with balance in all movement, including free-falls, through the nineteen to twenty-eight small articulating vertebrae.

These special landing qualities of the cat may have proved most useful in Ypres, in Belgium, in the famous live cat throwing ceremony that was held annually for 800 years until the last century. Cats that were thrown off a 200-foot-high tower down into the main square below usually survived and ran away quickly to the excitement of the crowds. It was an exercise begun in the year 962 to demonstrate that cat worshipping had ceased in the town. Though the spectacle is still enacted, live cats were not used after 1817 and toy cats are used in the more compassionate and less superstitious twentieth century.

For the sake of speed, the ankle joint of the cat's leg looks like a human knee in reverse and stability in running is given by a close arrangement of the bones of the paws. When we or dogs run, we use the extension of our legs to enable our feet to contact with the ground and push off for the next stride, with some unavoidable loss of momentum from the contact. The cat, by contrast, and with a complementarily designed shoulder, fully extends its forelimbs and then brings them down and back before the feet touch the ground so minimising any reduction in momentum. The strength behind the stride is maintained by the arching of the spine and push from the rear legs, which, because of the amazing flexibility of the spine, do not check the action of the forelegs much when the cat is running.

But once the prey is caught many of the larger cats also need to be extremely strong to be able to wrestle it to the ground, especially when it is heavier and larger than they are. Hence even the larger small cat species, such as the bobcat, are enormously strong. I well remember the grip around my neck of a 'tame-ish' bobcat that I was holding on a visit to the Cat Survival Trust in Hertfordshire. The power of his forelimbs was immense and when, affectionately, he decided to hold me in place to give me a little nip on the cheek, there was absolutely nothing I could do to move my face out of the way or detach his grip without help. While pet cats can also be strong, most of their hold seems to be mediated through their grip with their claws and paws, but the bobcat's strength seemed to come purely from his forequarters and forelimbs. Had I been a tasty prey item, or even a female bobcat, I suspect that escape would not have been possible!

Cats can jump in many ways, both to suit requirements in climbing and reaching high vantage points and in the final pounce to capture their prey. They can jump more than five times their own height through a prepared vertical spring, surprise backwards leap, or forwards leap when making a fast escape from a threat such as a dog in hot pursuit. They can also perform a semi-vertical semi-forward hunting pounce that gives their prey little time to escape, the power for which comes from the compression of that flexible spine and muscular tension in those strong rear legs exploding from the crouch and launching the cat into the air. Climbing is a combination of upwards thrusting from the back legs and use of the claws in the front paws as crampons, usually after an initial leap up the tree to get a good start and build up some momentum. But cats get stuck up trees, especially when experimenting as kittens, because descent is more difficult with backwards pointing crampons and no support from the back legs. So, if they get too high up to jump down, they either stay up the tree until someone comes with a ladder (at which point they usually take fright and run further up the tree, needing the fire brigade to retrieve them from the top) or slide down ungracefully and leap off at the last moment to avoid banging their face on the ground!

Claws

The claws of the cat are surely the most representative symbols of the feline physique and character and hence were chosen as the title of this book. The main weaponry of the cat is ever-ready, sharp and instantly releasable to enable the cat to grip and climb or, more devastatingly, to grab and hold prey. Yet these deadly sharp weapons are held in, apparently harmless in everyday life. Each claw is hidden and attached to the side of its toe by a ligament and held in a protective sheath.

Strangely, in the dog-eat-dog world of the African plains, the claws of the fastest cat, the cheetah, are not very retractable, being used more as running spikes than weapons at the kill. A dog's claws are not retractable and are used for balance in running down their prey, a strategy also adopted by the cheetah, hence its more dog-like claws. But in most cats, the claws are kept latent in their bunkers, ready to be propelled forwards out of the sheath and across on to the front of the toe by individual flexor muscles. The tension in the muscles of the paw during a strike also flattens and aligns the bones of the paw into a more rigid formation for the claws to pivot against.

The main claws used in gripping and holding prey are the four on each forepaw. The fifth, which is a dew-claw, is usually only used if it comes into contact with the moving body of small prey in the process of immobilisation, or when the cat is dealing with larger victims. Its main function seems to be more as a side grapple when the cat is climbing. The four claws on each back paw are only employed if the cat is tackling even larger prey, or in a fight with another cat, when they are used for making kicking more deadly. A cat can inflict severe injuries to a struggling large rabbit or another cat using the claws on each back paw to deliver rapid alternating slicing kicks to the the soft stomach area.

The whole body of the cat and the claws are supported on the damper system of the pads on the base of the paws. The pads enable the cat to move silently when stalking his prey and, though soft and spongy, the skin on the surface is tough and relatively thick at 1/20 inch. It becomes hardened through use to give protection when walking on rough surfaces and provide good grip on slippery ones. The cat also uses his paws to test the temperature, texture, size and shape of unfamiliar objects so, despite their adaptation for walking and killing, they remain highly sensitive to touch. It's very interesting to compare the waxy soft pads of a permanently indoor cat who lives his

66

life on carpets with the very different hardened and often cracked pads of the cat who spends his days in the undergrowth and his nights on the tiles. Remember to check for any abrasions after allowing young cats, or older cats which have never been out before, into the garden for the first time. While the larger heavier cats or urban feral cats often have hardened paw pads through use on rough surfaces, others are protected from harsher environments. Some have fur all round the feet to protect the pads against extremes of cold, such as the Canadian Lynx in the frozen Arctic Circle. The Sand Cat's furry feet protect it against the heat and spread the load on the paws in the unstable sands of the Sahara.

Interestingly some cats are polydactyl, having up to ten extra non-functional toes, usually situated above the actual paw around the dew-claw. Polydactylism certainly seems to be an inherited feature as there have been several reports of whole groups of feral cats, which are known to be closely related, having extra toes and claws. The genes for extra toes seem particularly prevalent in Boston, Massachusetts where fifteen per cent of cats are polydactyl, according to biologists Michael Konecny and Barbara Sleeper, and so one might presume that the mutation arose there. The claws of these extra toes are non-retractable and the toes are not directable but they must make the paw look like a vast inescapable net of talons to any mouse that strays near.

Like a prized sword, the claws must all be kept in good condition and ready for use, hence cats scratch their claws on rough surfaces such as on the bark of trees or fenceposts. More annoyingly, many pet cats use the three-piece suite or areas of carpet in the house. In scratching, it is not the point of the claw that is sharpened, rather the whole outer layer of the claw is shed to expose a new claw surface with a new sharp point underneath. If you check on your cat's favourite scratch post, be it a tree in the garden or one that you have bought for him to use indoors, you can often find discarded outer layers of claw embedded in the surface.

On the subject of scratching areas for cats, I always find it amusing that so many manufacturers market posts made from carpet. This surely only teaches the cat to enjoy using carpet and to become more widespread in his choice of scratching posts of other and perhaps more valuable carpets around the house, which rather defeats the purpose! Better to play safe and provide your cat with a string wrapped pole or genuine tree bark on which to keep his weapons in trim.

Head, teeth and tongue

The cat's head is also perfectly evolved for the predatory lifestyle. The jaws are short and (relative to many other carnivores) they have a short muscle to close the jaws and so have a powerful bite in gripping or chewing their prey. The skull also has built-up bone arches for those strong jaw muscles to pivot against. The shorter jaw means that the cat has fewer teeth than many predators, having twenty-eight or thirty compared with the forty-two, for example, of the closely related civet. Along the jaws are lined the impressive teeth of a killer. Most apparent, and particularly renowned in that famous extinct cat the sabre-toothed tiger, are the canine teeth. It is interesting to note that the canines are stronger and more impressive in the cat than the dog, from which they took their name. Longer than all the other teeth, the canines are used by larger cats to grip their larger quarry and enable them to suffocate them to death. There is a gap behind these killing teeth to allow them to sink even deeper into the victim. In smaller cats feeding mainly on a diet of small rodents the canines are used to penetrate the skin and dislocate the neck vertebrae in classic nape bite style. The blade-like edges of the carnassial teeth midway along the sides of the jaws are specialised for slicing through skin and muscle with the fourth upper premolar and first lower molar being particularly sharp. These teeth are easily found if you run your fingers along the the jaw of any pet, though go carefully! There is also a ridge or notch on the carnassials to help hold the flesh while it is sliced up, and if you've ever wondered why, for once, cats seem to be rather awkward when chewing with those teeth, it's because they can only chew with one side at a time and so it helps to angle the head to keep bulkier or tougher food in the right place on the chosen side. The smaller incisors at the front of the mouth are used for pulling fur and feathers from the dead prey.

The cat's tongue is famous for its roughness and abrasive feel, even when the cat licks us in affection. The roughness is caused by backward-pointing spikes which help grip and break up the food and then transport it to the back of the mouth for swallowing. These spikes also help the cat pick up softer food and to lap water or milk, which is further aided by the cat's ability to form a small cup-like depression in its tongue and 'spoon' up the liquid. The spikes on the tongue also act as a very effective flexible comb for use in grooming, enabling the cat to keep the coat clean by removing dust, scurf and parasites, layer its coat as an insulator and evenly spread waterproofing oils produced by the skin. Loose dead hair is removed most efficiently by the tongue so the cat retains not only a marvellously sleek shiny appearance, but also a streamlined form of reduced wind resistance ideal for quick silent movement in stalking their prey.

Digestive system

As well as having the outward appearance and design of a hunter, the cat's digestive system is also totally geared towards processing a meat diet. Though cats may also consume some vegetable matter, this is generally thought to have other more mechanical purposes, such as enabling easier vomiting of parasitic worms or assisting in the grinding up of meat and gristle which may be otherwise slow to digest. Cats simply cannot sustain themselves on an entirely vegetable diet, and there are even certain essential amino acids, the building blocks of protein, which the cat's body cannot produce for itself and which must be obtained from the flesh of other animals . . . hence the fraudulent nature of any pet food company that tries to appeal to our increasing emphasis on vegetarianism by marketing solely vegetarian diets for cats. Cats have shorter digestive systems than other predators because they tend to feed on more easily digestible meat, though it is believed that the system is less efficient as a result, even though there may be advantages in streamlining and weight reduction from having less of a digestive system to carry about. Pet cats and lions vary little in their efficiency at energy conversion of their prey at about eighty per cent but this is about ten per cent less efficient than the scavenging omnivorous dog or the exclusively scavenging vulture. The implication is that like sports cars, cats can perform faster but need constant refilling with higher quality fuel. The fuel is burnt less effectively to achieve that high performance compared with the average family get-you-there car which burns fuel more efficiently and will cruise all day, but won't ever find the power to overtake going up a hill.

4
The hunting cat

'In the dark, all cats are grey' Proverb

Hunting is essentially a simple response of controlled, targeted predatory aggression on to a moving target, a response that is expressed because of a strongly motivated inborn urge and then refined through acquired hunting skills. These skills are based on early learning when a mother cat will bring home half-dead victims for her kittens to play with and learn, by trial and error, how to handle and despatch them. From very young, the cat's progressive experimentation with its developing sensory and physical capabilities in exploring objects, and reacting with its mother and littermates in its immediate surrounding environment all improve and co-ordinate hunting skills. They are further honed by the gradual extension of interest and abilities to fulfil the demands of independently feeding itself once weaned and after it has left its mother.

The strategy

Cats are described generally as opportunistic hunters and scavengers. Hunting consists of the search for potential prey through an investigation of the environment with all senses fully functioning. In cats, the search may comprise an active range through grasslands, fields or forests with frequent stops to investigate the immediate surroundings more acutely. This is referred to by biologists as a mobile or M-hunting strategy. Hunting may alternatively comprise a visit to a known successful hunting area, such as a 'run' used by mice in a hedgerow or beneath an active bird nest, and a patient wait until something scurries past or attempts a first flight. This is known as the 'sit and wait' or S-hunting strategy. In the latter case, the cat will approach the centre of the productive hunting zone, say an entrance to a mouse burrow, very cautiously so as not to announce his arrival, and then sit motionless waiting for the first sign of activity. Clearly, cats can employ both strategies and, while some wild species may prefer to use only one type depending on the prey that is available to them, the hunting pet cat uses both. But whether the M- or the S-strategy is used, the stalk or pounce of the hunt and the precise application of all that design for being a predator and sharp reflexes will be triggered by the arrival or detection of any prey. Few studies have examined which strategy suits which cats in different environments, or whether either strategy is better suited when hunting various types of prey at different times of the year. However, domestic cats have been shown to be more successful at hunting rabbits using the M-strategy than the S-. Much depends also on the history of previous success, and many cats do head along certain hunting walkways for their M-type hunting and go to specific areas of burrows or runs for the S-type. Cats will also often head towards a recently disturbed area in their normal hunting range presumably because rodents will be still learning how best to stay concealed and will not have organised escape routes and will therefore be vulnerable to being detected by the alert predator. Such areas may be explored with a deliberate zig-zag strategy or with a less organised M-type meander.

The stalk

The cat's highly developed senses of sight and hearing are all fully operative in the search and thoroughly alert across their respectively enormous capacities in the detection of any slight movement or sound that may identify the presence of any suitable prey. Once identified, the stalk begins, perfectly judged and controlled. During the fascinating stalk of prey identified at distance, the cat moves deliberately and slowly with dramatic silent and controlled bursts of speed in approach, perhaps heading in stages to temporary cover or halted after a few yards in a body 'freeze'. This is especially the case when stalking birds which usually have almost all-round vision and can spot a predator

71

from any direction. The cat keeps his head low in the stalk and his shoulders and body crouched, sometimes even so low as to give the appearance of slithering along the ground like a snake. Once within the range of that upward and forward pounce, the cat waits and sets itself, co-ordinating its senses and body for the final assault. This may be described as the 'lie and wait ambush' and be an extension of the sit and wait S-hunting strategy, but this is when biologists are going rather overboard on classifying every component of what an animal does and put at risk the pure magic and lethal beauty of the hunting cat.

The kill

With every sense focused on the target ... ears pricked, pupils dilated, whiskers spread wide and set forward, rear legs stepping silently on the spot and with bottom raised and swaying menacingly from side to side, it is surely to do the cat a disservice to try to classify such exciting nervous tension. But, for the sake of argument, it is at this co-ordination stage that many stalks fail, right at the last, as the detection systems of the target animal locate the danger. Alarmed, the potential victim makes a rapid escape to survive another day and leaves the cat to move on to another area or wait patiently for the next opportunity at an established mouse run or near a well-stocked bird table! But for those less aware of the danger, their doom is usually assured as the cat's forepaws grasp them and, held in those grappling claws, they are instantly (with an experienced adult small cat like Bullet, at least) despatched with a penetrating bite to the nape of the neck which dislocates their spine. If the bite is unsuccessful or the prey is too big to be despatched in this way, or the cat is inexperienced, then he may temporarily release the prey and immediately pounce on him again, or shake the wretched creature to disorientate him and then try again. With larger and perhaps more resistant and well-armed victims such as rats, the smaller cats may soften them up first wiith plenty of batting and quick throwing with a clawed paw, and only attempt the nape bite when the victim is weak and a clear aim at the neck is possible. For this, the rat, for example, may be held firmly on the ground with one paw with the bite aimed at the neck held just in front of the paw. In all his successes, or even any failures at tackling rats, the diminutive Bullet has never once shown any evidence of a bite or injury sustained in the process, so his tactics must be right, even when he has tackled some that are nearly as big as he is. Large Bullets, like cheetahs and lions, deal with their larger prey of antelope not by nape bites and paw holds but with a throttling grip of the throat, suffocating their victim to death in a much less direct method and one which will make the cat wait before he can consume his meal.

Bullet's hunting grounds

Bullet has several relatively static hunting areas around my garden where he employs the S-strategy. There is a bank along one side where pygmy shrews abound and, during the daytime in spring and summer, Bullet is especially patient at waiting on the lawn just at the base of the bank listening acutely for an ultrasonic squeak or rustle in the grass. He inflicts great carnage on the population, catching five or more on some days and rarely having a shrew-free day. The shrews seem to be unpleasant to taste, however, for like many cats, he never eats them. He either dumps them dead on the lawn or in the kitchen or brings young ones in, still alive for his Siamese girlfriends to play with. At dawn and dusk he wanders off into the more wooded areas and waits, listening for mice. At night throughout the year, he wanders down to that fateful railway where Scribble met her sad end and hunts using the M-strategy, for rats. These are also brought home, but eaten or half eaten with relish and often washed down with a midnight snack of a bat taken mid-air from the rear of the house where they circle in great numbers on warm insect-laden nights.

In winter, Bullet switches his strategy to lurking at various vantage points around our two bird-tables. Despite moving the mobile one several times he still manages to contrive a successful strategy, sometimes crouched low beneath the rocks of the terrace before making an explosive dash of three or four yards followed by a frantic leap. He has dispensed with the wait prior to the pounce as he would be too much in the open and easily spotted. As a result, his success rate is poor and he probably only serves to keep the local bird population free of stupid, blind or deaf members which fail to spot his most uncat-like clumsy assaults. His tactics at the other static table are more typically controlled and far more productive. There he exploits the cover afforded by a stone wall to enable him to set himself close by and make the typical stalk and bottom waggle refining the aim of the pounce on any bird dallying too long or relaxing its vigilance. Sadly, robins seem too trusting at man-made bird-tables and regularly fall victim to Bullet, though only once each of course!

Clearly Bullet is not alone at employing varying hunting strategies to deal with different types of prey, most noticeably to deal with flying or ground-based victims. Many cats are poor at catching birds because the stalk and pounce tactic is less effective against a normally observant prey which can effect a vertical escape, but when they are caught, they are usually despatched with a bite to the shoulder and the nape bite is delayed until the bird is already dead or very nearly so. Naturally one might expect most cats to favour prey which is unable to fly away and some cats are reported to be so poor at catching birds that they give up hunting them altogether in favour of looking for rodents. However, it is felt unlikely that any cat becomes so specific in its hunting as only to pursue one species unless forced to do so because there is only one type of victim available or one particular species is so simple to catch that other species are largely ignored. This perhaps may only occur when cats find themselves among the relatively impoverished fauna of some islands and have to feed exclusively on reptiles or choose to feed on helpless ground nesting birds for example. Bullet, however, did learn that just because a bird looks ungainly when confined to an existence on the ground and apparently easy prey, a cat will not always succeed with his stalk and pounce. Certainly the day he tried to nail my new young but hefty Muscovy duck was the day he learnt to stick to smaller birds as he felt the rough end of Hissing Sid's beak batter his head! Bullet slid away, just quickly enough to effect escape but hoping that he appeared untroubled and nonchalant to any onlookers when Sid and the other duck, a lighter and faster but nonetheless well-beaked Indian runner, decided to remove his presence from their immediate proximity!

One of the founding fathers of the study of cat behaviour, Paul Leyhausen, who had the good fortune to be an early student of the great Konrad Lorenz, suggested in 1979 that cats do not have a mind's eye view (or schema as he called it) of what a prey item looks like or does. So after Bullet's attention has been drawn by a sound or movement, he will be attracted towards any moving object in his field of vision that is of an appropriate format. It must be small enough to fit into the field of vision without being too small, and moving approximately along a straight path. Hence the freeze mechanism of some small rodents when they sense danger is very clearly designed to downgrade the predatory interest of movement-sensitive predators such as cats, as well as helping them to camouflage themselves. In turn the cat may have evolved to compensate for this, as we saw earlier, by wiggling his bottom to provide alternating fields of vision and give the impression to his brain that the mouse is moving and so help him aim his strike better. Cats clearly respond to movement of their prey rather than its smell, and without early recognition and a waggling bottom, hunting stalks may cease if the prey stops and remains motionless. The cat faced with a prey that has disappeared may learn to approach in roughly the direction of its previous course and it may then get close enough to it to disturb it and cause it to bolt, whereupon the chase, stalk and pounce may begin afresh. Interestingly, Bullet and many other cats already in possession of a dead or inactive mouse may abandon it to pursue another which runs past, or sometimes to chase a decoy moving target of a small ball of newspaper rolled nearby by a distraught owner anxious to rescue the mouse. It's usually a more successful policy than chasing the cat, who may dart for cover and usually manage to take his victim with him.

Eating to live – wild feline diets around the world

Generally small wild cat species are like Bullet and also feed on a wide range of prey, though they can survive well if they are limited to only a few types at certain times of year, or live in harsher environments where species variation may be lower. An excellent account of what is known of the diet of small wild cats and their larger cousins can be found in *The Natural History of Wild Cats* by Dr Andrew Kitchener, published in association with the Mammal Society of Great Britain in 1991. Diets range from predominantly rodents such as various mice, rats and voles preyed on by ocelots in South America, by African Wild Cats in Botswana, by Sand Cats in Russia, by European Wild Cats in Italy and France compared with Scottish Wild Cats which favour rabbit instead. Birds appear to make up a maximum of about ten to fifteen per cent of the diet of any of these small cat species.

Many cats in sparser environments, such as the Sand Cat, have also been shown to prey on reptiles such as geckoes and snakes, as well as insects, and the African Wild Cat has been found to consume spiders, frogs and even scorpions. Clearly some very clever prey handling went into the despatch and consumption of those! While the size of prey taken is rather dependent on the size of the cat, larger prey such as hares and squirrels are taken regularly by the European Wild

Cat and the only recently discovered (in 1967) Iriomote Cat of Japan has been found to have consumed fruit bats and wild pig along with a wide range of birds from herons to owls. The Iriomote Cat also regularly eats no less than thirty-nine species of beetle, and insects account for about one third of all items consumed, though this doesn't amount to much of the total energy intake. The Fishing Cat of India has a specialised method of catching its prey. It lies on an overhanging branch above a river with its nose held just above the water until an unwary fish passes underneath and is quickly dived on and grabbed. The cat uses its mouth rather than its paws, as might a pet cat stalking a goldfish in a neighbour's pond. However, while most cats will exploit whatever is available and catchable, for sheer diversity of prey species taken and the ability to adapt to survive on bizarre or restricted numbers of prey species, few of the small wild cat species can match the free-living domestic cat, as we shall see in Chapter 16.

In the drive for survival, cats, like many predators, are also by no means averse to taking advantage of a free meal if, in their wanderings, they happen across suitable carrion. The occasional free meal may be a welcome supplement for the wild cat, especially during winter when natural live prey may be scarce, but a deliberate strategy of scavenging has also enabled many feral cats almost to give up hunting altogether. They may learn instead to lie around wastebins of hotels or restaurants waiting for fresh supplies or to cadge from well-meaning human providers in urban areas. But whichever strategy is used to obtain their prey, cats the world over are extremely effective at hunting, as one might expect from such a perfected design and their ability to use their senses, physique, patience, stealth and cunning to launch a surprise attack on their prey. The violent aggression of predation is perfectly controlled and directed solely at the prey in order that the cat might feed itself. At nearly all other times, cats, especially pet cats, are decidedly non-aggressive and, aside from fights over territory or mates, largely avoid challenge and threat by running away or settle differences between themselves through gestures and vocal, scent and body language. We could learn much from the specific and purposeful application of such power, though, sadly, it is unlikely that man will stop developing ever larger and more deadly weapons to threaten his enemies with, or cease finding reasons for unnecessary hunting, violent fighting and war.

Many admire the relaxed life of the cat, which, like all predators, spends much of its day doing what cats do best . . . not hunting, but sleeping. Domestic cats may sleep up to eighteen hours per day, over twice as much as we do or would even like to do, given the chance. Lions may sleep or rest for up to twenty hours per day at certain times of the year, waking only to groom themselves and each other, stretch and flex their bodies and then relax before the concentrated activity of looking for food. People who dislike cats often describe them as lazy but, as most have evolved to hunt at times when their prey is active, at dawn, dusk and at night, there would be little point in them being active during the day looking for prey which isn't there. In any case, because the meat diet of cats is rich, they need to consume much less food than the herbivore, which requires long periods of grazing to get enough energy from vegetable matter, or even the omnivore, such as man, with his mixed diet of fruit, meat and veg.

SECTION THREE

A Wild Pet

5
Small cats in history, a virtually unchanged blueprint

'The cat was a creature of absolute convictions, and his faith in his deductions never varied'   Mary E Williams

About thirty-five million years ago, feline forerunners appeared on the earth, but the first recognisable cat-like creature didn't evolve until another ten million years later. Several forms of a generalised cat known as Pseudolurus were found in what is now Europe and North America about twenty million years ago but cats more in the style of present-day types only first appeared about ten million years ago in what is now Europe and Asia. The larger species of the same group such as modern day lions and leopards only arose about two million years ago in Europe and perhaps in Africa. The most famous forerunner of the cat is, of course, the sabre-toothed tiger, and this evolved on no less than four different occasions in different eras. Clearly the world was just waiting to perfect the design of the predatory cat. Generally the fossil record of cats is not very good with most small species leaving few traces of their existence. Several scientists have tried to piece together what material is available to propose theories of how the cats we find today evolved from which ancestors and when, and how they are all related. However, all cats are remarkably similar in form and so there is still some disagreement about exactly how many species there are, and certainly about how they arose.

It is accepted by most that there are twenty-six species of small wild cat to be found around the world today along with eleven larger cats. While most of us could probably name all eleven larger models, lion, tiger, puma, jaguar, etc, the smaller cats are far less well-known and far less frequently brought to public attention through television natural history programmes or commercial advertising and product naming by multinational companies. Part of this focus arises from the impact of the sheer power of the large cats in helping to impress sales of petrol or cars on people but, while the usually more stealthy secretive lifestyle of the smaller species may have less commercial value, pound for pound they are probably just as powerful.

The naming of cats

'Set down my name, Sir'   John Bunyan

The twenty-six smaller species all belong to the genus or scientific group known as Felis. The domestic cat, named by Linnaeus, the great man who established the most widely used system of biological classification, is known as *Felis catus,* the European Wild Cat as *Felis sylvestris*, and the Sand Cat, somewhat boozily, as *Felis margarita.* The second part of the biological name is used to define the species within the genus described by the first name. When, subsequently, what was thought to be a single species is found to comprise differing individuals in a species, then a sub-species name may be added. For example, because the Scottish Wild Cat is rather more heavily striped and darker in colour than the wild cat species of Europe, and he is now geographically isolated from mainland Europe, he is now often known as *Felis sylvestris grampia* to distinguish him.

But just what is a species? No group of animals begs the question of definition more than the family of small cats. Man's urge to classify living things and prescribe a name to each has led to all sorts of measurements to find differences between one and another. Size and colour and locality of existence are obvious features but, with cats especially, the classification scientists, known usually as taxonomists, have even had to measure skulls and relative proportions of certain parts of the skull on dead animals to find names for the living. Most small cats are remarkably similar to one another so they have taken to arguing among themselves as to whether there are twenty genera (a genus is a group of closely related species) or as few as six!

81

Even while taxonomists are painstakingly looking for physical differences between species, the process of evolution is constantly producing new forms. Presumably the divine job is still underway, so there will always be creatures evolving in response to changing environmental conditions placing new selective pressures on their present design. Measuring those changes in some individuals may inspire some taxonomists to identify a new species, while others will simply claim that the specimen before them is a variant of an already classified one. With such an opportunistic predator as the small cat, the game of survival, and therefore survival of its genes, depends on its adaptability and response to circumstances. So it is hardly surprising to find that their genetic make-up is very fluid to enable each species to evolve and continue to evolve to suit many different and changing environments. And just when we think we have a system of classification we discover that one 'species' in one part of the world can happily interbreed with a different species in another part, implying a common and recent ancestor. One of the fundamental definitions of a species is often that it shouldn't be able to interbreed with near relatives or, at least, as with the different species of the horse and the donkey mating to produce a mule, not produce fertile offspring.

Our mistake was to have assumed that because the first cat didn't look much like the second, they were of different species with different genetic make-up, instead of incorporating a better knowledge of adaptation and the history of radiation of the first cat. What is a species? It's usually defined as a group of individuals within a genus that have common and observable outward characteristics and which can interbreed and perpetuate those specific characteristics and remain distinct from other species within their genus. The problem is that small cats seem, as so often in their relations with us, to resist such order and classification and definition of a species for such a wide-ranging and highly adaptable genus as *Felis* is naturally perplexing!

Where did the pet cat come from?

Such scientific definitions have little relevance in any case to the casual observer of cats, as we generally use the common name rather than the Latin one to identify any wild cat that we may be lucky enough to see. However, because of its special relationship with man, there has long been much debate about the origins of the pet cat named *Felis catus*. Just where did this highly successful cat come from and who were his original ancestors?

It has generally been assumed that the ancestor of all our pet cats is the African Wild Cat, known as *Felis lybica*, though under some classifications it is often referred to as the amenable sub-species of the European Wild Cat and called *Felis sylvestris lybica*. It is often also suggested, though without any firm evidence, that the modern cat also contains elements of other related small cats from Africa such as the Jungle Cat, *Felis chaus,* and from elsewhere such as the Asiatic Wild Cat, *Felis ornata.* The supposition is based on the fact that these species can all interbreed with each other and with the pet cat and therefore must be related, a curious piece of double-talk in the search to delineate one species of cat from another!

In the development of the pet cat it has also been suggested that perhaps there has been some crossbreeding with Pallas's Cat, *Felis manul,* which is found in mountainous country from Iran to the western side of China and the Sand Cat, *Felis margarita,* found from the Sahara to Baluchistan, to produce the domestic Persian strains. The Asian Golden Cat, *Felis temminkii,* found in the forests from south China to Sumatra and the Leopard Cat *Felis bengalensis* found from eastern Siberia to South-east Asia have also been proposed as having some input in the development of the Oriental cats such as the Siamese and Korat breeds that we know today in the Cat Fancy.

However, most of these suggestions are based on the physical appearance of the modern pet cat and are attempts to try to explain how the African Wild Cat, *Felis lybica*, could have given rise to the modern pet cat in such a variety of shapes and hair types even though he himself is usually brown-sandy-grey in colour. Closer examination of actual specimens and detailed measurements of the bones and brain size of pet cats and wild cats has revealed that, in fact, the modern pet cat, be he a Persian, Siamese or short-haired moggy, is very similar only to the African Wild Cat and the Asiatic Wild Cat.

Later, as analytical techniques advanced, it was found that the African Wild Cat, the Asian Golden Cat, Pallas's Cat and the Leopard Cat all have nineteen pairs of chromosomes, the same number as the pet cat, adding weight to the argument that one or more of these was involved in the production of the pet cat, *Felis catus.*

The African Wild Cat is nowadays found throughout Africa and Arabia in savannah and bush regions though it is absent from pure rain forest or desert environments. Physically the African Wild Cat is described as having a coat that varies from a pale sandy colour to yellow/brown to dark grey with tabby-like lines on the face, wavy stripes on the sides and spots on the forepaws and lower chest. The tail tapers and has two or three clearly defined rings and a black tip. They are rarely seen or studied though they are thought to produce litters of two or three kittens usually, and only occasionally four or five. But although the cat is reported as being shy, there are also many anecdotal and well-documented reports of local people befriending kittens and keeping them as tame pets into adulthood.

The nineteenth-century explorer George Schweinfurth, while on an expedition in North Africa, certainly recorded local people catching and rearing young African Wild Cats and keeping them around their huts and enclosures as pets. The cats presumably stayed around because they wanted to and similar events are even occasionally reported in modern times in northern Africa and Arabia. The Azande tribe of southern Sudan have lived in tolerant proximity with the African Wild Cat for centuries without actually taking it into their homes and hearts. The cat is content to find shelter and scavenge around the tribal settlements and shows little fear of people. The relative docility of the African Wild Cat and ease of comparison with the 'pet cat' was noted subsequently by Schweinfurth and by many others. So it is perfectly reasonable on grounds of its past and present willingness to adopt a life with and around man without being held in captivity, that the African Wild Cat could be the ancestor of the modern pet cat. In short, my suggestion is that the African Wild Cat pre-domesticated itself and moved alongside man, rather than being held captive first and then domesticated by man. The tolerance of the African Wild Cat, compared with the usual fearful and withdrawn nature of its relatives, in the face of man seems to me to be a crucial difference in trying to tease apart all the influences that have been suggested as having an input into our pet cat curled up asleep in front of the fire. Pre-domestication, and the cat's extraordinary adaptability, which enabled him to encompass the presence of man in his immediate environment, seem to be the crucial elements that explain best just how the cat has become so successful.

A German scientist called Hemmer, who must have had all the painstaking patience in the world, discovered that the brain size of any domesticated animal is always smaller than that of its original wild ancestor and that a sub-species that ultimately gives rise to a domestic species has a smaller brain relative to the rest of the species.

One might infer that the process of domestication and living with man is fuelled by decreased intelligence, an interesting proposal as Hemmer did indeed find that the African Wild Cat has a smaller brain than the European Wild Cat. This may also answer the conundrum of why more carnivores than the cat and dog haven't become sociable with man. After all, most carnivores are social to their own kind, but only the dog and the cat can really live as our pets. In short, the sociability of other animals with their own kind only continues because it suits the survival of that particular species. All other large mammalian species will either be regarded by them as prey to hunt and eat, or threats to be avoided, like man – as neither one thing nor the other – and ignored. Only our modified wolf – the dog – and the pre-modified cat have made it as pets, and this is largely due to their ability to regard us as neutrals or of benefit to their social set-up and survival, rather than threats.

6

The Egyptian connection

'In Egypt the cats afford evidence that animal nature is not altogether intractable'   Aelian

Clearly any study of the origins of any domestic animal must consider what is known of the animal's relations with man throughout history by looking at archaeological and historical records. As every cat lover knows, it is well-documented that the Ancient Egyptians were the first people to leave evidence of living closely with cats, though remains of cats perhaps eaten by prehistoric man have been found in much earlier excavations. The earliest definite record is of a 9,000-year-old cat's tooth of an unidentified species found in Neolithic excavations in Jericho and, interestingly, 7,000-year-old remains of a cat have been discovered in Cyprus. That cat was an African Wild Cat and must have been transported there by man, as there have never been any indigenous cat species in Cyprus even though the island is well populated by free-living domestic cats today.

According to Dr Juliet Clutton-Brock at the Natural History Museum in London, cats were living alongside man or 'domesticated' at an extremely late age compared with other species. There are no records of cats from the Old Kingdom (2686-2181 BC) of Ancient Egypt and only pictures of cats from the Middle Kingdom, which could be of wild species rather than cats living in people's homes or palaces. The cat only appears for certain to be living in harmony with the Ancient Egyptians in the New Kingdom from 1567 BC onwards. However, it is likely that the cat was 'domesticated' a little earlier, perhaps around 2000 BC, because some time would have needed to elapse before it was a big enough part of life to be depicted in pictures of everyday home life with people and their other pets, such as monkeys. Cats in the New Kingdom are depicted on painted reliefs and paintings in the tombs of noblemen, in the home, often seated under a chair of the wife or couple.

Domestic cats at this time were almost certainly specimens of *Felis lybica,* which moved into centres of human population from the surrounding lands in Ancient Egypt, where they were, and still are, indigenous. They were probably attracted to human settlements pursuing concentrations of their natural prey of rodents, which doubtless abounded around the grain stores of the Ancient Egyptians. The earliest paintings by the Ancient Egyptians which include cats certainly depict specimens which are very similar to the African Wild Cat living in close contact with humans. By 450 BC in Ancient Egypt, cats and all animals, both wild and domesticated, were regarded as sacred with the death penalty or severe fines imposed by priests for anyone who killed one. Cats, like many other animals and, of course, people, were often embalmed after death, mummified in linen wraps and buried in large cemeteries. The number of mummies of animals such as cats, is notable according to Dr Clutton-Brock. The most abundant animal mummies were cats, mongooses . . . and crocodiles!

At the end of the nineteenth century mummified cats were excavated mainly from an enormous cat cemetery at the cat temple of Pakhet and shipped to the UK in 1889 on the steamer *Pharos and Thebes*. After landing in Liverpool, they were auctioned and ended up being irreverently ground down for use as fertiliser and as ballast on ships. Farmers bought the mummies for the equivalent of £4.25 per ton . . . what a way to treat such valuable relics! The keeping of cats must have been intense in Ancient Egypt as one consignment of feline mummies weighed nineteen and a half tons! It is hard to describe the thrill of actually holding a mummified cat from Ancient Egypt, but I was lucky enough to do so while filming a video at a superb exhibition about cats held at Salisbury Museum in 1990/91. It was amazing actually to hold in my hands an example of the first friendly cats to walk with man on earth. It was an experience matched in my 'cat and dog' life only by sitting and touching live, wild but captive friendly-ish cheetahs and African hunting dogs at a breeding station in the bush in South Africa in 1990 and keeping a European wolf for a while when running an animal shelter in Greece in the 1980s!

But back to Ancient Egypt. Of all the hundreds of thousands of mummies shipped to England to be pulverised from that nineteen-and-a-half-ton consignment from Beni Hasan, only one skull was kept. This is now housed in the Natural History Museum in London, along with 190 skulls dating from 600 to 200 BC collected from another burial site at Gizah. Of these, 187 have been clearly identified as belonging to *Felis lybica* with the other three belonging to the Jungle Cat, *Felis chaus*, which was probably kept in captivity but not bred as a domesticated animal. Despite the appearance of the Jungle Cat here and the discovery of a few of their bones at other more recently discovered sites, the Jungle Cat is thought to have contributed little, or probably nothing at all, to the development of the domestication of the cat. After all, it was and still is shy of man. Though it may have been captured and held successfully in captivity by the Ancient Egyptians and even interbred with its relative, the African Wild Cat, any hybrid kittens are more likely to have been on the wild side of their parentage and behaved fearfully, like the Jungle Cat parent, rather than be tolerant or friendly towards man like the other parent. This would have militated against either the Jungle Cat or such hybrids being taken in as pets when there were obviously thousands of friendlier African Wild Cats around. So, despite the fact that the range of the Jungle Cat overlaps the range of the African Wild Cat in Egypt and elsewhere in north Africa, suggesting that it has contributed to the make-up of the pet cat is not a very scientific approach just because remains of a very small number have been found along with extensive remains of African Wild Cats. Nor is the theory enhanced by the presence of tomb wall paintings of the Jungle Cat because the Egyptians featured many wild and domestic animals in such murals. Indeed, the suggestion that the shy Jungle Cat contributed to genes of the pet cat has not been corroborated by any firm evidence. In law, being identified at the scene of a crime does not mean you are guilty!

However, many of the mummified *Felis lybica* cats of Ancient Egypt are noticeably larger than the modern day species which suggests either, to add horribly to the confusion, that they belonged to a different species than *Felis lybica*, or that the smaller examples were already showing a typical response to domestication, or perhaps in this case, captive breeding, of becoming reduced in size. It also shouldn't be discounted that the standard of nutrition plays a large role in the development and ultimate size of any animal. The larger mummies may have been of cats that were caught in the wild or particularly well cared-for specimens and the smaller ones could be the bodies of cats bred in captivity that were rather malnourished, especially as kittens, and so hadn't grown so large when they ultimately met their fate as juveniles or adults. After all, the Egyptians must have had little idea of how to feed kittens and cats in captivity and there are certainly no records of mouse farms for them, nor of prepared cat food. However, one might also suggest that some of the more assertive temple cats perhaps received more food than their captive colleagues or wild counterparts and, what with reduced energy demands for hunting, tended to grow larger earlier, thus accounting better for discoveries of that larger version of the African Wild Cat than uncorroborated suggestions of cross-breeding with other species in captivity.

In 1982, a new find of large quantities of cat mummies was made by a French archaeologist beyond the west bank of the Nile at Saqqara and in 1990 the British cat specialist, Roger Tabor, discovered a hitherto unknown 'seam' of mummies and remains at Pakhet's Temple at Beni Hasan. There is a sufficient wealth of material here to make up for the ravages on the earlier discoveries and studies will hopefully reveal more about the first cats that lived with and around man in Ancient Egypt.

Cats of both sexes were held as sacred by 664 BC and kept in sanctuaries or breeding catteries alongside temples. Females were sacred because of their fertility and mothering ability in honour of the goddess of fertility, Bast (also known as Bastet or Pasht), who was depicted as having the head of a cat. The cult of Bast was the most important one associated with cats in Egypt and reached its peak sometime after 2000 BC, with temple cats being venerated in special courts at the one-time capital of Egypt, Bubastis (nowadays known as Zagazig) in the Nile Delta, north of Cairo. About half a million people flocked every year to Bubastis to celebrate the fertility festival of Bast, surely still the most popular cat show of all time, even if the judging was of a rather terminal kind compared with the modern day rosettes handed to selected cats! But while female cats represented fertility, males were held in honour of Ra, the sun god, because they especially were thought to carry the sun's glow in their eyes at night and carry the gods' power against the forces of darkness. It wasn't a bad assumption considering that they didn't know about the *tapetum*, that reflecting layer of cells in the retina at the back of the eye.

The sacred cats were nurtured, albeit perhaps on a less than ideal diet, until they were about one to four months of age, whereupon their necks were broken and their bodies eviscerated, dried and then covered in resin. They were then wrapped in linen bandages and sold by the guardians of the temples to be used as offerings to the deity in question by visiting worshippers. They were offered to the temples, taken back by the priests and then ritually buried in the often vast nearby cemeteries. Older cats discovered of nine to twelve months of age had probably grown too big to be fashionably desirable as offerings, or were excess non-breeding males that were killed and sold off cheaply to poorer worshippers. Later it became more common to dedicate a small bronze cat statue to the temple as an act of religious worship, doubtless to the relief of any watching live cats!

By the time cats were being ritually strangled, the captive keeping of cats was well-established and the effects of this 'forced domestication' were probably already altering the original wild ancestor, *Felis lybica*. The constraints of captivity were quite likely making the cat smaller and of smaller brain capacity even within a few generations. The rearing of young kittens to at least juvenile age will also have ensured that some became extremely friendly and will have avoided their religious destiny by being kept longer in the sanctuaries or even taken home to become house pets.

But the Egyptians didn't just keep cats for religious sacrifice. There is ample evidence from writers of the time that cats were kept in houses too. Indeed, many subscribe to the theory that the African Wild Cat's tolerance of man was first evident in the towns rather than the temples of Ancient Egypt. Among the narrow busy streets of worker townships such as Deir el Medina near the Valley of the Kings at Luxor, cats were scavenging for a living and learning the art of begging from the townspeople who were building the Pharaohs' tombs. The suggestion is that this type of interaction led to cats entering man's home as a pet to take up their place on his lap, by his fire and to be fed from bowls, events all recorded clearly on the wall paintings of the humble workers' tombs.

Surely it was in the towns that the first pet aggregation occurred on a large scale between man and the cat from the desert. After all, man had been storing grain in Egypt and elsewhere within the African Wild Cat's natural home range for some 7,000 years prior to the date of the first evidence of a relationship developing between them. It is quite likely that the African Wild Cat and man had had, as is still seen across its 'wild' range today, a close mutual tolerance of each other and that occasional closer relations were simply not recorded as relevant in ages prior to this when day-to-day survival was more important. Perhaps it took the growth of human civilisation to want to record the nature of home life, including the presence of domesticated, wild and semi-wild animals before the cat could be recorded as relevant. After all, the cat was never likely to be the prey of man the hunter and feature in descriptions or drawings of hunts. Perhaps it took a growing religious respect for the cat in Ancient Egypt for it to be valued enough to be worthy of mention, even after centuries of being around man.

As a result of easier living in the towns, cats were able to build up far denser populations than the surrounding lands could ever support. They could also do this quickly. The fertility, fecundity and mothering ability of cats, recognised by the Egyptians, are the keys to quick rapid colonisation of new habitats for many species. This is a phenomenon known as the 'r-strategy' to ecologists. By contrast, 'k-strategists' are animals (or plants) that take longer to reach and colonise a new habitat, but establish firm enduring roots in it, with individuals living long and raising fewer, slow-growing and carefully nurtured offspring. A tom cat can sire his own offspring before he is a year old and can continue to do so all his life. While few free-living cats would reach such an age, pet cats of sixteen years of age have been known to father kittens. Females can also reproduce in their first year and have two or three litters of usually about three to four kittens. The record for a single litter is held by two queens in the 1970s who produced fourteen kittens each, and the record for the number produced in a lifetime is 420 kittens by a tabby cat called Dusty from Texas. With the care and attention lavished on kittens by their mums helping to ensure that as many as possible survive to adulthood, it's not hard to see how or why cat populations can colonise new areas or new lands so quickly.

As is still seen around the resorts of the Mediterranean today, cats which learn to accept close human proximity in towns and hotels, and which learn to cadge and beg, will often do better than the pure scavengers. So one can presume that there has always been fairly heavy selective pressure in favour of friendly cats above tolerant ones in the towns and that this was occurring even before the upper sections of Ancient Egyptian society incorporated cats into religious rituals.

Either way, by the time the cat had become a doubtless unwilling part of the religious scene in Ancient Egypt, a definite 'us and them' distinction had arisen with regard to how cats were treated. Contrasting with the huge scale of killing of cats for religious purposes, any private person who killed a cat was likely to be sentenced to death and if a pet cat died, the owners would have to shave their eyebrows off as a mark of respect and perform detailed funeral rites, including embalming the deceased pet's body and burying it in one of the large cat cemeteries.

7
The flight from Egypt and the necessity of man

'A creature which makes clear that it will pledge no permanent loyalty cannot be accused of breaking its vows'　　　　　Bernard Levin

The Ancient Egyptians were highly protective of their cats to the point of prohibiting their export and pursuing any that were taken out of the country to bring them back. That policy failed because by 1000 BC the practise of keeping cats had travelled northwards across the Mediterranean on board ships – perhaps those of the Phoenician traders – and arrived in Europe. They were then found progressively eastwards and taken to China via land and sea-trading routes, and later into Japan, where they were kept to help protect the valuable cocoons of the silkworm industry from rats. As well as being happy to leave the Egyptians and their African homelands behind and migrate with other peoples, these early migrant African Wild Cats were interestingly put into battle against the Egyptians when their army was confronted by the Persians near Pelusium in 525 BC. The Persian army are said by Polyaenus to have paraded cats and other animals sacred to their enemy in front of their infantry as protection. A devious trick, but the Egyptians didn't dare launch their missiles or spears for fear of offending their gods, and so lost the battle.

The Romans regarded the cat as a rare and exotic pet although later the cat's larger cousin, the lion, was to play a greater role in the lifestyle of the Empire, paraded as a power symbol by emperors and

93

used in the amphitheatre to rip up Christians and other dangerous religious activists, and to combat gladiators. While some believe that the pet cat arrived in the United Kingdom with the Phoenicians, who were known to trade with the tin-mine owners of Cornwall, most believe that it was the Romans, some time before 4 AD, who brought cats with them to the edge of their empire. The cat proved to be yet another civilising influence that they imposed on the primitives they found there! The discovery of cat footprints on a tile from Roman Silchester (modern day Chelmsford) and the feline skeletons found under the floor of a Roman house in Colchester indicate that it was friendly cats, African Wild Cats far from home, that were kept as pets. The indigenous wild cat, the European Wild Cat (or 'Scottish' when in Britain) was and still is far too shy and fearful of man to be skulking around a tile or brick factory or human habitation. And when the Romans left British shores, they left behind their cats, who, by virtue of their adaptability in new environments and continuing tolerance of man, had firmly established their right to stay and were already outdoing their European cousin for rights of occupation.

By 1700 BC the cat was depicted in domestic poses in art in Israel, and in Greece by 1400 BC. By 500 BC the cat seems to have become a regular feature of folklore and civilised life in southern Europe. Pliny mentioned the hunting of the cat, with both M- and S-strategies described though not named, in *Natural History* written in 77 AD and Palladius, another Roman writing later in the third century, recommended employing cats to catch moles, presumably with the S-strategy! The cat was also found in Roman religion being depicted at the feet of Diana, the goddess of light, in many art forms. It is quite likely that the cat was still kept and transported around this time predominantly to keep rats and mice down, both on board ship and then in newly settled towns around the world and also used as trade, to be sold and bartered for the same purposes.

Elsewhere in the world, the Mohics of Peru worshipped the god of copulation, Ai Apaec, who was represented in the form of a cat, and one of the Chinese gods of farming, Li-Shou, was worshipped in the form of a cat after the harvest to seek protection for the grain from rats and mice. Later, Siamese and Birman cats were venerated in Thailand and Burma as guardians of Buddhist temples. Both peoples believed that cats housed the spirits of the dead and there is even a sacred cat in Burma called Sinh. In Japan there is also an eighteenth-century temple consecrated to the cat in Tokyo and back in northern

Europe, early Celtic monks made beautiful illustrations and wrote poems for their loved pet cats in Ireland in the eighth or ninth century. So the religious connotations of the cat's association with man have been widespread in human culture and found in many important religions.

Dr Terry O'Connor, an archaeologist at Bradford University, suggests that cats were far more prevalent in the English countryside and around towns after the Norman Conquest in 1066, perhaps because they were being more deliberately kept as pets after the civilising influence of the French. Free-living cats were certainly common enough in the English countryside of the early Middle Ages for cat hunting to be authorised by Henry III to control numbers and provide fur for monks to wear. Dr O'Connor also manages to find an occasional cat skeleton to examine from the wells of Middle Ages England because 'abandoned wells were used to get rid of rubbish'. Dead cats, live ones thrown in, or live ones that fell in while pursuing rodents? It's interesting that he should find them there anyway, in the light of the words of the nursery rhyme:

> *Ding, dong, bell,*
> *Pussy's in the well!*
> *Who put her in?*
> *Little Johnny Green.*
> *Who pulled her out?*
> *Little Tommy Stout.*
> *What a naughty boy was that*
> *To try to drown poor pussy cat,*
> *Who never did him any harm,*
> *And killed the mice in his father's barn.*

Without doubt, as early settlements and towns developed in Europe, the rat population developed too, especially until the region finally caught up with the ideas about sanitation first brought to them by the Romans over 1,500 years earlier! But while the black rat raided the grain stores and wallowed in the filth of man's existence, he also brought disease, spreading plague and Black Death via his fleas which decimated human populations. Over a quarter of London's population died in the 1660s from bubonic plague and the only ally man seemed to have against the rats was the natural enemy of rodents, the cat. The cat was certainly popular on one hand, but he

95

was originally blamed, along with the devil, for the Black Death in 1348 by the Lord Mayor of London who ordered that all cats should all be killed.

The cat was also persecuted for many hundreds of years because he was linked, particularly by the churches of Europe, with witchcraft and satanic influence. The association and persecution had begun before the Black Death in the thirteenth century and lasted for about 450 years. Throughout the sixteenth and seventeenth centuries especially, cats were cruelly tortured and killed, particularly during Lent when they were customarily thrown into bonfires to expunge the devil in them. The cat was simply a sad victim of being misunderstood by a superstitious people. They found unusual design features such as the cat's reflective eyes and high wailing voice as inexplicable in earthly terms and the queen's reproductive behaviour, in mating with several toms in succession if available, as promiscuous and therefore sinful and ungodly. With the rise of Lutherism and the Protestant religion, cats also became a hated symbol of Rome and the Catholic church, especially in Protestant strongholds such as Essex in the latter half of the 1500s. There, persecutions against witchcraft and anti-Pope feeling ran hand in hand and the Essex cat was regarded as a confusing mix of the devil on earth and the Pope. In nearby London, and right across Protestant Europe, basketwork effigies of the Pope were stuffed with live cats and roasted over huge fires. First it was the Egyptians strangling them as religious offerings and then the Europeans burning them for being associated with the 'wrong' religion and to exorcise themselves. Despite being worshipped at times, religion seems to have been fairly rotten to cats one way or another!

It wasn't until superstitions about cats being witches in different guises declined in the more enlightened Europe of the eighteenth century that it became a little more acceptable to be associated with cats again and the ritual burning of cats at midsummer fires ceased. (These midsummer cat burnings formed part of an old Celtic festival of the continuity of life and were included for no extra charge as part of later Christian ceremonies held at the same time.) However, the popularity of so-called 'sport' pits ensured that many cats were still used to train and bait fighting dogs.

The logical assumption is that until then, most cats tended to live as they had done in the worker towns of Ancient Egypt, by hunting and scavenging around man, but were no more likely to be kept as pets. Ordinary people at least would have been doing as much as possible to avoid any association with anything related to the occult or witchcraft. Indeed as superstitions persist for a long time in human cultures (we still regard a black cat crossing our path as being a good or bad portent, depending on whether you live in Britain or America), cats really only became acceptable again when, in the eighteenth century, the voracious brown rat invaded Europe from the east.

Far more opportunistic than the native black rat, the precocious brown rat was quite happy to exploit any source of food and shelter, and it seemed that only the cat could help man against this new threat. Suddenly it was acceptable to have a cat living in the house, shop or factory and curled up by the hearth taking a rest when not hunting. With Pasteur demonstrating in the nineteenth century that diseases were caused by microbes that thrived in filth and squalor, the cat's natural cleanliness, with all that washing and grooming, became respected. And this in an age when most other animals were being shunned and regarded as 'dirty' and even horses would only be handled with gloves in some areas of the country!

The cat's assimilation right into the home of recivilised man, as opposed to living simply around his settlements, was becoming established again after over 2,000 years and voyages in various directions around the world. That acceptance paved the way for much greater selection of the cat for docility and acceptance as a true pet, and then for beauty at cat shows and associated selection for type. But just what was the genetic make-up of the cat in the nineteenth century? I would suggest that the cat was still genetically very similar, if not identical to the African Wild Cat, *Felis lybica*. Any physical changes that had occurred to give variations in size, coat colour or even head shape were far more likely to have arisen because of their existence under different selective pressures in new lands. Maintenance of spontaneous mutations in the population from the original blueprint under those selective pressures would be far more likely to account for these physical changes than any great degree of cross-breeding with the indigenous Wild Cat, or deliberate selection for form, appearance or temperament by man.

So the cat that left its prints in the tile in Silchester in Roman Britain was probably still genetically an African Wild Cat, albeit already a smaller version than the original ancestor still found then in north Africa. He and all the early migrating small cats would not always have stayed on board their ships in port, nor with their new owners in faraway lands. They would have escaped, wandered away

97

and become established as a new addition to local fauna, perfectly equipped to survive in most new habitats they found themselves in.

Right up to and including the present time, some cats will undoubtedly have encountered, competed and interbred with the local wild cat species such as *Felis sylvestris* in Europe and, it is often suggested, given rise to a more heavily coated and more definitely marked cat than the original pale colour of the new immigrant from north Africa via southern Europe. Indeed it is presumed that this is how the present day north European moggy pet cat obtained his stockier, shorter-faced appearance and more crouched gait compared with the leaner, leggier, longer-faced African originator. Interestingly, the pet and free-living cats I have encountered around the Mediterranean, closer to their ancestral home, are far more similar in appearance to the leaner shape of their ancestor than pets and free-living moggy cats in northern Europe. Perhaps this is because they haven't encountered stockier cousins to interbreed with, or perhaps the climate and other influences select positively for the leaner appearance and larger stockier individuals are less able to survive under the prevailing conditions.

8
Mixing with Scottish cousins

'You've forgotten the greatest moral attribute of a Scotsman . . . that he'll do nothing which might damage his career'   Sir James Barrie

Whether any of the half-breeds resulting from matings between indigenous north European Wild Cats and the new immigrants, or even from early deliberate attempts by man to produce new colours and forms also produced 'handleable', friendly pets is unlikely. Such hybrids between wild cat species and pet cats today are usually rather spitty, unmanageable and, like Campbell, only behave as pets while they are very young. Caught between nature and nurture, they seem to respond to the call of their wild half far more than their pet portion and revert to a life on the wild side if given the chance. And herein lies the real conundrum that European Wild Cats, including the Scottish variant, are simply not tameable and do not make pets, and are only ever semi-approachable captive animals if restrained in cages. Any crossbreeding with pet cats does not placate their instincts for self-defence or increase their desire to be sociable with anything, let alone an upright primate who wants to mother them once they are beyond the age of needing to be mothered.

Scottish Wild Cats are normally solitary creatures except at mating time or when mothers are raising young, though several have been kept fairly amicably in enclosures, notably at the Highland Wildlife Park in Kingussie, Scotland. They behave amicably towards each other that is, but not towards even familiar people in any way. European Wild Cats have been bred in zoos at Prague and Berne, but

99

there is no record of instant tractability being achieved in the kittens produced!

In his splendid and fascinating account of captive breeding of Scottish Wild Cats over several years, called *Wild Cat Haven*, Mike Tomkies describes the difficulties of keeping the kittens raised in his remote cottage in the Highlands of Scotland. He managed to raise and release two litters of Scottish Wild Cats and one hybrid litter arising from a mating between a Wild Cat female and a free-living domestic cat. Despite a runt kitten called Liane maintaining a longer friendly relationship with him than the others, all the kittens ultimately rejected his friendship and left home to adopt a wild lifestyle. The domestic cat/Wild Cat hybrids behaved similarly, and 'regressed', if that is the word, in just the same way as Campbell had done with me in the less remote hinterland of Surrey.

The implication in behavioural terms is that deliberate crossbreeding of African Wild Cats transported around the world from Ancient Egypt is unlikely to have been pursued because the first crosses were already 'unhandleable' and would have been destroyed or fled human habitation to live in the wild. To obtain the colouring of the European Wild Cat species in a pet form without also introducing the wild temperament would surely have been as beyond the expertise of early man as it still is today, with all our improved knowledge of genetics and the importance of early handling of kittens on their subsequent behaviour as adults.

But surely there must have been some absorption of European Wild Cat genes into the pet cat genetic make-up if only to produce the darker colouring of the tabby cat of northern Europe? That would have made its appearance so much more similar to that of the European Wild Cat than its African cousin. Or was it just a chance mutation of the African Wild Cat that enhanced its survival prospects in new and colder environments? The European Wild Cat would certainly have been far more common in Europe around the time of Christ and even up to the seventeenth or eighteenth century, and so perhaps a slow intrusion of European Wild Cat genes could have occurred with the inevitable frequent interbreeding of half-breed cats living wild mating with pets to produce quarter wild cats, etc. But even the domestic cats living around human settlements would have been selected by Mother Nature to have shorter ears and tails, thicker coats and a colour that helped them blend with their rural or semi-rural environment. As a result they would tend to lose the appearance of the thinner coated, paler originator that evolved in the more open, warmer semi-desert of North Africa.

Such is the intractability of the European Wild Cat that any crossbreeding would have tended to make the African Wild Cat import more wild rather than the European version more tame. The tendency, as already suggested, would have been for cats to revert to a wild lifestyle unless restrained from doing so. And there is little evidence of specific breeding of cats by man for type, colour or character until the late nineteenth century when the first cat show was held in London under the auspices of cat fanatic Harrison Weir and the modern Cat Fancy was born.

The suggestion I am continuing to make is that it is the genes of the African Wild Cat, *Felis lybica*, that will have kept the small wild cat living in close harmony with man and so have been perpetuated wittingly or unwittingly by man's desire and the process of urbanisation of the environment. Contrastingly, the genes of indigenous *Felis sylvestris* that may have become integrated would always have forced the crossbreeds to seek a life away from man, less manipulated and less willing to pick up free or easy meals around his settlements. The more the friendly cats interbred around man or in his house, the more likely their genetic complement would have remained close to that of their original African ancestor. Any 'wildness' from the surrounding indigenous wild species would have tended to force those offspring out into the countryside ever further away from man's increasing domain. Kittens born to European Wild Cat mothers mated with pet cats would have been raised away from man and, never having had any contact, and with that all important fifty per cent wild input, grown up effectively like Campbell, as wild cats with their pet cat half suppressed.

Sadly, according to Nigel Easterbee, writing just before his untimely death, the nature of the biggest threat to the continuation of the Scottish Wild Cat as a species (or isolated population of the European Wild Cat) has changed. Initially the Scottish Wild Cat would have been better known as the British Wild Cat as it was found virtually throughout the country. But with the development of agriculture and the accompanying destruction of their natural wood and forest habitat, and hunting for fur, numbers were steadily reduced. The last Wild Cats in the south of England probably died out in the sixteenth century, though a few persisted in the north-east until the eighteenth century. Their numbers were then greatly reduced and their home range diminished to remote highland areas in Scotland through intense persecution by gamekeepers and farmers up to the First World War, at which time the population was at its lowest ever and restricted to the west of Scotland. With gamekeepers and other land workers packed off to the front to shoot at their fellow men in the trenches rather than at Scottish Wild Cats in defence of game birds for their masters to shoot at in the name of sport, the Wild Cat population recovered a little, particularly in eastern Scotland.

Nowadays, though they still avoid lowland areas which are farmed or managed intensively, Scottish Wild Cats are found in sporadic populations along the south-west and midwestern seaboard. However, they have not been able to traverse the industrial line between the major cities of Glasgow and Edinburgh and so will probably never return to other relatively recent habitats in northern England or to the forests of Wales. Persecution by man through trapping, snaring, poisoning and shooting is still high and obviously can have disastrous effects on small local populations, but Nigel felt that the main threat to the Scottish Wild Cat is now hybridisation, or crossbreeding with free-living domestic cats which produces fertile young. Like Campbell, the hybrids are then more likely to live a wild lifestyle and mate with other Wild Cats than with domestic cats. This further reduces the genetic integrity of the Scottish Wild Cat throughout its already much-reduced range.

In Nigel's extensive surveys, he found that free-living domestic cats and Wild Cat hybrids were widespread in Scotland, even in the remote areas left to the Wild Cat, but sadly he never lived to pursue his aim of locating and protecting the pure populations that still exist. He always fought shy of hazarding even a guess as to how many might remain. The Wild Cat of Europe is suffering the same challenge in its remaining natural open forest and steppe habitats in Greece, Italy, France, Russia and central Europe. Such is the adaptability of the African Wild Cat and its free-living domestic progeny compared with their native cousins that perhaps the Wild Cat of Europe will never again find safety and racial purity outside the walls of a zoo. It's ironic that such protection will only come about if action is taken by us, his more traditional foe, and quickly.

So, as well as going on to threaten the purity of their fathers' race, kittens raised in human company by pet cat mothers resulting from matings with European Wild Cat fathers are always likely to have developed like Campbell, and those raised by Mike Tomkies –

docile to some extent until adolescence instinctively drives them to adopt the wild life and move away from man, even with his free handouts. Man would surely be left with cats that perpetuated the African Wild Cat genes with little or no input from the indigenous population, that is those produced by domestic mothers mated by domestic fathers with no indigenous Wild Cat input, and it is from this stock that we continue to take and breed our pets.

9
Coats of many colours

'Under the fur, whatever colour it may be, there still lies, essentially unchanged, one of the world's free souls'   Eric Gurney

The most popular 'blue (grey or black) and white' cats of the seventeenth century, as quoted by Keith Thomas in *Man and the Natural World,* and predominance of black cats could have arisen in towns as a result of freedom for these colour mutations from the selective pressure that favours camouflage of tabby or agouti types in rural areas. Even today, black and black and white forms predominate in urban free-living cat colonies. The variety of coat colours observed in cats today is found because the genes that control colour in cats are very prone to change. Spontaneous simple mutations can occur at one or more of the six relevant gene sequences easily, and produce many colours and combinations of colours even on one cat. Then it's up to the selective pressure of the environment, including the effects of predation, climate, etc. to determine which colours survive best and where. For most true wild cat species and many other wild animals such as rabbits, the agouti-coloured hair predominates because it camouflages the animal best in woodland, light scrub or even field environments. The tabby pattern of many small wild cats further breaks up their outline and blends them into the shadows of the woodland when hunting at dawn or dusk, and more forest-dwelling species such as the European Wild Cat benefit further from even heavier striping in the murky grey light. Some, such as the leopard, are better blended into their background of shadows and shafts of bright light that penetrate thicker woodland and jungles by being spotted or dappled. Paler grey/sandy-coloured forms of the lightly striped tabby colouring are favoured to survive better in lighter backgrounds of semi-desert.

The gene that codes for agouti banding on the hair can now be relatively easily bred out by man through replacement with a recessive gene that codes for uniform colour such as black, red or white along the whole hair shaft. The implication is that spontaneous mutations are likely to have occurred in the African Wild Cat relatively frequently and this is indeed the case. While dark or bright new colours would not help the cat in its pale original north African environment, once the African Wild Cat found itself in new environments in Europe and elsewhere around the world by courtesy of man's transportation, he would be subject to new selective pressures. Those pressures of course meant that pale colouring was less of a guarantee of a long enough life to offer the chance to reproduce. Other colours, particularly the darker tabby and black forms, would then be at an increased advantage. As a result, these colours would start to permeate through the population and in turn be carried to new places to test their advantage under yet more local environmental conditions. A great combination of colours could therefore be produced in cats once those genes became established in an expanding cat population worldwide. That population is subject to such a huge range of selective pressures in so many different environments and so the original pale agouti colouring of the African Wild Cat has become dramatically altered to produce the variety of strikingly different-looking but otherwise fairly identical cats we know today.

Geneticists such as the American Neil Todd have attempted to look more closely at the genetics and spread of feline coat colours around the world implying that the more widespread any particular colour, then the longer it must be since that colour first arose as a mutation of the original agouti colour of the African Wild Cat type. He suggests that because the tabby, black, blue, ginger, white spotted and white cats are found worldwide, they must be the oldest colours, with the separate mutation for long hair being equally as old because it is found in cats of all those colours. By looking at the relative frequency of coat colours, he has tried to suggest when and where many of these mutations may first have occurred. Interestingly, for example, he suggests that single colour coats, especially black, first arose in the eastern Mediterranean region in the Classical period. Geneticists have also noted the high concentration of ginger cats in north Africa and along what corresponds to an ancient trade route from the Mediterranean region to London, implying that the cats either accompanied the traders or were items of trade themselves.

Certainly the agouti colouring of the hair of the wild cat species is rather fragile, genetically speaking. Among the spontaneously evolving black forms and other solid colours, orange cats, brown and silver tabbies etc., a relatively new tabby form, the 'blotched' tabby', has a special story. It arose, or rather was first recorded, in Italy and England in the fifteenth or sixteenth century. In fact, it probably mutated earlier in about the thirteenth century in the free-living cat population but went unrecorded until a passing nobleman spotted one. The blotched tabby became noticeable in the population because it afforded a survival advantage in the darker woodlands compared with even the usual brown striped tabby colouring. It is not perhaps surprising to find that the heavier, darker, joined striped markings of the blotched tabby evolved in northern Europe. After all, this colour resembled far more closely the markings of the indigenous wild cat species which had evolved to blend into the same environment under presumably the same selective pressures before the African Wild Cat arrived with the Romans many centuries earlier. But like the black cat, the blotched tabby was also at an advantage in the shadows of the human settlements and towns of the era compared with the striped tabby and camouflage may have been all important in an age when so many cats were being persecuted in witch hunts and anti-Catholic festivals.

But if the African Wild Cat in Britain mutated into a blotched colour pattern through 'natural' pressures, he had one more advantage because of man's opinions. The blotched tabby was soon discovered and came to be prized by man both for its appearance and because, as is often quoted today, it is often a very languid, easy to handle cat and doubtless this led to its popularity as a pet. But like that other perhaps more famous mutation, the Siamese, and many other breeds or colours of cat that evolved with the good fortune to be of slightly different appearance to the normal range, the blotched tabby was first valued and protected by the royal and the rich. As a result it then became more popular with the masses and so spread throughout the pet cat population. Later, it was to be shipped to all corners of the British Empire and establish itself in the cat populations of many countries colonised by the British, starting with America, then Canada and Australia. The frequency of blotched tabby markings is especially high in countries which had no small cat population prior to the arrival of British colonisers but especially low in cat populations of countries left uninvaded by the Brits.

Is feline temperament related to coat colour?

Black coats and blotched tabby markings, Todd suggests, survived better in the urban environment not just because of better camouflage but also because this colour is linked to a less assertive temperament, more placid character and better tolerance of crowding than the agouti coloured original. These are all factors which would have made black cats, and then much later, blotched tabby cats, better able to live with man in towns and better accepted as pets, rather than simply as free rat controllers. Black cats may be tolerant but may also have their limits. Many professional animal trainers find black cats as stubborn and single-minded as uncastrated toms and may be more difficult than most to train to walking on a lead and harness. Their association with good luck in Britain, however, may also have helped assure them of a little respect and affection, though in America, a black cat is often a sign of bad luck.

The modern pet cat's adrenal glands are a little smaller than the original African Wild Cat's, implying that over time, the pet may have come to produce steadily less adrenaline and other hormones which 'energise' the body for running away from challenge or fighting. The implication of this is that such cats would be less likely to run away so quickly from humans compared with the reclusive European Wild Cat and so habituate to their presence and be more likely to become pets. But it is not known whether the smaller adrenal glands could have evolved because of a reduced need to run away in the company of man rather than evolving first and then predisposing for the less reactive behaviour and enabling the cat to stay around man and survive better as a result. Perhaps the success of the black cat fills the former supposition while the later mutating friendly blotched tabby fulfils the latter. Either way, a lowered physiological response to challenge is the basis of tolerance in the behavioural sense and the role of the adrenal glands is probably crucial in the association of the cat with man.

Other colours aside from black and blotched tabby also seem to relate to a cat's temperament in some way. Subsequent interbreeding with other older colour mutants such as white, and later arising ones such as ginger (orange) from Asia Minor, could then steadily have given rise to the even greater variety that we enjoy today. Popularity of colour-related docility may have been harder to trace with the sometimes quoted hot temper of some tortoiseshell (especially the Old English variety in my limited experience!) and ginger cats. Though ginger cats are often also quoted as being calm and affable, when they are spitty and reactive, it can be time to take quick avoiding action. Such cats certainly fuel the old idea that, as with human red-heads and chestnut mares, genes coding for red hair may also give rise to fiery character. The curse of being 'blessed with ginger twins' was the ultimate punishment for a sinful life as far as my wife's grandfather was concerned. Though, sadly, he never lived to see his great-granddaughter, he would have been watching closely to see whether the present fine orangey-fair hair on her six-month-old head was turning full ginger to see just what sort of a life I've led and whether I really am a nice enough husband for his perfect blonde granddaughter!

But then, we can also find a fiery character attractive on occasion and would probably have deliberately incorporated the genes coding for red or orange into early cat breeding to produce a reactive as well as attractive cat. Tortoiseshell and ginger colouring are relatively easier to manage because they are sex-linked. Only some ten per cent of ginger cats are female and though male tortoisehells have been thought to be inviable and never born, there have been occasional reports of individuals turning up around the world. I have personally petted a very splendid and obviously male example at the veterinary school in Bristol, where I practise. He is currently undergoing a few harmless tests to see whether he is fertile and might pass on his unusualness!

Todd also suggests that as dark-coloured coats are more abundant in cities and where cats live closely with man, the earlier the urbanisation of any culture, the greater the proportion of dark forms, at least in the days before neutering of pets and of free-ranging cats became the norm in the Western world. He argues that cats were probably only brought to north-eastern America in the seventeenth century to combat rats in urban areas like Philadelphia. The greatest variability in coat colour will be found in the older industrial societies, he argues. The genetics of coat colour in colonial populations of cats in cities such as Philadelphia will have had less time to mutate and respond to new environmental selective pressures and so resemble the cat population of mid-seventeenth-century Europe in terms of colour variance. Hence the colours of the cats that first colonised the USA remained largely unchanged for many generations, despite the fact that the cats themselves were rapidly exploiting yet more new environments and ecological niches.

I would argue that these cats were still largely unaltered or perhaps even near-pure African Wild Cats, whose adaptable genes were being given further rein to spread and then respond as required to facilitate survival of the species under local conditions. And of course, having left in Ancient Egyptian times and evolved new forms, the African Wild Cat was perhaps even better able to colonise its original environment when it returned with the arrival of European settlers in north Africa in the seventeenth century! The free-living domestic cats living around the tourist hotels in Tunisia and Morocco are of the original lean and leggy variety rather than the stumpier, thicker-coated, free-living feral cats of New York, London and Amsterdam.

Genetic stretching . . . making new breeds

But what of the notably different breeds that we have today, such as the elegant Siamese and beautiful Longhairs or Persians? Surely, their physical and colour departures compared with the standard moggy could only have arisen through manipulation by man and they must be far removed from any link with the African Wild Cat? Not so. The Siamese is a very old breed, and arose from a natural mutation which survived. Originally, it is believed, Siamese cats were kept only by the Siamese royal family. The distinctive colouring of the Siamese derives from a reduction in the pigmentation of the hair in warmer parts of the body, while the pigment develops in cooler areas such as the ears, nose, feet and tail. These are the 'points' of the different varieties, though of course, if the pet Siamese cat is allowed outdoors in a British climate, the darker colouring can soon emerge virtually all over the coat. Show specimens that are presented for spaying at the vets are often operated on down the mid-line of the stomach rather than through the usual incision in the flank to hide the dark band of hair that grows over the scar underneath and keep the pale body appearance for as long as possible.

The British Consul-General to Siam was most honoured to be given a pair of Siamese cats in 1884 but the 'breed' had already reached Britain earlier in the century at the Crystal Palace Cat Show of 1871. The 'nightmare kind of cat', as it was described by one observer (cover your points, Bean and Flirty Bottom!) was of the Seal Point variety, though at least twenty point colours are now recognised in the Cat Fancy, including the popular Blue, Lilac, Chocolate and Red points, and more genetically complicated Blue Tabby Tortie (Patched Tabby or Torbie) or Chocolate Tabby (Lynx) Points. Interestingly, while Siamese breeders around the world have worked hard to establish and maintain the different coloured points, the Lilac and Tortie have evolved spontaneously and can be found in the free-living cat populations around some of the Buddhist temples in Thailand today. The very slim or 'Foreign' build of the Siamese has been accentuated in recent times as a result of deliberate selection by breeders. Originally the Siamese, and those which now live free around the Thai temples, were and are of the stockier 'normal' cat shape.

The Longhair mutation originally arose and became established in cold and often mountainous areas such as Angora (nowadays known as Ankara, the new capital of Turkey) where a thick coat was clearly an advantage against the elements. Angora gave its name to that particular Longhair variety and the Turkish Van, famous for its predilection for swimming, takes its name from its centre of origin, around Lake Van in Anatolia. However, the finer long coat of these breeds is different to the thicker coats found in the long-haired mutations of the colder north, such as the Norwegian Forest Cat and others that are similar in Scandinavia and Russia. They have double coats of a thick warm woolly layer protected by an upper layer of longer, coarser, more layered waterproof hair. Doubtless these Longhair mutations also became perpetuated in the free-living cat populations because they survived better under the prevailing conditions. It's a case of two similar successful mutations occurring in different parts of the world to help the cat survive in environments that are very different to the one the African Wild Cat originally evolved in, where a long or a long and thick double coat would have been a distinct disadvantage in the heat. If cats with such mutations had arisen, they would not have been likely to compete in the heat nor survive for long, hence the Longhair genes would not have permeated the cat genetic pool of the region.

The Longhair gene is romantically thought to have entered America via six Angora cats owned by Marie Antoinette on board a ship that was supposed to take her to safety as the revolution threatened in France. She missed the boat and lost her head, but many of her personal effects, including her cats, made it safely. The Angoras are thought to have interbred with other cats there, spread the Longhair mutation around a little and ultimately given rise to the beautiful dense-coated Maine Coon variety. More likely perhaps, given that the Maine Coon is a double-coated variety, is that the double-coated Longhairs had already arrived 500 years earlier via Scandinavian traders. Longhairs, incidentally, are known as Persians by the American Cat Fancy, a term that is also used commonly now in the United Kingdom, though the British Cat Fancy officially sticks to the original description of Longhairs. Nowadays three types of coat are recognised: the Angora, still with its long lank coat, the northern cats with their thick double coats and the modern Persian, which has been developed by selective breeding especially with the modern 'powder puff' coat and squashed-in broader face shape.

The white Angora came to the United Kingdom from France, and a little before the Siamese, but it had colour-linked deafness problems. Later introductions towards the end of the nineteenth century had no such problems. Other colours were soon developed in the breed and though the shortening of the face in the breed was noted in the early part of this century, it has really only become exacerbated in the seventy years or so since then, through selection by cat breeders trying to make something look different to the basic cat design. Thankfully, I suspect that the damage they can do with this type of breeding of modern Longhairs is limited compared to the disasters of dog breeding when it produces something as physically deformed as a Bulldog. Cat genes that code for anything other than colour or hair length are extremely difficult to manipulate.

The German Hemmer has spent much time looking at the skull size, brain capacity, behaviour, litter size and vocalisation patterns of the Siamese and Longhair breeds and found that there was no evidence to suggest that any other species of wild cat was involved in their development than the African Wild Cat. Even the yells and screams of the Siamese can also be heard in *Felis lybica*, albeit occupying a rarely used portion of their vocal range. The longer pregnancy of the Siamese compared with other breeds is simply a function of their producing larger litters and he found no evidence for the earlier cited suggestions that the hairier Pallas's Cat or hairy-footed Sand Cat had any involvement in the development of any of the Longhair breeds.

It would appear that even the very distinct pet strains were simply originally 'natural' mutations, some of which survived because of understandable natural advantages that man seized upon and then perpetuated for his own reasons and refined or developed to accentuate the recognisable differences. Recent examples are the Rex cats, which have non-shedding crinkly coats that especially find favour with people who are allergic to cat hair and dander. The Cornish Rex mutation arose from a single kitten born in 1950 to a farm cat mother in Cornwall. Mated back to its mother, a common if rather unnatural technique of animal breeders seeking to establish unusual characteristics, it bred true to form the Cornish Rex breed. A like mutation occured in Devon in the 1960s and produced a similar breed called, of course, the Devon Rex. These spontaneous mutations would have died out without man and another, the Siamese cat, would have been unlikely to spread naturally to or survived well in colder climates. But the Siamese has been taken around anyway because man wanted him all over the world as a cared-for pet. Similarly, while the Angoras and other Longhair mutations survived better by being warmer under their long coats, the artificially developed fine but long-haired modern cats need constant grooming to keep their beauty. Out in the wilds, they could not keep their coat layered, parasite free and waterproofed, and once their fur became damp and matted would not survive for long.

Selection by man has usually centred on perpetuating the rather occasional mutations that have occurred spontaneously in the cat such as head shape, absence of tail (for example the Manx breed), folded ears (for example the Scottish Fold), stumpy legs (the hideously deformed Munchkin which appeared in the 1980s in America) and the more frequent colour mutations. Even the unique appearance of the hairless Sphynx Cat in 1966, born to a litter produced by an ordinary black and white pet moggy, followed the same route as other cats which have mutated to be different from the usual blueprint. This sad mutation, destined never to stray far from a sunspot or radiator despite the fact that the rest of its genes tell it to go out and hunt, was seized upon and bred selectively by man. By the late 1980s, some breeders were asking £4,000 for a Sphynx kitten when surely in the interests of cat welfare, the first unfortunate little kitten mutation should never have been allowed to live in the first place.

In pursuit of notoriety, fashion and finance, it is man who has defined the one hundred or so breeds and varieties of cat based on spontaneous mutations in the hair length, colour and shape of the original African Wild Cat as it has spread around the world and responded to local environments and selective pressures. After seizing upon any 'natural' mutations man has subsequently worked at the most artificially modifiable feature of coat colour and incorporated different colours into all the other breeds as best he can. It's no surprise then that colour is used most widely to distinguish between breeds in cats, compared with various colours being identified within a single recognised breed of dog, such as the Greyhound, for example. It seems that even the most physically distinct varieties of cat from far-flung corners of the earth are still mutations and now enhanced adaptations of the original cat to enter into life around man, the African Wild Cat.

10
Pet cat = African Wild Cat.
The proof?

'Give her but a wavering leaf shadow of a breeze combing the grasses and she was back a million years, glaring with night-lit eyes in the thickets'   Paul Annixter

Just last year in 1991, while on a lecture tour for vets and others interested in pet behaviour in South Africa, I was fortunate enough to meet Eric Harley, Professor of Chemical Pathology at Cape Town University. He has the first evidence that just may corroborate all the implications made in Chapters 8 and 9. With his colleagues Faadiel Essop and Nomusa Mda, he has looked at the nucleic acid, DNA, of the mitochondria (those tiny parts of cells that produce energy) from a very small number of domestic pet cats including moggies and a pedigree strain of Siamese from the Cape Town area. He has also looked at four examples of *Felis lybica* taken from cats from the remote western Cape area (and therefore from as pure a population as possible with regard to any possible 'hidden' interbreeding with domestic cats). So far, Eric and his team have found the nature of this 'blueprint for the pet cat' genetic material to be identical in all of the pet cats and the African Wild Cats! The analytical techniques used involved a complicated structural DNA mapping technique and were, in some ways, similar to those now used in genetic fingerprinting. Genetic fingerprinting enables almost certain identification of individuals, such as suspects in criminal cases, from genetic material taken from skin or semen samples

114

because everyone's DNA is individual to them.

Because such biochemical techniques are now precise enough to identify individuals from their unique genetic blueprints, Professor Harley's findings can be said to represent the most advanced refinement in the classification of species since Linnaeus first began his daunting task. As we have seen, such definitions of species used to be based on straightforward physical appearance in relation to location and habitat, then on skull and skeletal measurements and, recently, by employing more complex techniques of hair analysis and immunological approaches using cell proteins.

Eric's work has also suggested that, more than being identical, the DNA samples taken from *Felis lybica* and pet cats are both also quite different from that of *Felis sylvestris*, the European Wild Cat. Although the results produced by Professor Harley's team are foolproof and clear-cut, they are endeavouring to obtain both African and European Wild Cat examples from a wider distribution before publishing their results officially in the academic press. Like all such revelations, it will take a lot more samples and tests to prove the case to the satisfaction of scientists such as Eric Harley and the rest of the academic community, but this early work is surely of absolutely fascinating interest to everyone whose life has become involved with the pet cat, and that includes every cat owner in the world.

At some point in history the African Wild Cat and European Wild Cat did have a common ancestor, it's just difficult to determine when, given the poor fossil record of small cats. Perhaps Eric can help here as well because by using even more complicated analysis of his data, barely comprehensible to an out-of-date biologist like me, he is suggesting that the European Wild Cat (*Felis sylvestris*) and the African Wild Cat (*Felis lybica*) diverged from their common ancestor about 700,000 years ago, about 696,000 years before the first evidence of cats living around man in Ancient Egypt.

By using surely the most precise and fundamental assessment of genetic integrity that can be made, Eric Harley and his colleagues are rewriting the definition of what constitutes a species at the nucleic acid level. What we currently describe as *Felis catus*, the domestic pet cat, is, in fact, so nearly exactly the same species as the African Wild Cat as there to be no grounds for differentiating between the two in terms of species. The pet cat is simply a reflection of a series of mutations into a wider range of forms and colours of the African Wild Cat. It is also clearly distinguishable from the European Wild Cat, the

Black-footed Cat of Africa and probably any other wild cat species, though obviously, they all need to be tested and compared.

The pet cat is apparently still a real original wild species that chooses to live with and around man. And if that raises all manner of questions about the resistance of genes and the nature of genetic analysis and species definition, at least it helps us answer far more satisfactorily just why the cat has remained the least domesticated, least manipulable 'domestic' species we have ever shared our lives with. It's because the cat still isn't domesticated genetically. He is still, in his genes, the same or almost the same as he was even before Ancient Egyptian times. The changes that have occurred in his colour, size and even his form have largely been natural mutations that have survived in the new environments that we have taken the cat to, or deliberately encouraged and enhanced for our own purposes. Even quite noticeable changes in the shape of the face, in the Peke-faced Persian for example, have only occurred very recently as a result of our direct and sustained artificial selection building on a previous natural mutation, and not as a result of any interbreeding with indigenous wild cat species in any country. The African Wild Cat would appear to have remained virtually pure with only a few fine edges alterable under any sort of selective process, natural or man-made, and is therefore quite literally a true wild cat in our living room. He is not domesticated, but domestic when he chooses. He is not some combination of several wild cat inputs combined with the effects of man's influence and desire, nor, as we have always known, is he fully compromised by his association with man.

Of course, one must now ask other searching questions. Why is it that *Felis lybica* is found in relatively constant form and colour in its natural north African environment? Why, if it is so adaptable, did it need man to transport the species to other environments before it could colonise them? Could the African Wild Cat not have migrated on his own? The answer, one suspects, is that there may have been climatic or geographical boundaries to prevent his migration from north Africa and that he evolved perfectly in terms of coat colour, size, etc. to suit conditions there. Hence mutations to, say, a black form would not have afforded any greater survival and reproductive advantage. In fact a different colour to the one evolved to camouflage him into his habitat would make him more conspicuous. He would then be more likely to be spotted by an enemy, especially when young and vulnerable and unaware that being black against a sandy background did not conceal him. Nor would being conspicuous assist at all in the stalking of prey. It would have perhaps required that little extra protection gained through his association with man and transport in his ships to enable the genetic adaptability of the species to be realised in all the new places he found himself in once he left the shores of Egypt.

Once arrived in a new world, the pale agouti colouring of the African Wild Cat would have suited the immigrant as well as it did the indigenous wild cat species in similar environments around the Mediterranean, although darker forms would soon have been selected for more shaded or wooded hunting grounds inland. In human settlements, a black mutation, one of the oldest recorded, would have been more likely to survive than in Africa, merging into the shadows of buildings.

In short, man could be regarded as a simple catalyst that allowed a veritable population explosion of this rather unique cat into all the areas that he himself was moving into. That cat, it appears from the archaeological evidence of those mummified specimens from Ancient Egypt, had perhaps already undergone a reduction in cranial capacity and brain size as well as body size as is usual in animals taken in and domesticated by man. These changes, however, didn't occur because of later man-made influences in keeping and watering down the wild nature of cats held in captivity. 'Domestication' had already happened as a single or series of spontaneous mutations of the African Wild Cat living in the wild in Ancient Egypt and it was this prior improvement in the cat's acceptance of man that enabled him to live in and around his settlements and later in his temples.

Perhaps it was when that reduction in brain capacity occurred that the African Wild Cat lost his fearful flight reactions towards man and became 'handleable' and stayed friendly even after kittenhood. Perhaps it was then that the 'friendly genes' we all enjoy today in our pet cats first apppeared. But whatever the true origin of the cat's change of character from the usual wild temperament of wild cats, the African Wild Cat has been successfully able to exploit the protection and food available around man ever since, and without ever losing the ability to fend for himself in the wild style if required.

By contrast, the indigenous wild cat species in Europe, Asia and elsewhere have responded to man like most wild animals, and retreat into the hinterland in the face of persecution through hunting, habitat destruction and environmental pollution. For the African Wild Cat, being even closer to man as his pet in certain circumstances has simply been to exploit the benefits that co-existence brings more fully. But being a pet is far from being a compromise on the cat's wild ancestry and has never been at the expense of losing his ability to survive alone through hunting if required to. Nor has man been able to disarm the cat of the hunting equipment of tooth and claw to make him safer to handle through selective breeding in the same way as dogs have been bred to have fewer teeth than their wolf ancestor. The old line about man having been domesticated by the cat rather than the cat by man seems to have some real truth in it if Professor Harley's remarkable findings can be fully substantiated.

In any case, according to Paul Leyhausen, there is a major conflict in viewing the success of the cat as having occurred as a result of even loose domestication by man. It makes the cat unique among 'domestic' animals in having shown such a huge diversity of social strategies within the contract. Some cats live solitary lives, others in small groups, yet others in enormous colonies. Some live apparently reasonably happily as pets in a forced dependent relationship on man because they live permanently inside his home and are not allowed outdoors. Most, of course, have a 'come and go as you please' arrangement with their 'owners' and choose to return for the most part. Many cats live a free-ranging life as what we describe as feral cats – 'domestic' cats which have 'reverted' to a free-living lifestyle. But if Eric Harley's theory is proven, the feral cat technically ceases to exist because the African Wild Cat can be said for certain never to have been domesticated in the first place!

As we have already discussed, after domestication, most animals show a loss of ancestral hunting abilities and specialised form as we start to select for production or for our own tasks. The cat never lost the original design for function. When other truly domesticated species such as pigs, dogs, sheep, goats or horses 'revert' and become feral, they fall back on what they can manage of the social system of their wild ancestors rather than developing new social systems, even though those old systems don't really suit their new lifestyle or habitat. And those original social systems are usually, as Leyhausen says, 'impoverished versions' of the wild ancestors' social set-up, hence the feral animals only rarely establish themselves as well as the wild ancestors.

The cat, by contrast, is unique in his adaptability when 'feral' because he shows an enrichment of his ancestral social behaviour to

118

adapt and survive so well in so many different habitats. As a population, cats can survive and thrive in environments as diverse as inner-city derelict building sites, oceanic islands, rural farms and suburban hospital sites and in temperatures ranging from the permanently freezing to the daytime heat of the desert. The problem is that we may always have been looking at things from the wrong perspective. The question is not why or how the cat has been able to show such enrichment in the face of the constraints of domestication, but how have those elastic ancestral African Wild Cat genes been able to hold him in such good stead in circumstances so far removed from the ones that they evolved in.

Leyhausen, writing in *The Domestic Cat - the biology of its behaviour,* said, 'The fact that domestic cats show a greater social diversity than their wild ancestors doesn't necessarily mean that they possess a greater potential. They have simply been exposed to far more extreme, not to say diametrically opposed conditions'. He is implying that the potential was always there in the total behavioural repertoire or generic behaviour (including social behavioural adaptability) of the African Wild Cat, and that it was passed on intact to the pet cat. It's just that the full elastic behavioural repertoire never met a large range of circumstances in Africa and so it wasn't expressed until man carried the cat around the world to be influenced by so many conditions and demands. The cat has then taken advantage of every brave new world he has encountered, only one of which has been to choose to live as man's pet.

The question then is how, in the African semi-desert, could such a creature have evolved to be so adaptive when he was already apparently so well-adapted to local conditions. I suspect the answer lies in that chance mutation that made the African Wild Cat willing to live his life close to man and even stay 'handleable' and sociable as an adult when other wild mammals, including all those other cousin species of wild cat in the rest of the world, nearly always revert to intractability as they approach maturity. Perhaps one might call it the spontaneous mutation of 'friendly' genes and perhaps it did appear late in Ancient Egypt in relation to the forced domestication of other species and only after thousands of years of the African Wild Cat living at a distance and retreating from man. Perhaps it was a lucky break for the African Wild Cat, for without it, he would never have been able to take advantage of the shelter, transport and food and reach all those new lands nor would he still be doing it today. And it's an interesting thought for a moment, to consider that perhaps the process didn't just happen once, but continues to happen continuously today as wild, free African Wild Cats mutate in the same way and make the same choice as their ancestors did, to move in with man.

Who domesticated whom and when may be only a question of semantics if you are curled up by the fire with your pet cat, but clearly, a total reappraisal of pet cat genetics, social behaviour, evolution and adaptation to environment will be required if he does prove to be genetically the same species as the African Wild Cat. It would certainly appear that the mutation to be friendly was, in a sense, all that was needed to facilitate the success of the cat. Thereafter, he has mutated little except at a tiny, albeit sometimes very noticeable, proportion of his genetic complement, and is highly resistant to being genetically manipulated by us. Has he really fooled us all along through his friendly behaviour and changes of coat colour that he was a domesticated species? Think about it as you cuddle him by the fire. Think of him as a wild animal. Forget about all those times when you wondered why he wouldn't do what you asked of him and went his own way, cocking a snook at what you expected from a 'domesticated' pet. Perhaps then you will come to see your relationship with him in a new and even more rewarding light.

SECTION FOUR

Feral Cats: A Life Still on the Wild Side

11
Life in a man's world

'He looked at me as I were some sort of unnecessary product which Cuthbert the Cat had brought in after a ramble among the local ash-cans'
                                                                    P.G.Wodehouse

I am lucky to have been able to spend much of my life since leaving university working with cats, and luckier still to have been able to earn a living from a life with animals, and cats in particular. Nowadays, most of that work is as a pet behaviour therapist, treating problem behaviour in pet cats and dogs. Dogs, as one might expect, are more likely to be problematic in behavioural terms than cats but, because my heart is basically feline, I try to concentrate on cats. I have 'three of each' at home, by the way, just in case dog owners try to accuse me of bias in my practice!

Most mammal biologists in their middle years end up concentrating on a single species or family of animals, fired by some irresistible attraction and curiosity even more than by the career structure that limited opportunities may force them to follow. The over-enthusiastic fascination with cats that I had as a small child probably forced my first pet cat, Lulu, to abandon ship and move in down the road, but it was rekindled by the opportunity to study cats shortly after leaving university. I owe an enormous debt to the feral cat for being there to be studied and for enabling me to start my professional career. I also owe an enormous debt to Dr Jenny Remfry, a vet and then Assistant Director of the Universities Federation for Animal Welfare, a highly learned and academic animal welfare society, for taking me on as Research Biologist. I was still wet behind the ears, clutching my degree certificate like so many others and desperately looking for a job that involved working with animals. It was Jenny who, slightly, I suspect, against the opinions of her colleagues, insisted that someone be taken on to carry out in-depth studies about the behaviour and welfare of feral cats and to promote their humane control.

It was supposed to be a three-month contract with UFAW, looking at the potential for the use of a chemosterilant derived from cotton, called gossypol, in the control of feral cats and dogs, followed by a literature review on the welfare of laboratory rodents prior to a symposium UFAW held in the early 1980s. I learnt a lot about broad animal welfare principles from the laboratory animal review project but it was cats, or more specifically feral cats, that began to grip me. As it turned out, gossypol, I discovered, wasn't to be of much help in the humane control of anything. Chinese studies using not only animals but also human 'volunteers' had shown that while the drug certainly reduced male fertility in some cases to zero, there were many side effects like total loss of libido, headaches, nausea and loss of co-ordination that meant it could not be safely prescribed. But the need for information about the feral cat remained, and I stayed with UFAW for over three years.

The first principle of any study is to 'know thine enemy' so I spent a lot of time reading up on what was known about feral cats to see how any method of population control might work. From then on I was hooked, not just on cats, but on the inordinate success of this domestic pet living rough. I started to look for and study feral cats everywhere I went, from the streets and parks of London to the farms around my home in semi-rural Hertfordshire, always wondering how it was that free-living cats were able to do so well. When I started working for UFAW, I viewed the feral cat as a victim of man's cruelty, an abandoned and pitiful creature that the mainstream animal welfare concerns seemed to be ignoring. But the more I studied the feral cat, the more it seemed to me that he was often doing okay and, in some cases, thriving without man.

Looking back ten years later and reassessing all that early work in the light of Professor Harley's research, many of the questions I was asking seem now to have clearer answers. There is perhaps no such thing as a feral cat, a domestic cat reverted to the wild. Instead all cats – feral, stray and pet – can be viewed as being the same species as their African Wild Cat ancestor, and the pet cat as simply exploiting an attractive opportunity. The 'normal' lifestyle is living around and with man, but not necessarily to the height of luxury that we offer him as a pet. Then the success of the cat 'living rough' and away from the direct care of man is that much easier to comprehend.

A self-supporting, solitary hunter such as the cat, which has the ability to adapt to a range of living conditions and diets would be better at living 'free' than a highly domesticated pack hunter such as the dog. It would also be far better able to survive as a free-living creature than any farm animal that has been drastically altered by man from its ancestral design in the pursuit of greater food production.

Despite the ability of the cat to survive without us, the feral cat was, and still is, a target for the attentions of animal welfarists. This is because in colour it looks exactly like the millions of cats that are kept in people's homes as pets and behaves rather like them in many respects too. Hence cat lovers and cat owners readily identify with the feral cat who keeps his distance from most people, yet lives around human habitations, parks and industrial estates. Though wary of most people, the free-living cat may take scraps of food from some trusted individuals and perhaps even allow them to touch or pick him up. Such 'cupboard love' from an otherwise fearful and 'wild' creature has made many people want to improve his living conditions, perhaps as far as trying to give every feral cat the same warm den and overflowing food bowls as their own cats enjoy at home. That he would be happier there than walking on the wild side in the urban jungle is beyond question to the cat welfarist. But in many city situations the free-living cat has also acquired pest status and faces demands for his control from those genuinely suffering from the effects of their smelly marking or noisy midnight fighting or courtship. They perhaps have a less pleasant fate in mind for the cat than a place by the fire.

Somehow a compromise had to be contrived and finding and developing one was UFAW's role. Since the society's foundation in the 1930s, it has been involved in so many real-life issues that have arisen between man and animals. Its studied concern for animal welfare and protection has always been balanced with an understanding of human needs and demands, however variable they may be. UFAW's role in the urban feral cat problem became my job. The more we studied and worked with feral cats, the deeper we became involved all round the world, looking at various feral cat types and strategies for survival, varying human demands and attitudes and realising the need to develop a humane approach to their interactions.

I couldn't have had a finer introduction to the wild side of the cat, nor to the realities of human attitudes towards cats, from ailurophobes (cat haters) to those who eat, sleep and breathe cats and little else. Work with pet cat owners and closer studies of the behaviour of pet cats and the pet cat/human relationship were to follow later in France and in the animal rescue shelter in Greece and through my feline behaviour therapy referral practice.

For the sake of tradition and rather than to keep referring to what I should perhaps otherwise be calling the 'free-living African Wild Cat', I'll continue to use the term 'feral cat' as meaning a free-living domestic cat. It's an easier term, though we may all have to review our conception of what a feral cat is, if Eric Harley proves to be correct. We may soon have to view the 'feral cat' as being the natural form of the African Wild Cat which has been able, through taking a ride with man, to extend its natural range, and concomitantly view the pet cat as a 'semi-domesticated' sub-species of the same thing.

Semantics again, but I make no apologies because it is now impossible for me to view the worldwide success of the feral cat as anything other than the result of colonisation of new ecological niches by a highly evolved predator. Indeed, these small cats are now the most widely distributed carnivore in the world, being found from latitudes of fifty-two degrees south to fifty-five degrees north and in conditions ranging from arid desert to sticky tropical rainforests and just about everywhere where man is found or has been. The domestic pet environment in our homes is surely just another one of those niches, the one most emphatically caused by man, and one that has been particularly successful for the cat at an individual level. The only price of such 'domestication', compared with the 'hitching a ride' approach the cat has assumed to reach other niches, is often to lose the individual ability to procreate because it suits us, the providers, better to have our pets sterilised. We now largely select who is fit to breed, not Mother Nature.

Free-living feral cats, on the other hand, do not have to make such personal compromises. For them, life, survival and the opportunity to procreate and pass on their genes to the next generation is a constant affair, dictated by their highly evolved abilities and the demands and whims of Mother Nature. It's a shorter life for most than when well-fed, vaccinated against killer diseases and then curled up asleep safe by the human hearth. While it's common now to hear of pet cats surviving to the age of twenty (the documented record is thirty-six years and a day!), even the best fed city feral cats start to look a bit ragged by the time they reach four or five years of age. Few reach the age of ten. The Humane Society of the United States estimates that the average lifespan for feral cats there is only eighteen months to two years for those that survive kittenhood. Most city feral cats do not fall prey to disease after kittenhood, nor do they die from exposure or fall prey to other animals or direct victimisation by man. They die mainly from the effects of non-consuming predation by motor cars. Up to 5,000 feral cats are estimated to die under the wheels of cars alone every year in Baltimore.

Despite this, it is quite likely that those feral cats in cities around the world which have learned to accept occasional free food hand-outs or have even been adopted by a regular feeder, and which have access to a warm shelter during cold and wet weather, are likely to survive to a greater age than the cat who is forced to hunt and scavenge his living on some remote island. Once living free, the cat is subject to all the survival pressures that any wild animal must face and populations of feral cats will vary throughout the year in relation to food availability, reproductive success, climate, disease, predation, competition between themselves and competition with other predators.

Fortunately or, more accurately, through the adaptable perfection of its design, the feral cat is able to survive long enough as an individual for the population to maintain itself in a large range of environments and under a wide range of conditions. This is largely because wherever the cat has been taken by man, or has found his own way, he has been able to feed himself as a free-living creature through one or more of three main feeding policies. He can hunt using the strategies of his cousins described earlier to cope with different types of prey available to him, or scavenge, be it on carrion or from man's waste-bins, or accept free handouts from man. As the cat can use one or a combination of these successful approaches, there will be few places indeed where one wouldn't expect to find cats.

Not surprisingly, the largest and most densely packed cat populations are usually found living in close association with man because of the greater access to the concentrations of food in his bins and associated rodents to hunt, as well the occasional free hand-out. Feral cats which genuinely hunt for themselves for most or all of their food will usually need a relatively much larger area from which to derive sufficient intake and so the population will be thinner on the ground, more territorially competitive between themselves and more responsive as a population to the seasonal availability of their prey.

12
Surviving and thriving everywhere

'Confront a child, a puppy and a kitten with sudden danger; the child
will instinctively turn for assistance, the puppy will grovel in abject
submission, the kitten will brace its tiny body for a frantic resistance'
Saki

The adaptability of the feral cat is probably nowhere better
demonstrated than on oceanic islands such as the Galapagos Islands
600 miles off the coast of Ecuador. This group of islands is famous
because it was here that Darwin recognised the hallmarks of adaptation
in his theory of evolution. He identified the slight variations between
the finches of one island and those of the next and described how each
adaptation enabled each type to exploit the local conditions of each
island that much better. Many of the bird and reptile populations
evolved under rather different conditions to those their ancestors left
on the mainland. Typically island species are fewer than on the
mainland and are often highly specialised to adapt to unusual or
unique conditions. In particular, many such species grow and evolve
without the presence of many predators and so are removed from the
selective pressure that their mainland counterparts live under and
evolve to deal with. As a result they invariably show little fear at the
approach of man or other non-indigenous predators because having to
recognise them as dangerous and avoiding them has never been
necessary. A particular example of this would be the safe evolution of
flightless birds such as the dodo on the Indian Ocean island of
Mauritius. The dodo was highly adapted and well-suited to local

conditions until hungry predatory sailors arrived and found it easy to catch and eat, as did their cats no doubt. The sailors, like the people who first took cats to some of the Galapagos Islands, could not have realized how fragile these island species were and how little able they were to resist predation even from relatively low populations of predator. The term 'dead as a dodo' could soon apply to many other island species, and many rare or unique species of the Galapagos Islands are now under threat both from man, who has hopefully at least learnt of their fragility before it is too late, and from introduced predators such as the feral cat, who being unaware of such issues, seeks only his next meal.

The domestic cat was brought to the black volcanic Galapagos Islands by man and soon set up a feral population, living alongside the feral pigs and feral dogs trying to survive on the wild side. Cats have been found living and breeding in the most arid and uncomfortable areas of some of these volcanic islands, taking shelter in the rough lava rock that even man has not been able to shape to his demands and where few other creatures choose to make their homes. From here the feral cat has been able to wreak havoc on the two species of frigate bird, three species of boobies and, on the island of San Cristobal, the unique swallow-tailed gull. These poor birds evolved to nest without the influence of any major predator, so now we find that sixty per cent of the chicks which hatch fall prey to one of the most highly effective predators the world has ever known. Cats strike mainly when the birds are nesting and most vulnerable and survive on a bird diet sufficiently well to establish a viable population.

Cats on nearby Charles Island pose a serious threat to the unique Charles Island mockingbird and on several other islands they threaten the survival of the Galapagos dove, flightless cormorant and penguin. On the island of Santa Cruz, by contrast, cats are surviving not on a diet of birds but largely insects, chiefly grasshoppers, and on young iguanas, the famous lizard of the islands. Others also even prey on the newly hatched famous Galapagos giant tortoises! A real Galapagos pasty! Sadly too, Darwin's finches are also frequent victims of the feral cat, a rather irreligious reminder to the founder of the theory of evolution that the pinnacle of the process, the cat, can devastate the island fauna that illustrate the very process of adaptive evolution so well.

Recent studies of two Galapagos colonies, one long established on Isabela Island and recorded by British explorers in 1869 and a more recent one on Santa Cruz, have shown that the cats exist at extremely low densities compared with city feral cat populations. Only two cats are found per square kilometre and toms reach an average age of just under seven years. Life is clearly harder on females as they only reach an average age of two and a half. Both sexes are roughly the same height and of the same dimensions as other feral cats elsewhere in the world but weigh appreciably less. Full-grown toms weigh on average just under six pounds and queens just over four and a half pounds (a normal pet cat at home weighs about eight pounds) and all are reported to be rather lean and underfed in appearance, despite the availability of many different sources of food from beetles and scorpions to newly hatched iguanas, finches and rats and mice.

Research on the Galapagos feral cats indicated that a cat's daily intake was only just enough for non-pregnant, non-lactating queens and well below that for toms or pregnant and lactating females. The answer to the conundrum of the cats' poor condition lay not in any local reduction in the cats' ability to use their ancestral hunting skills to cope with the range of prey before them but in the lack of availability of fresh water for nine months of the year. Cats have evolved to thrive on a high protein diet which requires a high water intake to accompany it for them to be able to process and excrete the nitrogenous breakdown products of the protein. When fresh drinking water is unavailable for so long cats may suffer physiological damage through retention in the body of those breakdown products and so they are forced to pursue prey with a higher water or lower protein content. While the Galapagos cat does indeed appear to select different prey to accommodate the lack of water, they are still unable to find enough water all year round to get the best out of even that poorer diet. As a result, the cats are smaller and live shorter lives and while the metabolism of mother cats works overtime to produce enough energy to feed and raise their kittens, the price on the mother's body is high and they die younger.

Although the cats' food sources may be locally or seasonally scarce in some areas or on some islands, the adaptable cat appears to have even modified its hunting strategies to cope. Though living largely solitary lives and still employing the M- or S-strategies to deal with the appropriate prey, pairs of cats have been observed hunting co-operatively with one driving lizards towards another to pounce on and then reversing the roles. Toms in the Galapagos Islands have also been observed guarding their kittens to allow their mother opportunity to hunt and keep her energy intake as high as possible. This has never been recorded anywhere else in the world as feral cat toms usually play no role in the raising of the litters they sire and may even pose a threat to them if they are passing and hungry! But it would appear that where conditions are severe, even the highly successful blueprint for survival of the cat can need a little alteration and in cat terms, these features are major adjustments. The only riposte on the Galapagos Islands, apart from the conservationists, comes from the unique Galapagos hawk, which has exploited the feral cat by swooping on kittens when it gets the chance. But, bearing in mind the inhospitable nature of the black lava shores and thorny vegetation of the Galapagos Islands, it is quite remarkable that cats have managed to gain such a foothold there and, despite everything, are maintaining a viable population.

Feral cats also had a pleasant landing on the reasonably barren Ascension Island in the South Atlantic Ocean around 1820. They soon filled the hitherto unoccupied niche of crepuscular/nocturnal predator of the several hundred thousand population of sooty terns and established themselves for good. Thankfully they did not have such a huge impact on these birds as on the noddy birds and petrels which the feral cat has all but wiped out from the parts of the island that it can reach. It is one of those quirks of fate that Darwin himself recorded their presence in his *Naturalists Voyage Around the World in HMS Beagle* published in 1860, writing 'Some cats which were originally turned out to the rats and mice have increased so as to become a great plague'. Despite this, he clearly didn't anticipate the impact that the same cat could have on his beloved Galapagos fauna.

Sooty terns on Jarvis Island in the central Pacific have also been greatly affected by the introduced feral cat for which they are the most important prey, though the cats also feed on other birds, mice, small reptiles and insects. Clearly dependence on one particular and vulnerable bird species does not mean that the other facets of the cat's hunting ability are in any way reduced in efficiency. Seasonal unavailability of, for example, nesting birds demands that cats turn to other less vulnerable sources of food at other times.

On Australia's sub-polar Macquarie Island in the South Pacific Ocean cats were reported to be living feral only ten years after the first pet cats were introduced with the discovery of the island in 1810. They found an ample year-round supply of rabbits to support them, but prey mostly on young ones in the summer ('summer' is rather meaningless as it seldom rises much above freezing at any time of year!) and only turn to other sources of food in the winter, such as white-headed petrels, a small number of rats, and seal carcasses washed up on the beach. Sadly, on Macquarie Island cats have already eradicated two easy prey bird species, a ground-dwelling parakeet and a flightless rail, and the grey petrel no longer breeds there.

Despite an apparent dependence on rabbits, however, it would appear that the cat is in balance with their population. Studies showed that while the entire population of some 375 cats consumed an astonishing 56,000 rabbits per year, this had no effect on the rabbit population. Like so many predator/prey interactions, the two populations are linked to each other and the predator effectively only harvests the prey without reducing it to zero. Such interactions often proceed in cycles with the abundance of prey, which responds also of course to its own food availability, climate, disease and other predators, determining the abundance of the predator rather than the other way around. Cats, after all, can only live and breed if food is available.

Interrelating population cycles seem to become established readily between cats and fast-breeding introduced prey such as rabbits and mice. The latter tailor their breeding season so that offspring are in abundance when their food supply is far in excess of the population's requirements. Cats, like any other predator, take full advantage and themselves breed slightly after the prey population has expanded. Indigenous island species on the other hand, despite being adapted to local food availability, will often be either slow breeding or raise their offspring in very accessible positions due to lack of challenge from any indigenous predator. As a result they are often so quickly preyed on by introduced predators such as cats or man that a predator/prey cycle never becomes established. By the time the island fauna has learnt to be wary of cats, man and other predators, or to select more secret breeding grounds, their population may already be perilously close to extinction or, like the dodo, already gone.

If conditions on the Galapagos Islands and others seem harsh enough for the cat, his sheer resilience is nowhere better demonstrated than on the volcanic Marion Island in the sub-Antarctic, south-east of South Africa. The island rises steeply from a submarine plateau and is almost constantly blustered by west winds and gales. More than 250 centimetres of rain and snow fall every year and when it isn't actually precipitating, it's damp and foggy. The average temperature is a mere five degrees centigrade and it rarely rises above seven and a half degrees even in midsummer.

While some cats that found their way there had been abandoned or jumped ship from American sealing vessels in the nineteenth century, five cats were deliberately introduced as biological controls in 1949 at the meteorological station to limit the rapidly expanded population of another, but accidentally introduced animal, the mouse. Alas, by 1976, Rudi van Aarde, who had been conducting long-term research on feral cats there, estimated their number as approaching 6,000, a growth rate of over twenty per cent per year. The cats had successfully learnt to shelter from the ravages of the weather in subterranean lava caves or even in abandoned breeding burrows of the petrels they had come to consume, as they soon adapted beyond feeding simply on the mice. The cats preyed successfully also on the various species of petrel according to seasonal availability, including prions which were taken throughout the year but especially in August/September, as well as scavenging from penguin and seal carcasses washed up on the shore.

An analysis of the contents of 125 feline stomachs revealed that cats are preying mainly on nocturnal burrowing petrels. Each cat was estimated, with slightly presumptive accuracy, to kill 213 burrowing petrels per year. The Marion Island cat population as a whole was estimated to account for 600,000 burrowing prions and petrels per year, though whether this is a level of predation that the birds can tolerate without long-term damage to the population has yet to be ascertained. However, in an effort to reduce the population of feral cats and protect the bird species from the perceived threat of the feral cats of Marion Island, the South African government deliberately introduced feline panleucopenia virus, one of the killer viruses that is commonly vaccinated against in our pet cats. But using a second biological control to arrest a rampantly over-successful first biological control produced a problem of its own. While there was an initial huge reduction in the number of cats, those that survived infection became resistant and quickly restored the numbers with non-susceptible cats. Humans 0 Cats 2! 'Give a cat an inch and he'll take a mile' – a thought to be borne in mind for the future whenever cats might be considered for use as biological pest controllers or tolerated where delicate bird life may be vulnerable.

To place all the blame for the depletion of vulnerable and unique island species of bird solely in the mouth of the feral cat may be unfair. My dear friend Ellen Perry Berkeley from Vermont in America is a veritable champion of the feral cat and authoress of the excellent book *Maverick Cats*. Ellen pointed out the inaccuracies of an article published in, of all things, *Animals Magazine*, the journal of the Massachusetts Society for the Protection of Animals. The article rather proposed cats as sole villains on islands while ignoring the opinions and research of many notable scientists who felt that while the cat was a contributor to the problem, most danger to flightless or ground nesting birds came from rats, destruction of habitat by man through farming or tourism or adaptation of the habitat by herbivores. Even on the Galapagos Islands, Ellen quotes a reliable source that cites rats, not cats as the primary predators of endangered ground nesting birds. Well-researched as ever, Ellen also wrote of the opinions of leading scientists who had suggested that competition from introduced birds as well as other introductions of other predators and rodents were also important factors in many cases and the dirty face of commercial specimen collectors and bloodsports could, sadly, be more important in terms of impact than the feral cat.

Some islands are simply too inhospitable for even the adaptable cat to survive on however. During an expedition to one of the Virgin Islands in 1987 to help establish a humane feral cat control programme in a very wealthy resort on Virgin Gorda, I arrived to find that until then, resort workers had been paid a bounty to catch cats by whatever means and dispose of them. Rather than kill them, which was thought to be unlucky, some of the workers shipped the few cats they could get by sea to nearby 'Cactus Island'. Though there were a few birds, doubtless a few rodents and occasional carcasses on the beach, there was no supply of fresh water on the island, hence its name, and so most cats dumped there met a horrible thirsty end.

13
Living closer to man

'A harmless, necessary cat'   William Shakespeare
                                                       (*The Merchant of Venice*)

Assuming fresh water is available – either through natural springs
or via frequent rain collecting for a while on the land surface – the
impact on rare or unique island fauna by cats has often been dramatic,
even if they are not the whole story. Though conservation battles rage
against the feral cat on many islands, on most it is a case of damage
limitation and species protection because it is unlikely that the wily
cat could ever be eradicated now that it is established and so well-
adapted to local conditions.

One of the most suitable types of local conditions for feral cats to
survive in has been the farmland areas in the temperate climates of
Europe and elsewhere. Not only is there often an abundant source of
rodent prey to hunt around the grain stores and waste to scavenge in,
but there are also places of shelter from harsher winter weather in
outbuildings and barns. Many farmers encourage feral cats as rodent
controllers while others do not actively persecute the cat, even
accepting that the occasional free-range chicken may fall prey to
them. Some go as far as to put out milk and food to help the cats
supplement their diet, particularly in winter when rodent populations
may fall. The old adage that hungry cats are better rodent killers is
not true as weakness will slow hunting ability, not sharpen it. The
best ratters are well-fed, but not overweight cats, as the interest in
their quarry is not, as we have discussed already, linked to appetite,

and a fit cat will be better able to respond to the sight or sound of a mouse or rabbit. A hungry cat is, in any case, more likely to move on to better pastures, but if numbers of cats around a farmyard do rise, then kittens may be taken in, tamed and found homes and numbers of adults may be culled with the traditional shotgun back to acceptable levels. Farmyard cats are a feature around many farms and, even under modern day intensive systems, are generally tolerated. In a survey of over 200 farms in the north of England the vast majority had farm cats. Eighty-eight per cent were felt not only to play a worthwhile role by the farmers, but were sufficiently good at the job for a fifth of the farmers not to employ any other form of rodent control. Only ten per cent of the farmers felt their farm cats to be useless at the job.

However, many cats do not choose to live so closely associated with man's settlements and live exclusively on the wild side. In Scotland, feral cats have been found to be highly successful at being wild animals and, as we have seen, actively outcompete the indigenous Scottish Wild Cat and drive it back to less and less hospitable areas through being able to exploit its ecological niche better. The feral cat adopts a similar social organisation and populates areas at about the same density as its truly wild cousin and also feeds predominantly on rabbits. Wild and feral cats do however both choose to feed their kittens on birds, if possible, despite the increased difficulties that most cats have in capturing birds compared with ground dwelling prey.

Despite this, ornithologists have complained for years of the effects that both pet cats and feral cats can have on bird populations. As far back as 1916, the subject was studied by the state ornithologist of Massachusetts in a treatise of obvious bias when one considers the title 'The Domestic cat: Bird Killer, Mouser and Destroyer of Wildlife'. He estimated that cats killed at least 700,000 birds per year in Massachusetts and more than three and a half million in New York State. His estimates were not based on accurate analysis of stomach or faecal contents, only on the observations of others who were no doubt coincidentally members of bird-watching clubs! More careful and less opinionated research carried out since has revealed that while cats do indeed take some birds, they mostly favour rodent prey. In 1949, one report called 'Farm Cat as a Predator' stated that over a period of eighteen months, one farm cat brought home 1,628 mammals and only sixty-two birds. In 1957, an analysis of 110 stomachs of feral cats killed on roads away from farms and towns found that they had fed four times as often on rodents as on rabbits, and nearly nine times as often as on birds. These figures correspond well with the predatory activities of cats around the world in other rural mainland environments.

In another American study in 1951, a further problem was highlighted that struck at the heart of those who use the countryside not for the purpose of making a living through farming, but for raising game birds to blast to death later in the name of sport. Cats in California were indeed found to prey predominantly on mammals (just over sixty-four per cent by volume) but estimated that feral cats would on average kill one game bird such as a pheasant or duck about every fifth day. The ensuing sentiment of many landowners who raise game birds to shoot, or the shooters themselves, is therefore to blast at any cats they see or instruct the gamekeeper to shoot or trap and kill them. A prime case of the pot calling the kettle black in my pacifist opinion!

From the point of view of the farmer worried about the effects a feral cat might have on farmed poultry such as chickens, geese, turkeys and ducks, concerns may be more justified. However, in the United States, feral dogs are thought to be a greater risk than cats because of their greater strength which enables them to enter coops and sheds. A properly designed and proofed enclosure will prevent such incursions and farmers whose stock is taken by cats, foxes or even dogs should surely blame themselves for not taking adequate precautions. Most do and, aside from localised incidents, it is generally felt that rural mainland feral cats have no significant impact on farmers' stock, nor on wildlife and bird populations. On occasion, and especially when their preferred rodent prey is in short suppply, they will, as they always have done, take advantage of whatever food may be available.

While the diets of island feral cats have been studied more extensively than their mainland rural counterparts, studies of the diet of forest-dwelling feral cats in Maryland, USA, showed that seventy-five per cent of their intake was of rodent origin. Studies in Australia have shown that cats living in bush areas consume mainly small indigenous bush rodents while those in farmed or semi-improved areas tend to prey on other introduced species such as rabbits and house mice, presumably because they are more abundant. In an area containing an assortment of wildlife one cat's stomach was found to contain three geckoes, two dragon lizards, two skink lizards, three grasshoppers, two centipedes, one stick insect and one mouse, but for the most part it seems that cats will choose to prey predominantly on mice, other rodents and rabbits but can turn to other prey if it appears before them or hunger demands a change of tactic.

In the UK, feral cats are significant predators competing alongside foxes and birds of prey for wild prey of rodents, rabbits and, to a lesser extent, small birds. In towns, foxes and cats are more likely to compete as urban scavengers for access to waste-containers. In the town and country, feral cats also prey on squirrels and were thought to have played a role in the decline of the British red squirrel. However, subsequent research has shown that the loss of soft woodland habitat is mainly to blame for the decline of this enchanting creature. The growth of the grey squirrel population introduced from America has also contributed as it is better than its red cousin at exploiting lower stocks of winter-time food. Perhaps, like the island fauna of the Galapagos, our red squirrel is another example of a 'soft' insular species that was bound to be driven back by a more gregarious introduced competitor, it's just that the island is bigger!

Feral cats in the UK take a wide range of mammalian species including squirrels and bats as well as a good array of mice, rats, voles, rabbits, the occasional hare (usually a youngster) and the killed but invariably uneaten insectivores, such as moles and shrews, which are thought to taste unpleasant. Snakes, of which there are only three species in the United Kingdom, are occasionally eaten by feral cats, though not in Ireland, where there are no snakes thanks to St Patrick, so the legend goes. Lizards, such as the legless and inaccurately named slow-worm (it is neither slow nor is it a worm!), and amphibians such as frogs are also killed by feral cats though perhaps more rarely eaten as they too can be bitter tasting and unpalatable. Feral cats may prey on fish if the opportunity arises, though this is more likely to be the preserve of individual domestic pet cats or urban feral cats who teach themselves how to hunt the goldfish in ornamental garden ponds. Insects such as grasshoppers, butterflies, flies, beetles and that slippery first victim of so many young cats, the earthworm, are also consumed as passing snacks by rural feral cats. Like pet cats and wild cat species, up to ten per cent of the feral cat's intake is in the form of vegetable matter. This is perhaps to provide roughage, as a ready source of certain vitamins and minerals, as a mechanical aid to digestion or as an emetic to help unburden them of any gastric worm load.

While the feral cat remains a threat to delicate island wildlife, it may also be a major threat to its mainland cousins such as the European Wild Cat as we have already seen. This threat arises partly because of the feral cat's ability to outcompete its cousin for what resources are available and because of the fundamental difference in the feral cat's tolerance of man compared with the retreat of the Wild Cat from urban areas and suburbia to less and less suitable habitats. In Victoria, Australia, the marsupial Native Cat is now either extremely rare or extinct in most parts. While it was thought to have declined due to competition from the feral cat that first arrived as a pet on the convict ships of 1788, like the Scottish Wild Cat, it may have declined more because of direct persecution by man and loss of habitat. The feral cat may simply have moved into the modified niches it left behind and prospered but, in so doing, took the blame for the decline of the Native Cat. The Scottish Wild Cat is most threatened however, in the opinion of Nigel Easterbee, not by direct competition for resources but by its ability to interbreed with the feral cat and so dilute its genetic purity, a far more insidious effect than the normal tactics in the Darwinian game of survival of the fittest. The Australian Native Cat at least is not threatened by this prospect.

14
Cats and urban man. 'Domestication' revisited

'I love their intelligence and their waywardness, their persistence and their willingness to abandon it if it should prove fruitless'

Bernard Levin

So much for the unleashed claws of the free-living cat, it is when the feral cat adopts a lifestyle alongside or in fairly close association with man that we naturally become most involved with him. And conflicts involving human concerns can soon develop about any cat away from the immediate and broader need to protect any indigenous species.

The ultimate source of many feral cat populations is not just from a few that have jumped ship or wandered away from the direct care of man after he has reached new lands or called in on oceanic islands. There is continuous recruitment to city, rural and human inhabited island populations from wandering or deliberately abandoned pets. They might technically be described as stray pets and soon readapt to life as a pet if fortunate enough to be picked up by a rescue society. However, if they are fertile queens and produce kittens which grow up unhandled by man, more 'truly feral' cats will have been added to the free-living and not easily tamed cat population. In many American towns there is almost an abandoned-cat population explosion every summer as students leave college to go home on vacation and, while most will be neutered pets, doubtless a fertile few will soon breed if not picked up quickly by the rescue services. The US

140

Department of Agriculture estimates that five million cats and dogs are dumped every year nationwide, and the practice has become so widespread in some places that established dumping spots have arisen, used in preference to the guilt-laden process of taking an unwanted pet to an animal rescue shelter.

The current population of pet cats in the US has now risen above sixty million and what with inner-city decay and the concomitant availability of derelict sites in which cats can shelter and hunt increasing numbers of rodents, one would expect the number of feral cats to have risen too. No accurate estimates of the US feral population have ever been made however. In the United Kingdom it was estimated in 1980 that the national population was about one and a quarter million feral cats, though experts now would probably regard this as an underestimate. It compares with a then population of pet cats of about five million which has now risen to nearly seven million.

Begging a living

Other feral populations have arisen ostensibly by chance, though purist welfarists would understandably blame man for the thousands of cats left homeless and reproducing in London after the blitz of the Second World War. Indeed, many argue that this was the major reason why there are so many feral cats in London today, though I would also suggest that the high population is maintained because of the traditional kind-heartedness of the British towards animals in providing food in such ample portions. London is also a particularly dirty city in places and rubbish abounds in many areas providing a rich scavenging ground for feral cats. Perhaps as London is slowly but surely cleaned up, the number of free-living stray and feral cats will fall as a result in years to come.

If I sound a little unpatriotic, I would also say that the cities and tourist resort developments and towns of many European countries bordering the Mediterranean are a lot shabbier and hence are often also home to many feral cats. One I have worked in is what is surely the worst city in Europe, Athens. Not only can feral cats survive there through scavenging and through handouts from the many kind-hearted people, but also, there is a continuous and large recruitment to the population from the pet population. Like many southern European countries there is a cultural resistance to having pets sterilised, particularly the males, because of misplaced macho attitudes

141

that persist throughout much of the society. So when an otherwise well-cared for pet produces a litter of kittens, they will often be looked after until able to fend for themselves and then dumped en masse in a local park. If they survive there to adulthood, they too will quickly go on to breed and cause the population to grow.

Tourists from northern Europe and America, unused to the sight of so many feral cats around the Greek island resorts or in the National Gardens in Athens, complain in their hundreds to tour operators about standards of animal welfare. The Greek government and that of other countries in the region which rely on tourism for a large portion of their gross national income would do well to address the fundamental attitude of their people to sterilisation of their pets. Many tourists are so upset by the number and condition of the feral cats they encounter that they never return to contribute further to the country's coffers.

There are many complaints too, not so much from tourists but from people concerned about the welfare of cats in all cities, including London. In his excellent book *The Wildlife of the Domestic Cat*, Roger Tabor estimates that there are well over half a million feral cats living in London alone. There may be up to 200 cats per square mile in many cities compared with six free-living cats per square mile in remote areas such as the Monach Isles to the west of Scotland or the Galapagos Islands. Tabor estimated that farm feral cats are found at an average population of one cat per twenty acres in the UK, but islands and rural areas are less densely packed with people and their waste and compassion, and so cats must rely on their own hunting skills.

In London, and probably all major cities of the world, the much higher cat density is only sustainable because of the free handouts and rich pickings available to be scavenged around human habitations. Many cats, if not most, will be beneficiaries of feeding by kind-hearted people on an occasional or regular basis and so the need to maintain a large territory to hunt in is reduced. Additionally, the ability of the urban ecological niche to support more animals at crucial lean times in winter is increased.

Indeed, one might argue as a biologist that such high numbers of cats in an otherwise grimy and unpleasant environment is only possible because of two reasons: one is the willingness of people to offer cats food, and the other is that our own lack of tidiness makes a waste food resource available for animals such as feral cats and foxes

142

to move into the city and survive. All they have to do is make the adaptation to a scavenging rather than a hunting lifestyle. For cats and, to a lesser extent, the fox, that transition is easy because scavenging has always been part of their *modus operandi*. The restriction on the expansion of the fox population in urban areas is probably related to its shyness and fear of man and insistence on crepuscular/nocturnal hunting and scavenging. But the cat, ever compromising, can cope with sharing his space much closer to man and relax his crepuscular/nocturnal hunting patterns to take advantage of day-round food availability and the handouts from feeders who, at best, appear in the early morning but leave the city to the cat at night. So, if ever an animal was equipped to take advantage of an urban opportunity, it was the feral cat. And, quite apart from their own breeding, densities of cats will always be higher in the city because of increased levels of abandonment and straying from the greater number of cats kept by people in the city, which constantly contribute to the feral population.

Behavioural adaptability

With food in such abundance it is more likely that the availability of shelter and suitable areas in which to raise kittens will often decide the number of cats that any particular local area can support. For some, this may mean a social strategy similar to that found by Oxford zoologist David MacDonald in some farm feral cat populations in the south-west, where queens establish breeding areas in a hunting range large enough to support themselves and any kittens. While related queens may share in the nursing and protection of each other's litters, usually the queens' territories are exclusive. They may, however, border one another and have overlapping areas and walkways that they are happy to share without conflict. Toms, on the other hand, will range across a much wider area, incorporating the ranges of many queens and generally be looking to mate wherever the opportunity arises and spread their genes around as widely as possible.

Such a system may prevail where food is limited in some city areas but many city feral colonies, in my experience, tend to mimic the social make-up of other farm groups studied later by MacDonald and his team. These groups tended to be collections of related queens gathered around a shelter resource, such as garages or derelict buildings, who were generally sociable with each other, shared sleeping areas and any food resources provided by man, and also shared the duties of raising kittens together. Communal nursing also has an interesting survival advantage for the kittens at the immunological level because they will benefit from a range of maternally derived antibodies via the colostrum and milk of all who nurse them. Mothers and acceptable aunties raising kittens usually defend their nests vigorously against all unfamiliar females and most toms.

Living at the edge of these feline societies were young or rather unassertive male offspring who clung to the protection of the group and were generally content to take the leftovers and play second fiddle to the females. As a result, they were often in rather poor condition and would tend to die off first in the event of disease striking the colony or during cold winters if they were unable to find shelter. They tended to live rather uninteresting lives and generally not mate with the females, an adaptation presumably evolved to prevent inbreeding. Such toms may be able to stay around the kittening area without apparent threat from nursing females. This is in contrast to the old idea that tom cats actively kill and eat any kittens they can find, perhaps a behaviour more likely to be restricted to the tougher itinerant toms. Like new males taking over a pride of female lions, their action may be to kill all kittens to remove the genetic investment of other males. It's a bloody policy designed to ensure that the queens come into season quickly again (often in only a matter of hours after the cubs are killed), are mated by the new male and go on to raise his genetic investment instead.

Colony queens in the countryside were usually mated by passing and more robust toms than the weaker hangers-on. Such toms are perhaps generally more secretive and less likely to be observed in association with the city colony. Despite the presumably greater concentration of groups of queeens to call on in the city, radio tracking data indicates that some of these toms patrol large areas on a regular basis. One Bristol tom walked no less than ten miles across the city every night calling in at sites occupied by colonies of queens and younger or less assertive males and stopping to scavenge at known sites of rich pickings. In contrast to the dull, hang-around, longer life of the weaker colony males, the independent toms of the city or farmland have a harder time finding enough food for themselves and fight more over territories with others of the same ilk. But they are able to walk straight past the colony toms unopposed and mate the queens at any opportunity. The price for the macho guys in farm studies is a much shorter, if more active, life even than the weaker colony-bound males. I wonder, if men were cats, which of the two strategies they would adopt if given the choice!

Perhaps, in human terms, we are looking at the choice of a long, peaceful and relatively plentiful family life in the suburbs rather than a faster and occasionally highly fruitful but exhausting life night-clubbing in the city! While most men fancy the fast and furious life with lots of 'mates' when they are young, most also end up adopting a more secure and safe life in a monogamous relationship later. Tom cats who want to breed don't have the opportunity to try the fast lane when young and become more sedate as they get older, they must respond to the demands of their genes, compete all the way and hope to hang on to life as long as possible. This concept of dual character in the tom cat may extend more subtly to queens as well and is an idea that we will return to in the next chapter when we look at the personality of the pet cat and how it relates to human 'owners'.

Paul Leyhausen's theory of the social life of the city feral cat was that all cats have a home-base territory in the city in which to rest, sleep and groom. This core is connected by regularly used pathways to shared hunting or scavenging grounds. Toms would also use these pathways to get to the home bases of queens during the breeding season and tough toms would have unopposed rights of access to anywhere in their range, including the territory of weaker males. Leyhausen described the social life of the city feral cat as a community or 'brotherhood' system, with more dominant or assertive males having rights of access at any time to any place and less dominant males having access perhaps to the same places but at different times. Females were thought to be less competitive and tolerant both of each other and of the presence of males, but all cats were thought to gather socially in the evening and at night with little conflict even between higher-ranking males.

In the light of my own studies of feral cat colonies in Regent's Park in London, and those of many others around the world, Leyhausen's model seems a little romantic, but it does serve to demonstrate once again the enormous social elasticity of the feral cat. It seems that the sociability of the African Wild Cat evolved to enable it to exploit the opportunities of the city even at high densities of cats and protect it as a species from the usual injurious interaggressive effects of crowding that one expects to find in other creatures. Seal colonies, for example, are full of festering, wounded and dying individuals when populations rise too high and personal space becomes limited but the cat seems to be able to accommodate a high density of other cats around him without fighting more.

Individual cat character and social behaviour is clearly highly adaptable. This, the variable hunting strategies described earlier and the cat's ability to survive on such a range of diets are the main features of the success of the species in so many varied environments. When the chips are down in harsher environments, cats all tend to be solitary and territorial, though when life is really harsh, related cats may even be forced to develop a communal approach to hunting and rearing each other's offspring to survive. The more relaxed the environmental constraints, the more sociable the cat can be and, in places of plenty, such as at some some inner-city areas where cats are fed daily by feeders, or in docklands packed with waste-bins, they can co-exist peacefully in huge numbers.

Dietary adaptability

Contrasting with the reputation of the pet cat as a fussy eater, the city feral cat is more like its cousins mentioned in Chapter 4 and will consume a wide range of food items, perhaps as an adaptation from the wide range of prey it might expect to encounter if living out in suburbia or still further out in the countryside. City cats will scavenge any meat or fish waste from bins and off the streets and will even consume apparently less attractive items for a predator, such as bread, chips and pasta. The effort of hunting live birds and mice seems naturally less attractive in the face of such easily scavenged pickings.

In England's cities and doubtless in many others around the world, it seems that every cat colony has at least one totally dedicated feeder. This is usually, but not always, a middle-aged or elderly lady who appears every morning and evening armed with baskets or trolleys of food for the cats. Much of the diet provided is left-overs from family meals or specially prepared 'stews' mixed with love and care to a special recipe, but usually supplemented with the best canned cat food money can buy. Some bring only commercially prepared cat food but, either way, the costs can be huge and many feeders make enormous sacrifices in their own lifestyles to be able to afford it all. For them the rewards are great. The cats soon come to recognise their feeder and allow her, or him, closer to them than anyone else and wait in the cold mornings to greet them with the characteristic tail-up strut, chirping their hellos. The cats impart a special exclusive affection at feeding time, with some even developing such trust as to allow their feeder to touch them. The cats soon get used to turning up on time for the often carefully prepared and highly nutritious meals.

While some, particularly the more vagrant toms, eat and then retreat to less public areas, others, particularly the queens and those younger and weaker males, may stay in the area and subsequently receive more meals from other regular callers, perhaps office workers at lunchtime. They will also hang around to receive occasional snacks from passers-by who just happen to be there and feel sorry enough for the cats to leave a half-eaten sandwich for them. Small wonder that some of the best looked after colonies comprise extremely portly cats in tip-top condition!

The diet of 200 feral cats in the famous Portsmouth Dockyards study carried out in the late 1970s and early 1980s comprised mainly items scavenged from waste containers. Indeed, the densely packed colony was divided into groups or 'prides' of two to seven closely related females and their young, each group based around the clumped food resource of a rubbish skip. Males tended to be solitary but moved among the female groups and defended their access to them against rival males. Most cats also received a good portion of their intake from the dockyard workers, many of whom brought food in on a daily basis for their groups of cats, or who were prepared to give up a portion of their lunch for them. It was felt that few cats relied on rodents for much of their intake as these were controlled by poison, not by cats, though one wonders how much secondary poisoning of cats occurred through them scavenging on dead rats and mice.

Without doubt, such a large population of cats was only sustainable in the dockyards, sealed off from local housing estates by walls on three sides and bounded by the sea on the other, because of the great availability of food. The population appeared to be at a maximum for the environment because while 400 kittens were born every year, only one eighth of them survived to adulthood. This was equivalent to the estimated number of adults which died in the same period.

While the dockyards are perhaps representative of a harsher life for the individual feral cat in man's industrial world, it is one where a form of 'natural' population regulation still occurs, mainly because the only compassionate contact the cats have with man is through the workers who give them food. People who may have been more concerned about the condition, health and lifestyle of the dockyard cats would be unable to influence their welfare or their population because of the restricted access of the general public to the dockyards. However, in more public areas where city feral cats gather, such as around hospital sites, city parks, small industrial areas and backstreets behind shops where restaurant and food shop waste may be left, the cats are more likely to be noticed.

Feral cats are also on view seasonally in the tourist resorts of the Mediterranean. There and in the more familiar cities of our homeland, we view the feral cat not as a wild creature fortunate enough to be able to cope with its chosen lifestyle and survive as a successful species, but as an abandoned pet who deserves our care at the individual level. When claws come with purrs in our city cats, we immediately become more forgiving of their hunting activities and antisocial habits than when they ravage rare island species. Lacking any fundamental compassion for the demise of local rats, we are then free to offer help and sympathise with the feral cat. Our emotions then go out to what is now seen as the sad victim of man's inhumanity especially, of course, when Mother Nature starts to take her toll on the kittens. After all, it's not their fault that they look exactly the same and come in the same array of colours as we find in our pet cats at home, in fact, once again, it can work to their advantage.

15
Managing feline success

'No matter how much cats fight, there always seem to be plenty of kittens'   Abraham Lincoln

Natural population control

As with all wild animals, few of the young born to any mother will survive to reach sexual maturity themselves. As we have seen even in the relatively well-fed feral cat world of Portsmouth Dockyards, many kittens are born only to die from disease or by falling foul of hungry predators before they can learn to fend for themselves. All animals overproduce to ensure the survival of the few and the rules of Mother Nature apply to the feral cat as much as any other creature.

Kittens born to pet cats of course, like our own children, have an inordinately greater chance of surviving to adulthood because we invest so much extra care and protection in them. Our kittens' mother is likely to be in the best of condition when mated and well-fed by us when she needs the extra energy to produce milk for her litter without the need to increase her hunting activities. Protected against disease by maternally-derived antibodies followed by vaccination before they become vulnerable again, most pet kittens are never challenged by the killer diseases of feline infectious enteritis and influenza that account for the death of so many city feral kittens.

Much of the interest in city feral cats and concern for their welfare arise understandably from people who are unused to the sight of Mother Nature at work culling off so many kittens to ensure the

149

survival of the fittest. The sight of sickly, helpless kittens in the undergrowth of the city park or railway embankment or lurking in the shadows of the industrial estate mewing for their mother is too much for us to bear and few can walk past without wanting to offer help. Sadly, by then, such care is invariably too late as the kittens' eyes and respiratory systems are often filled with mucus and the only reason that the kittens are so visible is because they have wandered away from their mother's care and are unaware of the dangers of being in the open. While some can pull through with intensive care and veterinary attention, many will die or survive only to join the queue of young cats looking for a home as a nurtured pet in a world where such homes are hard to find. It's sad that having survived the early threats, the wild-born feral kitten will often be at a disadvantage when it comes to finding that most comfortable of niches compared with his home-bred counterpart and will be left on the animal sanctuary shelf.

In so many cases, juvenile feral cats would have fared better if they had been left to take their chances on the wild side rather than put in the halfway house of an animal sanctuary for sometimes a lengthy, or even lifetime, sentence. Though they may be given the best of food and veterinary attention, it comes without the luxury of a home and loving owner to go with it. It's all a question of human values and viewpoints, of course. But for sure, if a feral-born kitten survives the major illnesses that account for most kitten deaths, it will usually have acquired sufficient immunity to local viruses to survive into adulthood and will be able to live on those highly evolved wits. It's just that it's unlikely to survive as long as a pet in a home or an inmate in a so-called sanctuary.

But of course any reasonable being could not be so dispassionate about the fate of creatures which, directly descended from the African Wild Cat or not, feral or not, and surviving as a population or not, still suffer so horribly at the hands of Mother Nature. In an ideal world, no creature would ever suffer such pressures and animals would not have to play the compulsory genetic game of overproduction to ensure that a few survive and maintain the population. Whether we understand and accept the theory of the selfish gene or not, it is also quite impossible for any cat lover not to identify with the plight of feral kittens or suffering adult cats and relate their problems to their own cats at home. The animal welfare argument for assisting feral cats is strong and no less justifiable because feral cats will, if left to their own devices, have their population regulated by natural processes. Those processes can be curtailed and suffering at an individual level – the one we identify with most readily because of the highly individual nature of each of our pet cats – can be alleviated if we choose to help.

Problems with cats

Then there's the other side of the coin. Whether we like it or not, not everyone likes cats and they may become disturbed at the sight of so many in a city colony or lurking around the open restaurant in their holiday hotel. We all have to share our world with each other and the people who dislike cats, loath though I am to say it about these strange types, have a right to control them when they are a nuisance. While farm feral cats or those leading entirely free lives unrelated to man may be pests for other reasons, the urban cat colony can become a problem simply because a gathering of cats around an area naturally causes a concentration of feline behaviour patterns, not all of which are sociable or clean.

Some people, unused to the sight of so many cats in one place, may simply complain about the size of the local population or what they perceive as a disease risk. Most complaints from the anti-cat lobby concern the noise of tom cats particularly, fighting over territories, and the usually very loud calling of queens on heat attracting mates. Unfortunately, both types of row usually occur at night, thus keeping good honest citizens awake. Then there's the very pungent and unforgettable smell of tom cat spray, often used liberally to anoint the trees, fenceposts and buildings around the cats' feeding areas and to announce their presence when the queens start to call. Add to that the smell of cats choosing or being forced to use perhaps a rather scanty patch of soil or even bare concrete continually as a toileting area and complaints about the presence of some feral cats in the city seem perfectly reasonable. Whether the concerns about the risk of disease to man from cats are justifiable is open to question as fleas will usually stay on the cat and intestinal worms are not normally derived from touching the cat, even assuming one got the chance. Ringworm, which is a frequently found condition in feral cats, can be contracted from handling the cats but the disease risk is thought to be minimal for the general public and probably less than that encountered in a poorly kept pet that is handled on a regular basis.

One of the major concerns about feral cats in many parts of the world is the risk of rabies, which most definitely can pass from cat to man through a bite or a lick on an open wound. However, in England we are fortunate that rabies has not been endemic since it disappeared in the 1920s and the government spends much time and money trying to ensure that it stays that way. The feral cat, therefore, is in the Ministry of Agriculture's contingency plans for control in the event of an outbreak of rabies. Having contributed something to those plans myself during the course of several meetings with their man in charge of cats some years ago, I have to say that I think the urban feral cat does present a serious risk in the potential spread of the disease because of the high density of many populations and their intermingling with pet cats and general proximity to people. However, I supect the British Government, despite the slightly half-hearted attitude towards cats that I encountered several years ago, will rise to the challenge of feral cat control if ever it becomes necessary in the event of a rabies outbreak. How humane that control will be is perhaps open to question, though that won't be too high on the list of public concerns if rabid animals are on the loose for the first time in decades.

Population management

So, in many cases, the urban feral cat clearly warrants management on welfare grounds and frequently requires numbers to be controlled if he is to live in reasonable harmony with his human neighbours. The price of moving in on man's habitat is that man may call the tune. Where numbers need controlling, there are three options. One is to carry on letting Mother Nature regulate the population and expect cat lovers to put up with it. This is not on, as we have discussed. The second is to attempt to cull all the cats, and many pest control companies attempt to do just that with traps and, illegally, by using poison and guns. Many pest control companies have then found to their cost, when they are discovered at their grisly work, that many local cat lovers are galvanised by the feral cat feeders and come forth in droves to protect their cats. I have even met pest controllers who have been assaulted, had their van tyres slashed and bottles thrown at them by otherwise gentle old ladies who want nothing more than to be able to feed and care for 'their' cats. Fortunately the pest control attitude to cats has, in recent years, become more wary and more professional. I have had the pleasure for a number of years to lecture to delegates on the annual training course of the British Pest Control Association on the delicate subject of the humane control of feral cats. The realisation that a pest controller can be a Pied-Piper hero one day for clearing a site of the universally loathed rat, but a social outcast with a black eye the next for killing or taking away the cats that used to eat the rats, is quite a thought. I'm sure many of the delegates go away from the courses determined to avoid cats for their entire professional lives!

This brings us to the third option for control of feral cats which in turn brings us back to my first professional involvement with cats. I spent three very happy years with UFAW developing and promoting a system of management for cats. It is a classic example of compromise, and a great success story in terms of getting people to divorce the physical presence of a pest animal from the problems it causes. In short, killing cats to solve the largely behavioural problems that most people complain about may work, but only temporarily. 'Nature abhors a vacuum' and there are surely few mammals to beat the cat at filling an opportunity to occupy the niche left empty by those killed. This is why culling feral cats is a pointless exercise in most city situations. There are simply too many other stray and feral cats on the move who will take their place. In my experience, where culling has been carried out, it takes no more than six months in London to repopulate the site with new cats, even in winter when there are unlikely to be many kittens growing up. Most importantly from the point of view of the people who paid for the extermination of the colony, not to mention the reputation of the pest controller, the numbers and all the problems return with the cats and they are back to square one.

Instead, a system of trapping, neutering and returning healthy cats to their site has been tested and proven to be effective not only at controlling the size of the population but also at alleviating the problems that most people are likely to complain about. After castration at the vets, neutered toms may still spray but the urine is much less pungent, and they are less likely to fight. Sterilised females no longer come into season and so no longer call to attract mates and people can enjoy a good night's sleep again. Overall, the colony becomes more peaceable and my own research demonstrated that cats are healthier, live longer and are more friendly to one another after neutering. Yet they are still able to act as a buffer to those local strays and feral cats

153

hoping to join the group and so a stable population is maintained. Research carried out by my good friend Dr John Bradshaw at the University of Southampton in recent years suggests that perhaps neutered colonies aren't so able at defending their resources as we had previously thought, largely because spayed females are subsequently no longer so aggressive towards unfamiliar cats in defence of their nesting areas and others may therefore move in. This may cause the population to grow, but providing the site managers quickly neuter all new immigrants and restrict food and shelter availability as far as possible to match the numbers present or desired, John feels that the colony will nonetheless remain stable in number.

One of my original study groups in underground garages in Wandsworth – from where I obtained my lovely silver tabby kitten of the same name – has never fluctuated by more than two cats up or down in the ten years since I trapped and neutered the colony of nineteen cats. All but three of the original colony have now gone but the group remains viable and healthy under the splendid care and site management of the two feeders, Betty and Charmian. Best of all is that many of the council officers on the great concrete housing estate where these cats live have also grown to love the cats, and not just because they haven't had to spend any money there on rodent control for so many years. They are proud of their occasional appearances on national television which has certainly helped advertise them as a caring council. The cat colony acts as a nice piece of pleasantness for everyone in an otherwise typically depressed, grey and sometimes violent inner-city area. The council have even generously donated one of the garages for the ladies to feed their cats in safety and put up warm resting and sleeping boxes for them.

Dinky – a smelly reminder of a survivor

I have another reason for remembering this particular colony with affection, though passengers in my old estate car might take issue with my wry smile. For four years, one particularly canny tom cat called 'Dinky' by the feeders resisted all my efforts to catch him. I even tried all night once with a radio-controlled trap made by my old friend and expert feral cat handling equipment manufacturer, Melvin Driver of MD Components of Luton. Despite that vigil with the latest in technology, Dinky wouldn't enter the trap and, after years of seeing the distinctive tabby-and-white face of Dinky eyeing me from a safe perch whenever I arrived to trap his companions or chat to the feeders, I had long given up any hope of arranging for his neutering at the local vet's. I came to regard him as the feline personification of the theory of 'survival of the canniest'.

Finally his wits let him down when, after all that time, he finally went into one of Melvin's automatic traps that I had set one evening to catch a couple of young cats which had recently arrived in the colony. Dinky looked more embarrassed than angry in the trap, but I was over the moon at my good fortune. He was duly emasculated by the vet, ear-tipped like all the others to identify him as neutered and given a good once-over to ensure that he went back to the site in the best of condition.

I collected him early the following morning in his carrying basket and put him carefully in the back of my car for the mile drive to the garages. Throughout the whole procedure at the vet's he must have saved a gallon of the most noxious-smelling urine for that return in my car. It went everywhere; all between the flattened seats of my estate car and into the seats themselves and all the way down on to the material lining of the floor. It sloshed into the rear light fittings and out of the tailgate where it stripped the top layer of paint off on its way out to the road! When I let him out at the garages, I'm sure he had a smile on his face and muttered something about having the last laugh as he shot, none the worse for his operation, over the nearest six-feet-high garage door to safety.

Dinky had left me a permanent reminder that the smell of tom cat's urine is one of the most pungent and persistent things on earth. I must have tried to clean the car a thousand times with a hundred different cleaners, all to no avail. Even on cold days, it was obligatory to have at least one window open, but in the summer, or if ever the heater was needed, the smell was utterly unbearable and all the windows had to be fully wound down! Girlfriends of the time refused point-blank ever to get in the car again after one drive, and so going out always meant a taxi! The atmosphere in that car remained until, tired of the pong and unable to sell the car at any price even on to another cat person, I scrapped it, well before its time. Even the scrapyard owner complained about the smell as, for once, he was able to drive an otherwise working car into the heap, well away from his cabin at the entrance to the yard! Last word to Dinky!

During the initial trapping of any feral cat colony, numbers returned have to be agreed with the landowner and most would not accept having all the cats returned. Fortunately there are always some that are actually friendly stray pets, which, along with any kittens, can be tamed or retamed and found new homes as pets. There will also be elderly, sick or injured adults for whom life as a feral has been harsh and who could not humanely be put back on site. These are usually kindly put to sleep at the advice of the vet so helping to return a smaller but entirely healthy colony to site.

Many groups such as the Cat Action Trust have a 'no euthanasia' policy and would rather treat sick or injured cats, and along with the older ones and those excess to requirements at the site, try to tame them for rehoming as pets or send them off to spend the rest of their days in a sanctuary. I don't feel that this is particularly kind, as most such sanctuaries are overcrowded and cats simply live their lives in a cage, hardly much of a prospect for a feral cat used to a life on the tiles. I favour euthanasia as a kinder option in such circumstances and also in preference to trying to tame adult feral cats which, though it can sometimes be done, can be a long and initially traumatic process for the cat. Most genuinely feral cats, as opposed to once tame strays or abandoned pets, are, in my experience, not at all easy to tame and rarely adjust well to life as a pet. However, those involved with management schemes must make their own decisions about such matters. Usually the all-caring approach for every cat can be maintained in small colonies where the cats are not causing too many problems to local people. For larger, more problematic colonies one has to think in terms of pest control rather than animal welfare to be able to get the job from the industrial estate, dockland or hospital authority. Laudable principles of keeping every cat alive may have to be abandoned for the sake of being able to sustain a managed colony of a healthy few and simply to be able to use humane techniques in trapping and dealing with sometimes hundreds of cats from a single site.

Of course, such methods depend on the landowner, or hospital authority, or whatever, accepting as inevitable the fact that they will always have some cats on site unless they are prepared to remove all the resources that attract them there in the first place. This can be more difficult than managing the cats, as to remove access to all the wastebins can be expensive if cat-proof bins have to be bought, stopping dedicated cat feeders from doing what they've always done is virtually impossible and removing any more natural prey such as rodents and birds can be even more costly.

So, having a calmer, cleaner, friendlier neutered group of cats around can be the best option providing, of course, that the cats continue to be fed and cared for. Feeders are usually more than happy to drop an occasional worming tablet into the cats' food and even treat their more accessible sleeping areas with anti-flea spray to keep the cats healthy. And the better ones will also agree to regulate the amount of food they provide so as only to feed the agreed number of cats adequately and not leave large amounts of uneaten food around which might enable others to join the group or decay and attract rats and flies.

The key to the success of such management schemes has been the level of after-care, indeed the neutering and return-to-site policy can only be recommended on welfare grounds if that care is assured. All cats, especially in city colonies where many will be black or similarly marked, are identified permanently as having been neutered and as part of the colony by removing a tip or notch from one ear, usually the left, at the time the cat is under anaesthetic at the vets. Then any new members can be readily identified, trapped and neutered themselves and existing cats need not mistakenly be trapped a second time and presented for unnecessary surgery. Of course, all members of the group will die in time or even occasionally wander off to pastures new to be replaced by new fertile cats. These must be identified and trapped and neutered quickly if the colony is to remain stable and problem free. Any new immigrants usually integrate much quicker and establish tolerant or friendly relations with existing members after neutering.

As a method of population control, well-organised mangement systems work extremely well. Although the initial costs of neutering by the vet may be quite high, in the long term my own research has shown the method to be quickly cost effective compared with continuous or sporadic culling of an ever-reforming colony, even if priced as a commercial operation.

Populations do remain stable and healthy and, of course, continue to act as free rodent controllers, though probably less than is sometimes thought. They continue to give great pleasure to those who care for them and feed them and complaints about them certainly fall away when they are healthier, quieter and less smelly and Mother Nature no longer has to regulate their population so cruelly in front of the eyes of local cat-lovers. Kittens just aren't born any more simply to die from distressing diseases.

157

SNIP!

Most schemes are carried out not by pest controllers but by local cat-welfare groups who often spend much time and their own hard-raised cash to fund their activities. Indeed there are many voluntary organisations around the world now dedicated to the welfare and humane control of the feral cat, in urban, industrial and rural areas. Many local governments are happy to allow such local welfare groups to deal with all the feral cats in their area, having learnt that their own environmental health officers and pest control teams find it tough going to deal with feral cats, and especially their supporters. Some, such as the London boroughs of Wandsworth in the south (the largest borough in the city) and Islington to the north, are even prepared to allocate funds to help enable these organisations care for and manage cat colonies. In Islington the job has been extremely well co-ordinated by Dr Kate Horne for many years. She and the borough's professional full-time animal warden have the situation well under control with excellent records of all the colonies they have neutered and subsequently manage through the local feeders. Kate's organisation goes by the marvellous name of SNIP – the Society for Neutering Islington's Pussies – and the whole deal for cats there and in many other areas of Britain has a marvellous community feel about it. Certainly the whole system of managing feral cats by this method is extremely rewarding for all who get involved. For me, there is little more pleasurable than going back to a site some years after having neutered the colony and meeting or at least seeing an old feline friend, still well cared for and living out a peaceful happy life on the wild side, loved by some of the local people and no longer hated by others.

The price of life with modern man

The city feral cat can continue to survive because we let him, though the price is the loss of the chance to reproduce at the individual level for those in such managed colonies. But if management by neutering has proved so successful in so many places around the world, one might expect a reduction in numbers of feral cats overall. But somehow, one often never quite manages to catch all the cats in a group and so many others remain active and fertile without joining a colony to attract complaint or the interests of animal welfarists. It's almost reassuring to know, despite the fact that I've spent so much of my life working with feral cats and establishing humane control schemes all over the world, that the urban feral cat will probably be with us for ever. He'll always be there, living on the wits he never gave up when he moved in to share our city lifestyles just as the African Wild Cat has been doing for so many centuries in so many parts of the world.

Management schemes have proved extremely successful in tourist resorts around the world. I have helped set up control schemes with local animal welfare groups and vets in places as culturally diverse as the West Indies, Israel, Kenya, Greece and Tunisia where tourism forms a large part part of the national income. Hotel managers are harangued during the tourist season about cats. Typically around the Mediterranean resorts the English, Americans, French and Dutch complain about the state or lifestyle of the cats eking out a living around the hotel wastebins and begging food from holidaymakers dining outdoors in the sun. They demand that the hotel looks after them better, while the Germans and Swedes (in my experience . . . my apologies to all those cat-loving Scandinavians and Germans!) complain and demand that all these unhygienic cats are removed from the hotel immediately. If the hotel manager tries to trap the cats or poison them, he gets into very hot water indeed with the cat-loving guests. If he does nothing, a steady stream of complaints continues to flow from guests and the tour operators.

How nice it is to be able to talk these managers so quickly into accepting a smaller, stable number of identified neutered cats that he can tell the Germans are healthy, wormed, vaccinated against rabies and feline diseases and kept on the books as rodent controllers. And how nice it is too to have set up special feeding areas, called cat cafés, some distance away from the restaurant areas so that those who want to feed the cats can take portions, or sometimes all of their meals to the cats and not upset the cat haters! As one emotional Belgian cat lover said to me in Kenya in a heavy Flemish accent, *'You bring ze kids all zis vay for a holiday on ze beach in ze sun and zey spend ze whole day playing wis ze cats around zer little house!'*. But even that didn't top the reaction of the manager of one Tunisian hotel who just couldn't express his gratitude enough and burst into floods of tears when we gave him a certificate of commendation from the Society for the Protection of Animals of Tunisia to put on his office wall and a poster explaining the hotel cat control system in four languages for the reception area. Perhaps he had been about to lose a valuable tour operator customer due to complaints about the cats!

Feral cats living so close to man in such situations clearly do bring out very strong caring and protective feelings in people. They do see them very much as unwanted helpless pets despite their survival as a population and despite their very successful adaptations to life as a scavenger and beggar in preference to the harder life of a hunter. People want to offer help because the cats convince them, just by being there and adopting what in human terms would be a rather miserable existence, that they are suffering. They arouse the emotions of each and every cat lover and pet cat owner. The nature of those emotions and the relationship between people and their cats is something we shall explore in the final section of this book when we look at the cat as a pet, that most refined of all the ecological niches he has come to fill since he first left Egypt with the help of man and set about colonising the world.

'The Cat. He walked by himself, and all places were alike to him'
In *Just So Stories* by Rudyard Kipling

SECTION FIVE

Cat the Pet

16
. . . but he still hunts!

*'The cat's mind works in its own ways and the objectives are not always
apparent to us'*
Dr Bruce Fogle

The ultimate sheltered biological niche in the world must be as a pet
in man's den. After all, it is really only man who has managed to
control his immediate environment to suit his exact requirements,
even beyond actual survival needs. The den the cat shares with him
is warm in winter, cool in summer, draught-proof and full of soft
comfortable resting places, not to mention the food that miraculously
appears to replenish empty food dishes. Additionally man improves
the survival chances of his pet cat by keeping him healthier through
worming pills, vaccinations against disease and expert veterinary
attention as required so it's really no wonder that cats look so
contented in our homes and live such healthy lengthy lives.

But while the often sumptuous living conditions of the seven
million or so pet cats in the UK, and an estimated sixty million cats
in the USA, are unlikely to be contrived independently by even the
wiliest of feral or wild cats, the price of this success at the individual
level usually defeats the purpose of natural selection. Most pet
cats are sterilised and so are unable to pass on their individual
success to ensuing generations. The only pets lucky enough to escape
the vet's scalpel are of types or breeds which pass on not so much the
fittest attributes of feline survival, but those features which appeal to

their keepers or the cat-buying market. But while this artificial selection for conformation, clarity of marking and colour of hair is designed to produce ever more beautiful cats of any breed, the fundamental nature of the cat remains fairly unshakeable and barely altered in any cat from the original genetic make-up of the African Wild Cat.

Indeed it is a source of great frustration for owners of valuable, apparently highly bred pedigree cats with recorded lineages a mile long and those of many humble moggies alike that their pets are still so 'wild' in nature. I get literally hundreds of calls per year, especially around springtime, from owners sickened by the carnage their sometimes very financially valuable and usually well-fed cats inflict on the local wildlife. While few bother to complain when the cat catches an occasional mouse, and I've yet to have a call complaining about the death of a rat, people leap for the cat shrink when the first damp-feathered dead songbird fledglings are brought in by the cat in spring.

'How do we stop him? Is there nothing we can do short of keeping him indoors?' The short answer would be 'No. Goodbye!' Undoing thirteen million years of perfected evolutionary process is beyond the ken of this cat shrink and all others to my knowledge. If I could devise a way of stopping cats hunting I would be a very much richer man, for I would have solved the only real enduring problem that people experience in their cats and thus would render them all utterly perfect! Alas, beyond intensive socialisation as a tiny kitten with all likely future prey species (too late by the time the problem is evident!), keeping the cat indoors, or boarding him at a cattery during the bird nesting season, I have little to offer. All I can suggest is not to let the cat out at dawn, dusk or at night during the nesting season and to place a bell on a collar around his neck in the hope that the birds may hear him coming. However, this smacks of the attempts to curfew cats that have been attempted to protect rare indigenous wildlife in Australia. In Sherbrooke, near Melbourne in the State of Victoria, all pet cats must be taken indoors by their owners at dusk and kept indoors until dawn to reduce the threat they pose to wildlife such as possums and the rare lyrebird. Owners face a $1,000 fine if they fail to adhere to the law though the Sherbrooke council do kindly suggest that the curfew also actually helps cats by saving them from being run over by cars. Given the choice, I'm sure most cats would prefer to run that risk to be able to hunt. They would probably also rather that a really daft law still on the statute in Ohio, USA was abolished, that's if anyone takes any notice of it. The law requires all domestic animals, including cats, to wear tail-lights to be seen and prevent accidents. The more real impact of predation on local wildlife by cats was also once tackled elsewhere in America, in Illinois, with a local bylaw requiring cats to be kept on leashes, a repetition of a much earlier Japanese law. That one was revoked in 1602 by the Kyoto government who sensibly ordered the unleashing of cats.

In England, at least, there is no evidence to suggest that the occasional high mortality of birds due to pet cats has had any damaging effect on even one species of bird, however distressing to birds, bird lovers and cat owners that predation may be. As for bells around necks ... well, I have witnessed my own dear Bullet adjust his stalking approach and postures towards birds around the bird-table so as to keep his neck and head as still as possible and avoid ringing the bell. I'm also convinced that the birds he still catches are marginally more stupid than the average bird, or partially deaf, and don't hear the bell tolling for them.

In any case, as we have seen, the strategy used by cats for catching birds is not hugely successful at the best of times and only increases in efficiency when the birds stalked are more vulnerable or less able to escape. The total bird catch of cats comprises mainly young birds and those learning to fly, the sick and injured and those gathered hungrily around a bird-table in winter which are so intent on feeding to be less aware of nearby feline-shaped danger. The stealthy approach and last-minute dart are probably just as likely to be successful even if the cat does sound a rondo over the last few frantic yards of the final pounce and I'm sure the only bell that would be effective at saving birds would be one that was heavy enough to slow the cat down in all his movements ... but then a lead weight would do the job just as well, and quietly!

Many owners call me not just with an air of desperation about their cat's killing but also because they feel that, by indulging in such activities, the cat is implying to them that he isn't properly looked after. It's as if, in some way, he has reverted to responding to his instincts because he isn't being fed enough or properly. Weight for weight cats take in half as many calories again as do humans. The average cat is estimated to consume five to eight per cent of its own body weight in food per day (more if pregnant or lactating), equivalent to nearly 130,000 calories per year. This is nearly thirty times its own weight in food and about the same again in liquids. Most of that food for pet cats in the developed world comes in the form of prepared canned or dry food but topped up with table scraps and 'fresh' items caught outdoors. A passing indication of the size of the industry that serves the feeding requirements of cats is the fact that Americans currently spend about two billion dollars per year on their sixty million cats.

But pet cats can be socialised with species ordinarily regarded as prey and then not attempt to kill or eat them later. The earliest work in such areas was performed by a Chinese biologist, Zing Yang Kuo, in the late 1920s and early 1930s. He showed that when kittens were raised in the company of rats, they wouldn't kill either their rodent pen-mates or other similar unfamiliar rats. Zing Yang Kuo also raised kittens with a variety of other prey species such as rabbits and birds for ten months in large enclosures and achieved similar results.

He then looked at the reactions between single kittens raised with rats compared with the effects of one kitten being raised with another kitten. The distress expressed by a kitten on being isolated from its companion appeared to be no different whether the companion was a rat or a member of his own species. But the bonding, though apparently permanent and capable of overriding any genetically inspired motivation to hunt rodents, needs to be established early on in the kitten's development, probably beginning at no later than four weeks of age. However, such passive behaviour in the face of prey may not persist long into adulthood once the cat encounters a range of individual rodents of differing species in varying habitats when the young cat is free to roam and has to fend for himself.

A memorable client

One of my favourite clients over the past couple of years has been Brenda Farrell, who now lives in Kent, sometimes known as 'the garden of England'. It's been more like the 'hunting grounds of England' for Tutu and Norman, her pair of Burmese cats. Among many other problems in the past, not least a very changeable relationship between the two cats, every spring I know that Brenda will always be calling me up.

In 1990, when Brenda lived in a different home, it was Tutu who was the boss cat and the one who used to disappear for days at a time on prolonged hunting trips in the local countryside. He packed his claws and his kit-bag and went on safari, worrying Brenda to death and only returning when his failure at finding enough to feed himself, or the need for a decent sleep in comfort, drove him back to the warm home offered by Brenda. He usually arrived home in quite a dishevelled state and extremely tired. Fed and rested, he would go off again a few days later to local fields and woods and this would repeat itself through the summer. It was as if the good Lord said to Tutu, even as a high-born pedigree cat, 'remember that you are really an African Wild Cat'.

In fact Tutu's behaviour was probably triggered by some hormonal change in his pituitary gland brought on by temperature and day-length changes which awakened ancestral desires to feed himself up on the spring glut of rodents and perhaps roam in search of mates, despite the fact that he is neutered. Many neutered males continue to show certain male characteristics even after being castrated before puberty, presumably triggered by other hormones from other places than the testes. The adrenal gland, for example, also produces a small amount of male hormone.

Alas, one suspects that Tutu wasn't too good at feeding himself because he always returned in a much worse condition than when he left, and his thin pedigree single coat did little to keep him warm and protected on colder nights or in rougher places. Poor Brenda used to go out searching for him and would catch an occasional glimpse of him in the local fields. But he would never respond to her calls, moving off quietly into the undergrowth like some disturbed tiger.

I've subsequently had several such calls from owners of various types of cat who behave similarly come the spring, though many do seem for some reason to be Burmese. Perhaps their owners are more inclined to worry than those of other breeds or perhaps some strains within this breed have a greater disposition for following the free uncompromised life in spite of the genetic engineering that goes into their appearance. Certainly Burmese cats are also often referred to me for problems of assertiveness, despotic aggression towards other neighbourhood cats and indoor spraying, suggesting an above-average level of reactivity in the breed.

The interesting thing about Brenda's pair, however, has been that since he has recovered from being struck by a car, Tutu has been much more of a home-loving cat and rarely wanders far. Norman on the other hand, who used to be a real mummy's boy, has taken over as top cat and it is he who now disappears on long hunting trips in the local equivalent to the Hindu Kush! Poor Brenda has simply had to accept this role reversal. Loving, caring owner that she is, Brenda has come to realise that, every spring, one of her cats is likely to respond to some deep-seated motivation to break free of the basic comfortable trappings of life with man. The motivation lasts until the 'call of the wild' is superseded by being cold, tired and hungry!

It must all come a bit hard to owners like Brenda to read of cats like Murka and Rusty in Chapter 2 who are so bonded to their home that they travel many miles to return there after they've been moved away. Another cat to annoy Brenda was McCavity, a three-year-old tabby. Unsure of his new home in Cumbernauld in Scotland, he dashed the 500 miles back to his old home in Truro, Cornwall in only three weeks, much to the amazement but chagrin of his owners.

'O what is more blessed than to throw cares aside, as the mind puts down its burden and, weary with the labour of far journeys, we return home and rest on the couch that we longed for'　　　　Catullus

Why do pet cats need to kill anyway?

The common question of many pet cat owners is just why well-fed cats should need to kill anything at all. The answer may be that not everything a cat kills is required for food and so may be used for the purposes of practice. A cat's victim, for as long as it remains alive and moves and squeaks, may also fit the bill as a toy or item of interest to satisfy the demands for exercise of its captor's senses and expression of its reflexes. Perhaps, like many human hunters, and as seen in many dogs, there is a joy and an emotional high to be had in the hunting and grappling with a victim which is lost once it is dead. The only way for a cat to maintain the interest then is to make it 'come alive' again by throwing it around, but most cats lose interest quickly in dead prey and either then eat or simply abandon it and go off in pursuit of new live quarry.

Leyhausen found that prey hunting and killing occur independently of hunger in the cat. So highly specialised are the instincive drives, physical nature and senses that have evolved in the cat's development as a predator that the sum total has perhaps become detached from the original meaning for it all, to enable the cat to feed itself in order to survive and procreate. It's only when we, with our more moralistic approach to hunting and survival, find ourselves confronted with the highly specialised hunter as a pet, that such torture and killing surplus to survival requirements is questioned by anyone. But then, isn't the major crime of Western man, the most prolific pet cat keeper ever, that of obesity? Eating in excess of our requirements in the knowledge that so many of our own species are starving to death every day is surely a far greater crime than excess killing by the cat who is responding only to what its evolution has made it into and has no moral philosophy on life? Cats, by the way, are rarely obese unless ill or overfed by us.

Can we stop cats hunting?

We have already seen how varied Bullet's hunted quarry is (see Bullet's Hit List, page 40) and that he uses the two hunting strategies and a combination of them to pursue his furred and feathered victims. Bullet, as a domestic pet, does not have to hunt to feed himself yet because he still does it, demonstrates nicely how distinct hunger is from the instinct to hunt. After an evening, morning or night's butchering, he returns to his bowl of highly processed, perfectly balanced dry cat food, sent to the UK for British cats to enjoy all the way from America. Of course, from time to time, he does eat his kill, or some of it, and destroys all that effort at balancing his energy, vitamin and mineral intake invested by the manufacturers! But even if Bullet only hunts because his instinctive drives tell him to and because he has the opportunity, the list of thirty-eight species of mammal, bird and reptile that I have documented as having fallen prey to him, simply shows the diversity of his skills. While he might have been socialised to domestic mice and rats as a kitten and grown up not recognizing them as prey, the irresistible triggers of the wild rodent moving and squeaking through the grass and its very different smell to its domesticated cousins would mean that Bullet, 'pre-wired' to respond by stalking, would still have turned out exactly as he is.

Nonetheless, it is still a pleasant surprise giving rise to hopes of biblical fulfilment that the 'lion shall lie down with the lamb' when one hears of the occasional cat that seems totally uninterested in hunting anything, such as the story of Mr Snowy Farr of Cambridge. Every Saturday, Snowy takes his cat to the market and raises money for charity by putting him on his top hat along with a handful of mice on the brim. There's not a hint of violence from the cat, nor fear from the mice, and in ten years Snowy has raised enough money to donate seventeen guide dogs to the blind. Perhaps someone should tell the cat that the money donated in response to his peaceful performance is canine bound . . . it may change his attitude!

In an effort to deter their cats from hunting many owners take the bribery route and try offering their cat what they see as the very best of food. Fillet steak, chicken, prawns, etc. are all lovingly prepared for the smiling cat in the vain hope that he'll then lose the taste for mice, voles and birds. Alas, it's all to no avail. Unfortunately the motivations behind hunting and killing are genetically, not appetite inspired, so even feeding our pets to excess won't stop them hunting unless they are made obese and slower off the mark! One might slow them down a bit by using the 'Alcatraz tactic' by which the cat is deliberately made so overweight (and this can be inordinately difficult with most cats) that he can't hunt and make those final bursts of speed so well. Clearly this is never to be recommended on health grounds for cats, though interestingly, this tactic was used to help ensure that prisoners were less able to escape from the famous island prison in San Francisco Bay. By fattening them up on stodgy food, the authorities ensured that if anyone did break out, the chances would be that they would be totally unfit and wouldn't be able to swim across the bay – at least not quickly enough to escape the sharks!

Why do cats play with their victims?

Many owners of pet cats are rather disgusted at the way their pets appear to play with their prey of a mouse, apparently torturing it to death rather than ending its days quickly with a relatively humane but fatal nape bite. When prolonged, such play can be indicative of an incomplete learning programme when the cat was young, particularly in pets brought up in the house by a mother who didn't bring home half-dead mice for her kittens to practise on and develop their killing skills. Hence the cat bats and plays with his victim only as far as he used to bat and play with toys and objects, his littermates and his mother's tail when he was a kitten exploring the capacity of his physical abilities. The cat may also use the half-dead prey he has to practise his hunting abilities for the next time, safe in the knowledge

169

that this particular victim has already been taken and can be killed and consumed at any time. Additionally, the well-fed pet has never had to learn to kill his prey quickly in order to eat to relieve any great hunger.

The play angle may lie behind the urge of some cats to bring their half-dead or dead prey home to us. If some cats see us as a friend or perhaps even as a kitten in the shared den (a real role reversal from the idea that they see us as a mother figure!), then they may be bringing their quarry in for us to play with and learn how to kill, or to ensure that we maintain the ability to do so.

Sometimes playful and usually intensive attempts by some cats to cover uneaten food by raking the floor around the bowl are quite comical but presumably are exactly what the cat does outside once it has eaten some of a victim such as rabbit which is too large to consume at one sitting. In the absence of any vegetation around the food bowl in the kitchen, the cat may scratch around for some time or attempt to nudge the bowl with his nose, rather than his paws, to a sheltered corner of the kitchen – a process known as caching. Then he goes off hunting again with the only hope for the rodents and birds of the garden being that he may be stuffed to the gunnels for a while and less able to stalk and pounce so easily. Tigers are known to go a step further to make sure that a meal remains to be returned to later after a sleep or a spot of territory patrolling. As well as caching their prey, they will spray an uneaten carcass with urine to identify it as theirs and deter any rival tigers or scavengers, and perhaps to pickle it!

To eat or not to eat

Surplus killing by cats and playing with dead or half-dead victims may seem distasteful for us but things could be worse! A cat called Smudge, cited by Janice Anderson in her excellent book *Cat Calls,* was bought by a lady for company. She didn't need a mouser as she hadn't seen a mouse in or around her home for years. Smudge duly went a-hunting in the garden, found some and brought them back in through the cat flap still alive. Proudly presenting each one to his owner, he would then drop them and go off for a rest. Before long the house was overrun with Smudge's little pets and their many, many offspring, all of which Smudge paid no attention to! Perhaps Smudge simply lost interest in mice once he had stalked and captured them. He would bring them home perhaps with the intention of eating them in a safe place but lost interest quickly or felt more like other things when he arrived and abandoned them instead. If they hadn't already died of fright, they found themselves in a paradise of warmth, food scraps and friends and duly took advantage, while poor old Smudge just kept responding to the instinctive drive to go and look for more!

The problems of mistaken identity

However, the main problem for owners distressed at their cat's hunting excesses is that they feel that as a pet, he ought to be naturally more sociable towards living creatures and, simply by virtue of being what they see as domesticated, he ought to be a good step removed from the need to indulge in the tooth and claw of struggling to survive. The problem is one of attitude on their part, not the cat's, and arises because we have all traditionally come to view the cat as a domestic pet, a creature which ought to be friendly and docile to us and everything that we enjoy. Now it seems that we should think again and forget about expecting our cats to be 'domesticated' when they are not.

While most cat owners accept that hunting is just part of owning a cat, those who only want the cuddles and purrs have always been disappointed, especially when the nesting season arrives. Perhaps the thought that their cat is still indistinguishable from the African Wild Cat in Professor Harley's research will help them. Owners like Brenda Farrell may perhaps now come to understand that their cat is not rejecting their care or affection by clearing off every spring, nor is he underfed nor fed on food that he doesn't like. He's just responding in the same way as all wild cats do to the availability and presence of their prey. He is still predominantly a wild cat species, even if we have tweaked some surface genes to make him hairless or hairier, more colourful or to have beautiful colour points.

It's not just a case of cat owners having no responsibility or control over the outdoor hunting cat in suburbia or in the city, it's more a case of being wrong ever to have expected to have any at all. Being a pet is just another but cushier niche that the cat has come to adopt since he first needed man to transport him around the globe to new colonisable lands. First it was a case of loose association with man in the towns, then they came to share an outdoor territory and finally, lived together for some of the time in man's indoor den. No one ever said anything to the cat about having to give up any hardy 'wild' characteristics or hunting skills. We keep cats as they are, and as they always have been right from the days when the Ancient Egyptian workers shared their streets and homes with them, and their royal and noble employers first corralled them for use as religious offerings. Cats have been faithful to their evolution even in spite of our concerted efforts to shape them into a wider range of shapes, colours and sizes in more recent years.

Bullet's list of species victims is sad but impressive and by no means unique. Most British pet cats in rural or semi-rural areas probably take an even wider range of victims, depending on local opportunities. While the number of available prey species may be fewer in suburbia or in the city, approximately the same total number of victims will probably be taken by every pet cat, allowing for some individual variations in hunting skill and motivation. It is, of course, true that some cats show no inclination to hunt, or only hunt certain types of prey, which may be the most locally prevalent or vulnerable species. However, once such a species has been ravaged, as by the feral cats on islands mentioned in the last section, pet cats will usually soon turn to the next most exploitable edible creature.

A few cats are also utterly useless at hunting and though they may try hard, fail miserably. In the wild, such cats would be unable to feed themselves and would die out unless they were able to find a ready and permanent source of carrion or edible waste and survive by scavenging alone. Lucky owners can at least revel in their cat's apparent lack of hunting skills. Such a lack, even if not frequently encountered in the cat, does beg the question as to whether we might be able to breed from these individuals deliberately and ultimately produce litters of kittens which had no motivation to hunt. While we can artificially select and breed from nervous dogs or mice and produce consistently nervous animals within only a few generations, I suspect that we would not be able to breed the hunting instinct out of cats, though we may be able to reduce it over perhaps a great number of generations of controlled breeding. I tend to think that non-hunting cats, or poor hunters, are more likely to have arisen through lack of opportunity to develop their skills when young. For example, a hand-raised kitten may be at a disadvantage compared with one that has grown up in a playful litter experimenting with the manoeuvres of stalk and pounce with his brothers and sisters and mum's tail. Mum may also bring back half-killed prey or small toys for her kittens to learn to 'kill', a developmental stage that human surrogate mothers may avoid or neglect. Alternatively, the inability to hunt may simply be confused with inexperience because of a lack of opportunity to hunt rather than lack of ability. Many cats seem uninterested in hunting when only encountering birds on the outskirts of the city, but are just as effective hunters and killers of rodents as the next cat when they do finally encounter them.

The environmental impact of pet cats

The effect that pet cats can have on local wildlife is similar to that of feral cats or the receding wild cat species in Europe and elsewhere. The scale of that carnage was investigated in the United Kingdom by Churcher and Lawton in 1987. Owners of pet cats in 173 houses in the Bedfordshire village of Felmersham were asked to keep all the kills that their pets brought home, put them in plastic bags and store them in the freezer to await collection and identification. Despite the thought of the grisly culinary delights that may have mistakenly resulted from late night 'fry-ups' on returning from the local pub, hungry after a night of only excessive liquid intake, this research revealed some most interesting data.

From analysis of the victims, the cats of Felmersham, a largely rural village, were found to have caught mainly rodents (woodmice, bank voles and field voles) and the insectivores (common shrews and pygmy shrews), with only a few rabbits and other mammals taken. Birds featured relatively highly on the list, particularly the house sparrow, though the song-thrush, blackbird and robin which also frequent our gardens and are happy to feed from bird-tables and nest near our homes were also notably recorded. Of course such straight sampling takes little account of other variables such as the time of year, nesting season and population of the local prey, though the project did suggest that cats living at the edge of the village caught more than those towards the centre, presumably because of greater access to larger populations of prey in the fields and woods. The investigation is therefore of interest rather than of great scientific value and when one considers that an American study estimated that pet cats only bring about half of their kills home, the Felmersham figures will perhaps tend to underestimate the true picture.

But the most startling figure to emerge from the study is the

173

least scientific one of all. If one multiplies the results per Felmersham cat to represent the number of rodents and birds killed by the nation's nearly seven million cats, even allowing for a generous ten per cent which are kept permanently indoors and have no opportunity to hunt, and allowing for the prey that wasn't brought home to be counted, one arrives at an astounding estimate. It is that seventy-five to one hundred million small mammals and birds meet their end annually at the claws and teeth of an animal that we nurture and keep as a loving pet!

These pet cats in one village in Bedfordshire brought home nearly 1,100 dead bodies in one year, comprising 535 mammals, 297 birds and 258 other unidentified little cadavers. The number of victims per cat per year was just over fifteen and a half according to this survey, though it will undoubtedly be higher when one considers the number of victims which are totally consumed, and those perhaps fifty per cent abandoned away from the home. There will certainly be many, many cats who kill a far greater number of rodents and birds per year than this. Though I haven't actually counted, I would estimate Bullet's annual figure to be more in the region of fifty observable victims though as my two Siamese have so far respectively only managed one young mouse and a shrew which escaped unharmed under the bed to be rescued later (Bean), and nothing at all (Flirty Bottom), the household average is probably about the same as Peter Churcher's estimate.

It was also estimated that the pet cat accounts for between a third and one half of all sparrow deaths in Felmersham and that cats probably kill about twenty million of them every year in the United Kingdom! What is even more astounding is that so far, the populations of sparrows, mice and voles, etc. seem to be able to withstand this apparently enormous level of harvesting, or at least no one has shown otherwise. Indeed, one might argue that the pet cat is simply filling the predator's niche in the United Kingdom, a niche left for a small solitary carnivore with the withdrawal or decline through loss of habitat of the native Scottish Wild Cat and other small hunters of rodents such as stoats and weasels, which can't exist so well alongside man. Their usual prey of mice, voles and songbirds often find life attractive close to us in our gardens and so their populations continue to prosper, despite the presence of a pet African immigrant predator. What effect the cat may be having on foxes, owls and hawks which also pursue the same or similar quarry, will only be seen with time. In the

United States, one estimate put the carnage of rodents at five and a half US billion per year by ten million cats in the countryside and suggested that because cats were removing the main prey of hawks and kestrels, these raptors were in decline as a direct result of a high pet cat population.

The impact of a single pet cat on a single wild bird species is nowhere better demonstrated than by the pet cat which arrived on Stephens Island off the coast of New Zealand with the new lighthouse keeper. Until that time, the unique but flightless Stephens Island rock wren was unknown to man. Indeed, it only became known when the cat started bringing dead examples home to the lighthouse and so perhaps we should be grateful that the cat was of the type that likes to bring at least some of its victims back to the shared den! However, by the time everyone realised that the poor wren might be in danger from the effects of this unfamiliar and highly efficient predator, it was too late. In a few months the cat had caught and killed all of them and the Stephens Island Rock Wren was no more! No sooner found than gone, and for ever, thanks to one solitary cat exercising the hunting prowess his species evolved thousands of years ago on the other side of the world.

Contrastingly, we have prized the efforts of the pet or factory cat at controlling rodents and there are many highly successful cases noted in the record books. A tabby male cat called Mickey caught in excess of 22,000 mice up to his death in 1968, in a hunting career spanning twenty-three years with a firm called Shepherd and Sons of Burscough in Lancashire. Towser, a female cat, was actually born in the Glenturret whisky distillery near Crieff in Perthshire in Scotland and, up to her death in 1986, had caught an average of three mice per day, a lifetime working total of over 25,000! But even these feats are perhaps outweighed by the great ratting cats. In six years between 1927 and 1933, another female called Minnie caught 12,500 rats at the White City stadium in west London, but it isn't known whether any of these hunters actually ate all their victims or not.

In the early part of the century, pet cats were deliberately put into cold storage warehouses to control rats in a Chicago meat-packing plant with the initial result that four-fifths of them died. However, those that survived bred to produce smaller cold-resistant cats with thicker fur and shorter tails who went on to fulfil their intended role. Quick adaptation to local, if contrived conditions was again the key to the success of this cat population. But if abandoned ships' cats or those deliberately introduced as biological controls can survive the hail and gale-lashed sub-Antarctic islands, and the Norwegian Forest Cats, Maine Coons and Angoras can evolve in the cold, high areas of Eurasia, the cold stores of Chicago ought to have been well within the adaptability of the species. Perhaps the surprise is that even those elastic coat genes of the cat could alter so quickly to ensure survival.

These figures and reports of the hunting abilities of cats are all startling in themselves, but as I wrote in *Do Cats Need Shrinks?*, they are also rather paradoxical in terms of our view of our pets and the welfare of animals. While we tolerate, albeit disapprovingly, our pet cats while they butcher millions of rodents per year without even the need to feed themselves, we are outraged by the use of a contrastingly rather small figure of about three million rats and mice which are killed by man for experimental purposes under the UK Home Office Scientific Procedures Act. Cosmetic and weapons testing, drug development and physiological research are all aspects of human demands on rodents that stimulate an often marked response from many of us, even in defence of the rat. But while we're campaigning and writing to politicians to seek greater controls on experiments and reduce the numbers of animals used, our much-loved pet cats are out in the hunting grounds of the fields, woodlands, suburbia and city backstreets wiping out about thirty-five times as many!

17
More and more pet cats

'Bring in the cat and put out the dog!'   Adapted song line

In the developed world the number of all types of pet, including fish, stick-insects and exotic spiders, is rising, and the rate of increase of numbers of pet cats is outstripping that of dogs. Already in the United States, where the number of cats kept has risen by twenty per cent in five years, there are more cats than dogs. By the mid 1990s, the same will have happened in the United Kingdom and most of northern Europe. And even when we want to share affectionate relationships with dogs, in an increasingly urbanised and individually chaotic Western-style society, we choose small cat-sized varieties, such as Yorkshire Terriers and Lhasa Apsos, to be allowed into the inner sanctum of our homes to be nurtured. The larger breeds such as Dobermanns and German Shepherd Dogs, though still popular, suit us less and less in our smaller living space and are less required as guards in the age of hi-tech security alarms and surveillance systems. But it's there, in our homes, that cats are proving even more popular than those small, more easily managed dogs. While there may be an equable draw in the companionship each species can offer us, cats win 'paws down' when it comes to ease of management and convenience compared with the dog.

It's something of anomaly that the cat, so largely unaltered by us in terms of physical appearance and temperament, and genetically still the same as when he first moved in to our homes, finds himself now so tailor-made to suit our demands of a social pet. The dog, which we have shaped and moulded for thousands of years more than the cat,

177

and whose genes for size, shape, performance and temperament have been so manipulated by us, is now far less suitable. We just haven't been able to perfect the design, because whatever shape or type we make, dogs enjoy routines which we no longer have, and need to be cared for in terms of attention to toileting needs, and control in the human community. As one would expect from an animal that has been developed by man from the highly social wolf, dogs thrive on contact with the family, their substitutes for their canine pack society, a demand which we are less and less able to fulfil. The pet cat, on the other hand, is still a solitary spirit who can look after all his own needs if the facilities are provided. While he has the capacity to be sociable when we are around, he doesn't pine for company if he is left alone and so usually thrives whether we are at home or not.

But while socially cats and dogs have changed little since we started calling them 'companion animals', we certainly have. Gone are the days when the man went away from the den hunting or, in latter days, to work to feed his mate and offspring back home. Gone are the days when women married and then produced a family immediately with little thought for careers. The days of the traditional housewife are numbered in Western civilisation as women choose to follow their own careers. Now men and women are marrying later and delay in having a family until their late-twenties or early-thirties when their careers are established and the first home is settled. And in any case, buying or renting the smaller modern urban home usually takes two incomes, whichever city you live in around the world. It all adds up to a den with no one in it for much of the day which suits the dog less and less, while the cat can cope quite happily.

At the beginning of this century, four-fifths of Europe's population lived in rural villages and small towns, now the same proportion live in dense urban areas. In the United Kingdom the figure is greater. Nine out of ten people live in cities and the surrounding suburbia, although most areas are reasonably green and there are areas of tranquillity within the concrete jungle of the inner-city. Similarly, over eighty per cent of the human population in the United States lives in the city or surrounding suburbia. While most inhabitants dream of moving to more relaxed, greener rural areas in which to raise children, they are caught in the city because most employment and wealth opportunity lies there. Not only this but, of course, many enjoy the social opportunities that city theatres, clubs, restaurants and leisure centres afford and so spend much of their non-working time at weekends or after work still away from home, at least until they do decide to have a family.

Work patterns have also altered enormously in the last decade or two. Many people enjoy far greater freedom with flexible working hours compared with the traditional nine-to-five approach of their fathers. The successful career-minded people often originally marked out somewhat disparagingly as 'yuppies' may also choose to work very long hours in the furtherance of their income and career with the result that their home becomes little more than a hotel in which to sleep and grab an occasional meal. This reduced dependence on having a home in which to relax can be carried to the extreme – some Japanese city professionals devote their whole day to their work and rent a sleep tube in a honeycomb of underground tubes in which to pass the night and rest before the next work day. There's just enough space to lie down in a sleeping bag and keep a small hold-all of basic maintenance equipment handy – perhaps a change of clothes and a toothbrush.

Modern city psychology

Psychologically, city living can be disastrous for many people. In his recent book, *Back to Earth,* environmentalist James Clarke describes the case of an elderly man living in a city in South Africa who was suffering from 'terminal loneliness'. He was rich, living in a large spacious house in a prestigious suburban street. The street however had long ago been turned into a traffic highway and become an 'inhuman, grossly over-engineered noiseway'. Instead of being an area where people would meet, make friends and go about the business and discourse of life, the area had become one where 'mothers live in fear of their children going outside the gate' in case of road accidents and crime. The old man, a widower, sat all day in his armchair, afraid to go out and alone and miserable. He was probably expecting to spend his declining years as did the old folk of his youth, relaxing in a chair on the verandah of a safe town house, watching youngsters playing on the streets and known and respected as 'Gramps' by one and all. Instead, in the modern badly designed city, he was waiting and wanting to die.

But while architects are beginning at last to design city living areas for people, not cars, and take account of the views of psychologists, sociologists and criminologists, and not just the town planners and engineers, pets can at least help keep some of us sane by giving us something to care for. In the social shape of a cat or dog, a pet can be something that will love us and help keep us socialised as well, if we need it. The Japanese tube-dweller may even actually enjoy his routine or at least be able to justify it and the London upwardly mobile young man or woman may enjoy the vast array of professional and leisure opportunities in the city. But there is increasingly less place for pet dogs and cats in this sterile human lifestyle, quite apart from the understandable pressures against dogs from other city people who want to enjoy what green there is in the city parks without stepping in dog mess.

Even in more spacious suburbia, if mum and dad are away all day and there are no kids until much later, it all adds up to a less than ideal or even pleasant life for the social dog facing being left alone at home for long periods during the week. It doesn't need a pet behaviour therapist to identify the traumas faced by a poor Border Collie for example, who, having been selected to be active all day working with a handler to direct sheep, is expected to live his life in a human den of an eighth-floor apartment in the middle of a concrete city with his pack away at work all day. Some of these dogs have been estimated to run seventy-five miles in the course of a working day on the fells and while they may not need quite that much to lead a happy life in a family, it gives an idea of how far short we may be selling some of our 'soon to be former best friends'.

Enter the cat, or rather, rise to the surface with a reputation of self-reliance, and an extraordinarily adaptable individual character and behavioural repertoire. He can accommodate living with us and our unreasonable expectations. As we have seen throughout the preceding chapters, the cat is as blessed as ever with that single-minded approach to survival whichever environment he finds himself in. This mimics our own currently more individual approach to life far better than the dog does. The cat looks after himself and doesn't depend on a group for co-operative hunting or defence of a den. It is most unlikely that any cat would become so attached to us as to fall to pieces and scream or chew the curtains to shreds if we leave him at home alone while we work or stay away to play. He'll conveniently use a litter tray for the necessaries of life if we don't give him free access to use the outdoors and even there, he's neat. He'll dig a nice little hole in the soil for a toilet (often in someone else's garden!) and cover it up afterwards so as not to cause offence. He certainly doesn't need us to get home to take him out for exercise, lead in one hand, poop scoop in the other. The cat will largely regulate his own food intake safely and easily without risk of obesity or scoffing early and going hungry later if we put out his food as we leave for work. And he'll let himself in and out of the house quite happily if we give him a cat flap. A totally convenient pet that couldn't have been designed better for the more solitary lifestyle demanded by us of the freer living sociable pet in the home.

A recent survey of owners in America by the Pet Food Institute revealed why people choose to keep cats. Eighty-six per cent do so for companionship, seventy-five per cent for convenience, thirty-five per cent do so because cats were thought to be good for children and thirty per cent because they were thought to be good for one's health. Only seven per cent kept their cat as a rodent controller. Seventy-four per cent of American cats sleep on their owner's bed but the biggest drawback, quoted by sixty per cent of cat owners, was fur-shedding. The second biggest drawback, cited by forty-five per cent of owners, and hardly the cat's fault, was having to find someone to look after him when they went away!

Human psychology

One might still wonder why we keep any pets at all if we have so little opportunity to be with them nowadays and they no longer fill any direct utilitarian role. The answer, as many eminent psychologists around the world have explained, is that they do fulfil a useful role, not so much of benefit physically for us, but mentally. We now need to enjoy the company of our pets more than ever to keep ourselves sane in the often mad world that we are creating for ourselves. Our pets, especially the socially reactive ones such as dogs and cats, help us unwind, give us a link back with nature. They make us feel better emotionally, if nothing else because they always love us even if many of our own kind at the office don't. That freely-given commitment from the cat in his relationship with us , means that it's no huge surprise that so many people claim to love their cat more than any person in their lives.

Pets are important for the emotional development of our children too. A Cambridge study which compared two groups of children found that the group which came from pet-owning families had a better relationship with their parents and a happier life at home than the control group from non-pet-owning families. The more pets owned, the better the family relations, according to the survey. Physically, it's also been demonstrated that we pet owners are less likely to suffer from a range of common ailments, including backache and the common cold. We also tend to exercise more and are less likely to suffer from heart disease if we relax and spend at least some time nurturing and petting a dog or cat. As a result, we will probably live longer and in better health than non-pet owners. This is gratifying to remember at those rare times when your cat – or those more frequent times that your dog – drives you to such distraction that you think you're going to have a heart attack!

But there's much more to living with a cat than the convenience of owning an independent pet that doesn't soil our den if we don't get home in time. One of the most prized features of cats reported in owner surveys in the USA and Europe is their affection towards us. That tail-up greeting, purring and rubbing are all exactly what we need, a wonderful tonic in our rather crowded but unfriendly cities. The cat curls up contentedly by the fire or better still, on our laps, totally relaxed and totally relaxing. The cat sees us a surrogate mother figure throughout his life and maintains a whole range of relaxed kittenish behaviour as an adult, when, ordinarily, he would have swapped such social graces for independence and development as a solitary hunter. And we love all that affection and warmth, it brings out all those nurturing emotions that we find little opportunity to express in our working or leisure lives and don't get a chance to release on our children until we're older and have made the time and wealth to have them. The cat tells us constantly around the home that we are his mum and yet places none of the demands of care that our kids or the dog require. Purrfect!

Another prized aspect of the cat reported in many owner surveys, though more so in the United Kingdom than in the USA, is his playfulness. How we love to play with our cats, dangling string or rolling simple balls of paper for him to stalk, chase and pounce on so appealingly. Some cats, especially the Orientals, even go that slavish step further and, like a dog, retrieve the ball or toy and bring it back to us to throw again – a real endorsement of the cat's take-over in our hearts.

Cats, especially when young, often delight us with their imaginary play, chasing and swatting at some hallucinatory mouse or bird and sharpening all those reflexes and movements. The African Wild Cat kitten out in the semi-desert is just as playful and chases the same hallucinatory targets, as he learns to be ruthlessly efficient in pursuit of the mice that will determine his survival. And the adult African Wild Cat, like all other cats, still puts his reflexes through their paces away from the actual process of hunting in lethal but enchanting practice sessions with wind- blown leaves and other objects of fancy. So while we are enthralled at our African Wild Cat's speed in play, that play is often simply the practice or expression of his uncompromised evolution as a hunter. It's just a form of the hunting repertoire that we can enjoy without the guilt we may feel when he actually puts it all into bloody practice outdoors. A babe in our arms in the living room one minute; a playful but ruthless, top-of-the-food-chain and highly specialised predator in the garden the next. The claws and the purrs both have fascinating and irresistible appeal!

18
Who's keeping cats?

'I have noticed that what cats most appreciate in a human being is not the ability to produce food, which they take for granted, but his or her entertainment value'
Geoffrey Household

The cat population in the United Kingdom has grown by over forty per cent in the last decade, and continues to grow at nearly two per cent per year, more than twice the rate for dogs. The growth has occurred as a result of the rise in individual owner's wealth . . . it would have to as a recent report by *Wild About Animals* magazine suggested that it costs £6,000 – £10,000 to keep a cat for a thirteen-year lifespan! Wealth naturally brings associated lifestyle changes which can accommodate a cat or two, especially in homes where the owners are middle-aged and presumably sage enough to rationalise the pros and cons of taking on a pet. Such owners will tend to have a well-established family life of settled home and reasonable routine and so perhaps be in a better position to take on a cat or a dog and have it contribute to the 'balanced family' atmosphere.

Cat ownership is certainly most popular in the thirty-five to forty-four-year-old age bracket with over thirty-two per cent of all such households having at least one cat. Ownership also tends to increase with the presence of children in the family and more so as the children get older themselves and demand a pet off their parents. Cat lovers, but not necessarily cat owners, tend to be female, a factor more reflected in the make-up of we humans rather than the cat's. Desmond Morris, author of *The Naked Ape* and *Manwatching*, puts this down to the group hunting characteristics of men which militate against reacting with a solitary minded hunter like the cat. The 'pack mentality' is less marked in women who can therefore accommodate the cat better in their own psychology and allow other nurturing and social emotions to flow.

Certainly women tend to show cats more affection and attention than either men or children and so perhaps get more out of keeping cats as a result. The various talks on dogs that I give tend to attract audiences of men and women in roughly equal numbers while the more frequently requested ones on cat behaviour and feline behaviour therapy are to predominantly female audiences ... it's just dawned on me why I prefer talking about cats!

The number of single-person households is rising sharply from the 5.3 million figure of 1987 according to the Beta Petfoods Pet Futures Report. Single people also tend to keep a cat in preference to a dog because of the ease of management and for company and friendship, especially, as we have seen, if they are otherwise lonely in the big city or out in suburbia. The report suggests that single-household ownership of cats will therefore tend to rise consistently as more and more people develop careers, live alone and marry and have children later than in times past. Owners tend to be middle-class and cats are thus concentrated in suburbia in the more affluent south and east of the United Kingdom.

Interestingly, much of the growth in cat keeping in recent years has come from existing owners who have decided to take on more than one cat. Perhaps while the hunting side of the cat is always cited by cat haters as one of the main reason for their dislike, especially if they are bird watchers, it isn't such a worry for cat lovers who are prepared to ignore, tolerate or accept it.

For most owners, the cat is seen very much as a member of the family and so perhaps his indiscretions on the local wildlife are viewed similarly to the pranks and scrapes that kids get into! But the cat remains a nurtured family member that, when he's indoors, is like Peter Pan and never appears to grow up, and whom the owners have decided to care for until he dies. Cats will always be forgiven by their owners, especially as hunting and the rest of their uncompromised spirit is something that we all have to accept in each and every one of them.

Cat/people relations

'I should feel a bit of a . . . a bit of a cat person'
Alan Coren, adapted by Janice Anderson

As the recent growth in the number of pet behaviour therapists testifies all too well, there are problems with many of our dogs and a few of our cats in terms of compatibility. Often, these problems concern 'normal' pet behaviour going on in places or at times or to a level that an owner cannot tolerate rather than genuine neuroses, psychoses and neurological disorders which are more prevalent in human psychiatric practice. The common feature of most of my clients is a great desire to resolve their pet's problems so that they and their family can enjoy living with their pet better. As a practising pet behaviour therapist, I do see several noticeable differences in the attitudes between cat and dog owners seeking help. For example, dog owners tend to blame the dog for being difficult or see his behaviour as defiant or spiteful, while cat owners invariably blame themselves for their cat's behaviour problems. Accepting responsibility for a pet they can't control seems to be a rather generous attitude, but perhaps is just another example of how the cat is able always to get the best of all worlds and exploit any situation to the full without compromising an inch.

Most of us cat owners are, however, decidedly happy with the deal, perhaps because of the complexity of relationship we can enjoy with our cats. The Beta Petfoods Pet Futures Report listed several types of relationship from the human point of view. The first, somewhat coolly described as 'Love Displacement', indicated that women were most likely to love their cat with the same intensity as they would a man, while the cuddly 'baby' image of closely nurtured pets, ascribed to many human/pet relations of times past, is actually held more by older people or very young owners than the adult woman seeking a child substitute. Those who do treat the cat as a surrogate baby do fit the image, however, as they tend to be older, wealthier, lonely and female and readily indulge their cat with everything they feel it could possibly want. For many people who live alone, whether male or female and largely irrespective of their age, the cat is viewed as an 'only friend'. This is the consequence of modern city living and detachment from a close-knit human community and is perhaps the saddest type of 'love displacement'. Smaller, cat-sized breeds of dog

186

such as Toy Poodles or Chihuahuas may also be treated and viewed in the same way. The report found that working pet owners, as we already knew, prized the independence of cats and the ease of keeping them. Younger owners, free to develop less dictated lives and relationships prior to leaving full-time education, value the cat as an 'intelligent friend' within that independence. The cat is for them a sort of buddy whom they get to know on equal terms rather than as any form of psychological prop that can help protect or cure their parents from the strains of everyday living.

Women owners, particularly older ones without children, may come to regard their cat as a source or focus of their own identity. They may also see themselves as the cat's friend and protector, introducing the idea that the actual self-esteem of the lady cat owner may be being maintained by directing attention on to the cat rather than have their character projected naked and vulnerable into the human world. The cat is, after all, a traditional symbol of cultured, chic femininity with a hidden curled-up power, an image expounded by the advertisers who bombard our lives with 'desirable' images. Contrastingly, cats may even be disliked for maintaining their own individual character by some female owners who only keep one to impart that very air of sophistication, femininity and fashionability to their circle of friends. In other words, it is the image in human terms of the cat that is appreciated in these cases, not the reality of the cat itself.

For most of us, the relationship with our cats is far less complex or expedient, and the cat is seen simply as a sociable creature that helps make a house a home and a more diverse and pleasant social environment for us to live in and for the kids to grow up in. Most of us love our cat but tend not to dote on his every whim. We let him come and go as he pleases with just enough attention, feeding and care as necessary, punctuated by occasional indulgences and displays of affection. This, of course, is exactly what a cat wants from life and our investing much more time, care, affection and expensive toys and beds does not necessarily mean a happier cat. In fact, if excessive love starts to prevent the cat from doing what he wants to do, then it could be said to be seriously misplaced and even deleterious to the cat's state of mind.

The cat shares many types of human den but always as a cat, never as a poor version of a human. He has little role to play in fulfilling the demands or shortcomings of the human psyche or in ameliorating the problems that the owner may experience in the nature of their lifestyle, other than by being there and being a cat. A cat has no need himself to meet such demands from us, so long as his spirit and genes remain as essentially wild as they are. And as long as we can empathise with the cat as a cat, the more satisfying our relationship will be from both points of view. The relationship will always be dictated by the cat's view of life rather than our expectations, however much some owners would prefer or infer otherwise with all the attention and trappings that money can buy a pet cat. It's yet another case of quality not quantity being the important thing in life.

Living up to expectations

Most of us need look no further than our own cats to know just how good they can be as straightforward companions. African Wild Cats have an awful lot going for them as a species with us in our front rooms, yet each and every one of them is different in his relations with his family of owners. Clearly much of this difference lies in the variability of human personality, but much is also due to the individually variable nature of the cat. After being ignored or even ridiculed as less than serious science for years, people/pet relations are now fashionable in academic circles. Much closer studies of the personality of the pet cat and the varying types of relations it can have with its owners have been carried out in recent times.

My colleague in the Association of Pet Behaviour Counsellors, Dr Dennis Turner, an American in Zurich rather than Paris, has been especially active over the last few years studying relations between pet cats and their owners, and looking at owner's expectations of their cats. He studied the human/cat relationship in the home by asking 158 housewives, who owned 344 cats between them, to scale their cats and their relationships with them for thirty-one different traits to see whether they tied up with their expectations of the ideal cat.

For many, their relationship with their pet cat was very close to fulfilling their ideal with an average seventy-six per cent tie-up for the thirty-one traits, though some were as close as ninety-four per cent. The data, by the way, was collected by two assistants visiting in turn the 158 households to collect information on three consecutive days according to thirty-three quantifiable behavioural elements which could be exhibited by the cat, the owner or both. In short, the two assistants were paid to sit in cat owners' homes and watch what went on in order to pull habits out of cats!

One may justifiably wonder why such observations and in-depth science are necessary to examine the relationship between man and cat, or rather in this case, housewife and cat, but the fact that Dennis's research is mainly ultimately funded by one of the largest pet food manufacturers in the world indicates how important such information is from a commercial angle, as well as from the interest point of view.

The project recorded over 6,000 'intents to react', defined as when the cat or owner approached one another, and then how the target reacted. The results were examined in the light of various factors thought likely to influence the nature of the owner/cat relationship: the marital status of the woman (single, married, with or without children, etc.), the housing conditions of the cat (for example whether kept permanently indoors or how long allowed access to the outdoors), the number of cats kept, their breed, etc.

Dennis found that the more cats a woman had owned previously, the more demanding or particular she was about her present cat and the higher her expectations of their relationship. By contrast however, he has also found that cats are not nearly as particular about who their owners are and the nature of their housing conditions as their owners are thinking or hoping! But then, the African Wild Cat is programmed to take advantage to the absolute full of what is available, but not demand more. If there isn't enough to suit, or the environment needs improving, they simply move on. It's an all-or-nothing relationship dictated by the needs of any individual cat rather than the desires of any individual owner. The only way to insist that the cat receives whatever we want to foist on him is to shut the doors and make sure that he can't move on.

But back to the thirty-one traits of Dennis Turner's study. Whether a cat lived permanently indoors or was allowed access outdoors, and the number of cats kept, was found to affect the actual or the ideal relationship for each owner according to her own assessment. The marital status of the woman and the breed of cat were not found to be statistically relevant. So in this respect, the sometimes notable variation in breed character between the Siamese, Persian, Burmese, etc. is not relevant to owner perception of their relationship, an interesting finding in the light of the suggestion that even these cats are not markedly different from any other cat genetically, nor from the African Wild Cat.

Dennis also drew from his studies the fact that owners of exclusively indoor cats were perhaps less willing to accept cats as being independent creatures which decide for themselves the nature of their lifestyle and relations with their family or fellow house cats. Owners of indoor cats also were more tolerant of scratching of furniture and other destruction around the home by their ideal cat, but in reality, there was no difference in the actual destruction caused by indoor cats compared with those given access outdoors, a point I would concur with based on experience in my behaviour therapy practice.

Comparing one trait with another, cats which were highly affectionate towards their owners were in return much loved, more predictable in their behaviour, and clean. This is useful back-up to my general principles in practice treating behaviour problems – that owners should love and fuss over their cats more and establish contact and management routines to help settle the cat and improve the owner's enjoyment of it. Many owners felt their own cats to be rather disappointing because they weren't so fond of physical stroking and petting as their ideal. Cats which were restless at night tended to be cats with access to the outdoors who were demanding to be let out while indoor cats were quieter at night and less restless having learned to match their rest patterns around their human providers.

In conclusion, Dennis found that in his sample of 158 housewives and their cats, the ideal cat was either very independent and unlike people or very dependent and similar in its habits to people. In reality cats being human-like and independent do not go together, one either has an independent cat who does what he wants when he wants – presumably usually a cat with access to the outdoors – or a totally dependent character who is appealingly humanised but rather uncat-like – presumably usually a permanently indoor cat, one I would regard as not having had the chance to fulfil his feline capacity because of the life of satisfying human demands that has been forced on him. Encouragingly, the potential for becoming a fully expressed cat again seems merely to lie dormant in cats kept indoors all the time. In my experience, if the opportunity arises, they can soon find their true hunting ability and their activity patterns change to cope and they quickly learn to enjoy being allowed access to the outdoors. I have seen cats kept permanently indoors in London apartments to the age of eight and more, find their hunting prowess in a matter of hours following the opportunity to go outside when their owners move to safer suburbia or the countryside. It seems that the African Wild Cat blueprint is well and truly coded in the genes of our cats and can last undiminished for the cat's lifetime awaiting the window of opportunity for expression, yet without necessarily causing the cat to suffer or develop unusual behaviour patterns through lack of fulfilment. As ever, even in more restricted circumstances, the cat can adapt to cope and survive when new opportunities are presented. That, of course, is the very reason for the cat's success in colonising the world around man.

But if the cat is as individually variable in character as its owners, Dennis Turner's research would seem rather specific to those cats owned by those Swiss housewives in his studies. So just how individual is each cat and what determines his character and temperament? A cat can live permanently and apparently happily in man's den and mould his activity patterns and behavioural repertoire around our demands, yet retain all the hunting and territorial attributes of his freer living relations. To do this, his individual personality as well as his species characteristics must be highly adaptable.

19
Catsonality: scientific appreciation of feline emotions and personality

'A cat has absolute emotional honesty'   Ernest Hemingway

Dr Mike Mendl studied for his PhD at Cambridge University investigating personality variance in cats. All of us have a good idea about the characteristics and individuality of our own pets that distinguish them from others and we can probably all describe our own cat's personality well in human terms using words such as 'friendly', 'playful' or 'sensitive'. We learn to 'speak' cat using the presence or absence of certain behaviours and sounds that we have encountered in our own pet cats past and present, and then use this language to establish relationships with new cats that we meet or own subsequently. Dr Mendl has looked at this in more detail to see how the cat's responses to us may vary and, most importantly, to use this information to see how we might develop our relationship, language and understanding of our cats to benefit both sides of that relationship. He has also tried to establish scientifically what causes cats to develop their individual characters, especially in their relations with man. It's quite a momentous step. The cat has gone from being fundamentally a wild asocial creature living around man with the level of proximity dictated by the cat, to a more social one living in closer contact with us in the human den. There he usually retains freedom to come and go and be as he wants to be, though henceforth, the sociability of the cat may be more closely scrutinised so that we might select a 'better' type of character with respect to our demands.

In his research Dr Mendl considered using various techniques for measuring the features of cat character that he was interested in. 'Pure science' observer methods of measuring frequency and sequences of behaviour in uncontrolled situations, specific controlled tests of responses by cats to certain situations and observer ratings or guided opinions of levels of responses, such as friendliness towards a human, are all regularly employed in behavioural studies of animals and people. Such techniques may be good at measuring quantifiable things such as how much time a cat spends awake or asleep and how the waking hours are broken down into hunting, washing or feeding but do little to help define or assess personality traits such as friendliness or sensitivity. While controlled tests can unlock some of these mysteries, such as measuring the time taken for a cat to enter a new environment from a nest box to test confidence, the tests are likely to be relevant only to the conditions at the time and not necessarily reflect the cat's 'true' character as a pet at home.

Such are the limitations of science, yet for so long biologists, psychologists and animal behaviourists have stuck rigidly to using entirely measurable features of sometimes appallingly designed experiments so that they can produce figures and analyse them statistically at the end of it all. I have always fought shy of this limited approach which does not allow for any account to be taken of an animal's moods, emotions or variability day- to-day. To the hard-nosed scientist, animals couldn't have emotions or moods because they can't be measured. Yet every single cat owner knows their cat has good and bad days, good and bad moods and variable reactions according to preceding events and the time of day. Mike Mendl tried to account for these variations and should be applauded for doing so.

The technique Mike used to start to assess feline personality was to have two or more observers who knew the subject cat well, independently to rate its behaviour and responses using a series of previously agreed human language adjectives such as 'active', 'aggressive', 'agile', 'tense', 'equable', 'sociable', etc. These terms are all readily and largely equally comprehensible to humans and so cat behaviour can be described accurately and similarly by different observers. The results do not lend themselves to being processed in an entirely numerical fashion but who can seriously want to try to explain a personality solely in terms of statistics anyway? While pointers to elements in the psychological make-up of man or cat can be made with mathematics, most of us don't limit our view of, for example, our cat's playfulness or partner's mood in the morning on a simple scale of one to ten with ninety-five per cent confidence limits to reinforce the value of the score. It's about time that all animal behaviour studies followed Mike Mendl's example and accepted that every cat's and every experimenter's behaviour are different in enormous numbers of ways, not all of which can be honed down to some meaning-less probability value. Mike's types of observation are certainly no less valuable because they are descriptive or beg more difficult questions than can be tied down to the scientific safety of numbers in their answers. In fact they are a darn sight more comprehensible and useful to the end consumer . . . the cat owner!

The importance of early experience on feline character

'The trouble with a kitten is that eventually it becomes a cat'
Ogden Nash

Cats tend to be relatively stable in temperament even as they age but may show dramatic changes such as when a sick or injured cat is nursed intensively back to health or following surgical procedures that influence the cat's hormonal status. Pet cats that were previously shy or unwilling to be handled a lot, and even some vicious feral cats that have never been handled, can become affectionate doting humanised pets after intensive nursing, and stay that way for the rest of their lives. Most of us deliberately 'aim' for a friendlier more stay-at-home male cat by having them castrated at or around puberty, before natural secondary sexual responses develop. It is perfectly normal for a tom cat to establish and patrol a large territory, but we call this 'roaming' on the basis that the cat really ought to stay in our home more. Scrapping with other toms over the rights to the territory and the resources in it is normal but can cause expensive repair bills at the veterinary surgery if he keeps getting injured and developing abscesses in the wounds. For the territorial tom, there's also the natural job of spraying smelly urine around the home range, and perhaps the home as well, to endorse his presence . . . another normal but undesirable behaviour from the point of view of the human owner. Indoor spraying by an intact tom would not be acceptable for long for most owners though if he doesn't do it indoors they may put up with the roaming and fighting for a while. But if he's not a strong cat compared with local rivals, or if he gets less able to hold his own when older and less agile, he can suffer quite a lot in facing up to the high density of cats that we maintain in the cities and suburbia. If he's going to fit in peaceably with other cats and with the demands of our home, then he'll have to 'have 'em lopped off' and most owners don't think twice about it.

But the main reason for castration is not because most people have had experience of living with a fully intact warrior tom. They have their young male cat castrated because they know that he is quite likely to be far more friendly towards them and any other male cats at home or in the neighbourhood afterwards. It's a case of character manipulation that has become the necessary norm for male cats living in the human den. With a young tom, it's a way of altering the cat's developing character and the effects will be permanent, while sterilising a female will do little to alter her developing adult behaviour other than to stop her coming into season.

While surgery for male cats or the trauma of illness or accident for both sexes can permanently improve their friendliness towards us, we can also shape their character from the emotional development and psychological point of view. The concept of a 'sensitive period' of socialisation in the development of young puppies and kittens has long been recognised. Puppies need to be handled by man and socialised with many people and other dogs between four and about fourteen weeks of age in two separate critical periods as their psychological and physical development, curiosity and desire to explore progress. The friendliness of adult cats has also been shown scientifically to relate to the amount of handling they received as kittens. Their receptiveness to such socialisation begins at about two weeks and lasts only until they are about seven or eight weeks of age. Puppies not handled before about thirteen weeks of age are unlikely ever to make sociable friendly pet dogs and the same seems to apply largely to kittens. My experience with feral kittens is that it gets ever more difficult to tame them and make them 'handleable', pleasant, social family pets almost with every day after they reach about eight weeks of age.

Some cats, however, even despite receiving appropriate early handling, remain nervous and timid, demonstrating that the effects of early experience on adult cat personality are by no means the whole story in the success of the cat as a friendly pet. Also, many hand-reared kittens are often noticeably and perhaps surprisingly difficult to handle despite an apparent surfeit of handling in the sensitive period. Once older, they can be affectionate one moment but even with familiar humans, spitty and scratchy the next. This probably arises through a failure on our part to wean them behaviourally in the way that a mother cat would teach them new and more adult forms of communication at the same time as they are changed from a liquid diet at the milk bar to a solid diet in the food bowl. Solitary or 'single' kittens also often show marked precociousness towards humans and have a strong desire to explore away from the maternal nest at an earlier age than kittens brought up in litters. This is a logical compensatory reaction because there is less to occupy their expanding minds in the nest and they need a flow of influences on the outside to exercise their motivations. Their excitement at finding another being to react with can go a little over the top. In the face of assault, we cannot teach inhibition of bites or aggression as well as the responses of a fellow kitten or the kitten's own mother can do, so single kittens can sometimes turn out a little too assertive for comfort. It doesn't mean that they can't make good pets, only that it may take a little longer and a lot of patience for them to become the sort of pet you would want to cuddle all day!

Behaving in your genes

Dr Eileen Karsh from the USA believes that she can identify a fundamental variation in feline character even in young kittens, a difference which remains with them as they grow up and on into adulthood. She believes that kittens can be described as either excitable and reactive or slow and quiet. Under challenging situations the former group will tend to be anxious and agitated, while the latter group are more likely to be relaxed and unresponsive.

It has also been suggested by Dennis Turner and others that there may be two distinct character types in adult cats. One type needs plenty of social contact with humans and cats, the other may tolerate some social contact with other cats in the home and enjoy the company of some people, but is unlikely to develop strong bonds with any other cat. It is only likely to accept affection from its owners when it initiates the contact. If the owners try to initiate any interactions, they are actually likely to have less contact time with their cat because he may run away and avoid them. The more distant character type seems to need to hunt and play more alone rather than seek affection from other cats or people in physical terms. The implication is that some cats may need to live with other cats and be less competent socially on their own while others need to lead a solitary life and are unwilling and unable to socialise with their own kind.

Most owners can probably recognise these two types and, perhaps, some have blamed themselves unnecessarily because their cat doesn't seem to enjoy a cuddle with them, despite their every attention. The more they try to love their cat, the more he avoids them or removes himself from their company when approached, and the more the owners become upset, though it's probably not their fault. But then, we've always known that many of our cats only accept affection when they want to, so perhaps it is nice to know that when they reject us, it's not our fault. It's probably in his genes! However, such cats are clearly unlikely to be rewarding for owners who seek a close affectionate relationship with their pets based on physical contact and so more careful observation and selection of kittens than is normally practised may help prevent mismatches.

Perhaps these fundamental personality differences also help explain the two types of tom cat strategy for life described in farm feral cats in Chapter 14 but exactly how it all ties up with feline genetics and early experience is still very unclear. Excitability and timidity variations in character are thought to be caused by inherited differences, such as a variation in output of adrenaline when a cat encounters a sudden challenge. Adrenaline is a hormone released at such times to prime the cat for 'fight or flight', hence larger production is likely to produce a larger priming reaction. In turn, this may either produce a more quickly overtly fearful or a more aggressive cat in his responses to the challenge of, say, the presence of another cat or strange human in the front room.

We can perhaps identify fairly easily which of Turner's two categories our pets fall into and particularly if we can see both contrasting types in the feline faces around the home. It's certainly easy enough to see advantages of survival to both character types for the African Wild Cat living in the wild, and when the species established a life around man and ultimately started the world's population of pet cats. It has been suggested earlier that the African Wild Cat pre-domesticated itself through some genetic shift in the basis of its temperament prior to moving into man's settlements.

Perhaps this is it – the genes coding for the slow, quiet character may be the evidence for some or all of that process. It would be logical to expect these cats to be the more sociable ones which thrive on plenty of contact with other cats and people in adulthood identified by Turner because they don't 'overreact' to being pursued by people wanting to be friendly or the mere presence of other strange cats.

The alternative genes that pre-wire the cat to be reactive and excitable in the same circumstances may be the vestiges of the original 'wild type' that evolved before that self-domesticating mutation and which would still be found in the cat gene pool. These may be the largely asocial cats of Turner's research who shun attention unless they initiate it, are largely intolerant of strangers and which are aggressive or asocial with other cats. Clearly the cats with these dispositions would be the primed, high adrenaline output, quick reactors which would be precluded from feeling comfortable when other cats appear or man approaches, even familiar owners. They would perhaps be the ones who stayed more distant from man's activities and survived on the safer edges of towns but remained in greater territorial competition for fewer resources with other cats than those more relaxed cats which comfortably moved to the riches in the centre of town. The reactive type's survival has probably often depended on their ability to react if man or cat got too close, though they remained dependent on a life scavenging around man and so still contributed to the pet cat gene pool.

The behavioural variations described are not an 'all or nothing' response as some cats are very reactive and timid while others can be encouraged to be more confident and any reaction will be under the influence of far more than just two alternative sequences of genes. So while most pet cats will be in shades of grey between the two extremes, it is nonetheless remarkable that there is perhaps an identifiable genetic variation between the two types of adult pet discernable in kittens and persisting into adulthood. It is also remarkable that perhaps this variation has been identified in two very different types of investigation by Turner and Karsh.

The findings are also backed up to some extent by the observations of Dr John Bradshaw at the University of Southampton. He has studied the behaviour of long-stay rescue cats held in catteries where the density of cats sharing a pen can often be quite high. On arrival and after being neutered, new cats will often simply sit and watch the others for a while, gauging how they will integrate into this new social environment. They establish a personal space and become tolerant of other cats moving around them. A few, presumably the reactive types, defend that space vigorously, and though they calm down a little if held for many years, they continue to be largely unsociable towards all other cats and form few, if any, friendships. They rarely approach other cats and are never seen to groom, rub or wash others or make any friendly social gestures, no matter how long they remain in the pen. The more relaxed type, after an initial settling-in period, do tend to spend time in social contact with others of the same attitude and they may rub and groom each other and make close and lasting friendships. This latter type presumably enjoy a far more comfortable life and cope with the pressures of captivity far better than their alternatively minded colleagues.

It is further remarkable that this apparent difference can still be seen in our pet cats today and that the two types seem largely unalterable through experiences in the freer and more relaxed environment of the home, especially once cats are adult. What is needed now is some new research to see whether Turner and Karsh were indeed looking at observable effects of the same thing by following a character analysis of plenty of kittens from two weeks of age to life as a full-grown adult as a pet cat in the home.

Certain other behavioural characteristics may be pre-wired in a cat's genes in the sense that we may, for example, describe many individuals in some of the cat breeds as having certain 'temperament' characteristics. We imply, therefore, that that level of expression of those characteristics is inheritable. Siamese cats, for example, are often described as sensitive, vocal and affectionate, Burmese as assertive and outgoing, Persians as placid, etc. As suggested in Chapter 9, there may also be some link between colour and character, but we all know of too many exceptions, too many by far to 'prove the rule', to be able to accept an absolute genetic basis to any link.

Behaviour is, after all, the expression of an action or a response to a stimulus afforded by the capacity for that action in the genes in the cat's physical design. The level of that response is determined by the learning and development of the individual and in response to the intensity of the stimulus and other stimuli occurring at the time. That rather lengthy definition of behaviour at least serves to explain why we all behave differently, because every parameter varies between individuals in response to the same stimulus and its perception. 'Identical' twins may be genetically identical but as soon as they are born, they receive different stimuli and experiences and each learns some things faster than the other. Their temperaments may ultimately turn out as different as chalk and cheese just as no two kittens in a litter will ever be the same in their behaviour. Similar maybe, simply because they are all cats and many of their genes will be the same, but never identical. In itself, that accounts for some of the great appeal of the cat as a pet. While we can have trouble determining character variations in a mouse or goldfish, they are as clear as day between one cat and another and we can therefore value their individualism as much as we do in our human friends.

The mechanism of how genes determine and affect behaviour is by no means clearly defined. I feel it is easier to assume that genes code for the potential to react or behave in a certain way in certain situations. Whether that behaviour is ever expressed and to what level will then depend in any individual animal on its experiences, previous learning, circumstances prevailing at the time of the event and its state of mind and body at the time due to preceding experiences. In early support of this approach, for example, Mike Mendl and his colleagues have found that litters of kittens with the same mother but sired by different fathers showed differing levels of friendliness towards humans, despite being brought up under the 'same' circumstances, and despite never having met their fathers. Each is thus uninfluenced by observation of its father's behaviour, only by his genes.

Getting the best from every pet cat

The best we can hope for with our pet African Wild Cats and all their genes is to minimise the risk of problems with them as pets by careful breeding and avoiding 'nervous' or 'aggressive' strains, giving them plenty of early handling between two and seven weeks of age and ensuring that kittens are brought up in as stimulating an environment as possible. Then they will get the best out of their genetic potential and have the experience and learning to cope with later challenges. Careful observation even at this age may help the would-be owner select the type of cat that will suit them. Some may prefer the reactive, less demanding type to keep as an only cat in a busy, often absent-from-home lifestyle while others will prefer the social warmth of the more relaxed type, especially if he or she will be expected to share resources with other cats at home. All kittens should be taken on by their new owners as soon as possible after weaning to give them as much chance as possible to socialise and form good bonds with their new owners. This is especially important in breeds with rather more heavily pre-wired temperament characteristics of 'timidity' or 'assertiveness'.

Alas, the regulatory body for pedigree cat breeders and showers in the United Kingdom, the Governing Council of the Cat Fancy (GCCF), stipulates that kittens must be at least twelve weeks of age and fully vaccinated before they can be homed. As a result they may miss out on going to their new home when they are best able to assimilate into it. Doubtless this is one reason why, in my practice, I see such a disproportionate number of pedigree strains for problems such as nervousness and indoor spraying or urination related to incompetence, compared with their far more prevalent moggy counterparts. Moggies tend to be homed as soon as a new owner can be found after they are weaned. The bias may also be due to genetic predispositions such as the greater 'sensitivity' of Siamese cats and 'assertiveness' of Burmese cats, which tend to be referred for problems of aggression towards owners or other local cats and need careful attention to be treated. I often wonder how many of their problems need never have arisen if they had been socialised better as kittens and homed earlier.

Of course, one must balance the greater financial value of pedigree cats and the breeder's need to ensure their protection through vaccination before they are homed. Vaccination courses are not fully complete before about twelve to fourteen weeks of age but the minimal increased risk of a compromise in sending a partially vaccinated cat (having had only one of a course of two jabs) is probably justified. An alternative would be for breeders to invest heavily in offering every kitten a wide range of experiences and novelty and plenty of handling by clean strangers to reduce the chances of their kittens missing out in the learning process. Surely it is just as important to consider a kitten's emotional development as well as its physical well-being when early experience is so much of an influence on ultimate adult character. Most breeders would rightly say that the majority of kittens are brought up in perfectly stimulating environments and only a tiny proportion ever go on to cause problems or dissatisfaction to their new owners after being homed even at twelve weeks of age. However, for the sake of the tiny minority and for those GCCF registered breeders not doing it right in the behavioural sense, it's important to know now and change their ways, especially if they are raising and selling kittens from close family interbred strains of timid or assertive types. Beauty is more than a pretty face!

The final lesson. Living with the claws and purrs

'As one whom his mother comforteth, so will I comfort you'
Isaiah 66:13

The first year of life is hazardous for a cat living the free life, as we saw in Chapter 11, but the same is true even for the more nurtured pet. Taking into account those that die before they reach one year of age, the average life expectancy of British pet cats is eight years. However, if it manages to survive its first year, a cat will have an average life expectancy of twelve years. Currently, twenty-seven per cent of all UK cats are under two years of age and seventy-five per cent are under eight, showing that, despite the love and care we lavish on our cats, few will survive to reach old age. Only about six per cent are presently over fourteen years old, though doubtless this figure will rise as increasing numbers of cats are kept permanently indoors protected from the dangers of the outside world, and in response to rapidly advancing veterinary treatment.

Sex differences in feline behaviour are less variable than in dogs and the full development of male behaviour, as we have seen, is muted by the usual neutering of tom cats before puberty. Interestingly, the bias in sex distribution of many wild species of small cat, and particularly the feral cat populations on the islands, is also reflected in the UK pet cat population. It is estimated that fifty-three per cent are female and forty-seven per cent male, indicating that the more risk-filled behaviour of wild species or feral toms persists in the pet population. Life tends to be harder on the more itinerant males compared with the females, who tend to settle in a sheltered area to raise their kittens, surrounded by a more compact hunting range. (The sex ratio of dogs contrastingly is approximately equal in the UK as both males and bitches adopt a more settled pack approach to life centred around the human den with group excursions for exercise and mock hunting forays.) As a result, the life expectancy of male cats is lower than females. By wandering further and more often, in solitary excursions from the home, they are more likely to encounter serious challenges, such as falling prey to the main predator of the pet cat, the motor car.

A cat-loving and cat-keeping society we may be, but the appeal of the playful kitten is still a far greater attraction than even the convenient friendly comfort of older cats. In 1990/91, there has even been a shortage of kittens in Britain to adopt as pets, so well has the message got across about the need for sterilization to prevent unwanted births. But if it appears that this has gone too far and there aren't enough wanted births to meet the demand, it should also be borne in mind that the RSPCA alone has to destroy about 12,000 unwanted cats per year and overall, perhaps some 3,000 are destroyed every day by animal welfare agencies because there simply aren't enough homes to go round. Of course, few of those will be of the pedigree strains, though the blue-blooded varieties still only make up about eight per cent of the national total. It seems that we all still prefer the African Wild Cat in his original clothes, or at least only in changes that he's made for himself and not those bred or 'refined' by our fellow man.

Doubtless the cost of purchasing a pedigree pet cat deters many. Some can cost many hundreds of pounds and I still baulk a little myself when I think that I handed over good money, and a lot of it, for Scribble, Bean and Flirty Bottom, my Siamese cats, when all the others have come free. While I've loved them all dearly, Bullet, my ex-feral black and white moggy from the back of the Polytechnic in south London, cost me nothing and has proved to be everything that anyone could ever want from a cat. But then, if he'd come from a rescue centre, he rightly would have had a price attached. We can't really expect to get all that companionship or all that perfected design in something so remarkable as an African Wild Cat in Britain for nothing any more. Most of us spend far more money kitting out our cat with the necessary things of life than we do on buying the pet himself, even if he is an expensive 'aristocat'. Bowls, beds, food, veterinary care all add up to many thousands of pounds over the cat's lifetime and in that context, whether one pays lots for a Flirty Bottom or nothing for a Bullet is hardly relevant.

Our desire to spend on our cats can go to amazing and sometimes absurd lengths. Silver-plated feeding bowls at £100, solid mahogany four-poster beds at £600 and diamond-studded collars at over £5,000 mean little to the cat, after all. And a video, *Cool for Cats* – and made for cats, not their owners – that I became involved with recently may be carrying the cat further into a technical age that he understands little, even if he is a permanent modern apartment-dweller! Mind you, if I were one, I'd quite like to watch pictures of mice, garden birds, pheasants, rabbits, fish, fast-moving balls and other objects accompanied by the sound and ultrasound of the prey my senses had evolved to pursue. In fact, I got involved with the video because it seemed to me that it might even help a lot of cats in flats or rescue homes enjoy life a bit more (see appendix for further details!)

If this all seems a bit far removed from what ought to be reality if the pet cat is still genetically wild, the level of care that we now offer our pet cats of any breed is rising, as is the cost of it. It contrasts ever increasingly with the traditional way that we have lived with cats until recent times, and that looser association, which first occurred in Ancient Egypt, is still observed in less structured and technological societies. Instead of living in an amicable relationship with man around his den, but not in it, like the pet cats of my father's youth, the British cat is most likely now to live actually in our den. Some ten per cent never even get to leave the forced comforts of home, a figure that may be as high as thirty per cent elsewhere in Europe.

The cat in our homes is more likely to receive care and attention as required simply because we spend more time with him and can spot trouble quickly and early. That we should want to care is natural, having let the cat become part of the family, but the real motivation for it lies in the closeness of the relationship between man or woman and cat and all their varied personalities when they are together.

When our cats are curled up with us indoors, when they have put away their teeth and their claws and are lounging around the den they have chosen to share with their people, they are at their most relaxed. And we are probably at our most relaxed when we choose to cuddle them or lie with them. The reason for it all is that in such circumstances, our African Wild Cat pets view us as maternal figures and give over their trust and friendship as they initially learnt to do with their own mother. With such regression, kittenish-type behaviour returns. It returns in the pet cat's willingness to relax totally with us in a way that would be lost to itinerant toms in the wild or feral state and only continue with queens when they had produced kittens. It is also evident in those many demonstrations of kittenish friendship, solicitation of affection and in anticipation of being fed. Hence even old or tough independent territorial tom cats may purr wildly when being cuddled, and tread up and down on their owner's laps or simply

204

in the air as an early conditioned teat-treading response designed to promote milk flow from their mothers many years ago. Some even salivate and dribble all over us as an early conditioned response in anticipation of that feed. And, of course, with our stroking and petting and soft words, we reinforce not only our friendly bond with our pet cat, but also all those appealing trusting kittenish responses (well, except over-enthusiastic treading with claws out or excessive dribbling!).

If each cat can happily view some or all of the people with whom he shares his den and even a few of their friends as maternal figures and be confident enough to revert to a relaxed kittenish outlook, it's no surprise that he invokes a nurturing maternal attitude from us. It doesn't matter whether we are sensitive housewives and mothers, hefty single working chaps or even little children in the process of learning about care and future demands of parenthood through observing our parents, keeping pets and role playing. But to describe the relationship as purely a regressive kitten/nurturing mother relationship is, of course, too simplistic. Cats are our friends, playmates, confidantes, our company, part of the family. They are friendly when they want to be just for the pleasure that friendship can bring. Stroking, grooming, touching are all good for us and our cats, and an essential feature of successful relationships for any social animal. Such interactions cause the release of endorphins in our brains, the self-produced legal pleasure drugs. Such pleasures help us to relax, stay healthy, fight illness and psychological upsets, feel better and live longer, happier lives. Through allowing itself to accept such social contact from man, the African Wild Cat is deriving exactly the same benefits! And while anti-cruelty laws have been passed in more recent times to protect the cat from the persecutions of old, it must have come as a real boost when Ronald Reagan, then Governor of California, went out of his way to make it a law that anyone kicking or injuring another's cat could be sent to prison! Doubtless he was lobbied steadily by his own three feline advisors back home!

The relationship we enjoy with our cats is all the more enhanced by their willingness to play with us and demonstrate their hunting abilities in the pursuit of rolled paper balls and dangled string, with claws (usually) retracted and bites (usually) inhibited when we play more physically with them. It's no wonder that we develop such bonds with our pet cats, and small wonder indeed, with all the other advantages of cleanliness, independence, etc., that they are rapidly becoming the most popular larger pet of modern man. And it's all done apparently with the same amount of compromise of the wild hunting side of his evolution that he has ever made. None. The cat has carried his soul intact, along with all of his original genetic complement, into life as a feral free-living cat in so many varied places. His relationship with man is surely simply the successful occupation of yet another environmental niche on the planet. It's the fine end of a relationship that the African Wild Cat has exploited since the first one moved in with the Ancient Egyptians.

It's the end result, perhaps, of a long process that began when later cats took a ride with the trading ships to reach all those new environments alongside man, and then branched out from the towns into the nearby countryside to exploit local prey and outcompete any indigenous small cat species. With a little help from us, the African Wild Cat, in the form of the moggy, has conquered the world and paid virtually no price at all for his colonisation and exploitation. The only price for him to pay has been as a pet cat to man, where a few already changeable genes or natural mutations have been seized upon and perpetuated to make pedigree strains. Some of those mutations have been made to persist by us in defiance of the laws of nature that the cat has otherwise generally obeyed and learnt to profit from. And there's also the individual price paid by some free-living cats and most pets of being sterilised so that some of the natural, wilder edges of their behaviour and reproductive potential can be better made to fit into our homes and lifestyles.

The cat is, as he has always been, a highly evolved, highly adaptable, highly successful predator but with an enormous capacity to be sociable. Understanding why a cat is a cat, how a cat is a cat and why the claws are inextricably bound to the purrs can only improve our love for the cats who choose to share our lives as pets and respect for those who live more on the edge of our world. Claws and purrs together are their success and the reason why, according to one French study, there are an estimated 400 million African Wild Cats in the world today!

DO DOGS NEED SHRINKS?

The internationally best-selling book on canine behaviour and problem treatment

By leading
pet behaviourist

Peter Neville

308 pages

In this book, Peter Neville examines the relationship between dogs and people and explains what dogs and their owners need to enjoy a harmonious relationship. Using case histories from his files he describes the problems that can occur – ranging from the commonplace to the incredible, from the moving to the hilarious – and then outlines the reasons behind them and develops plans for treatment. Packed with practical information and insights into our our dogs' thoughts, this book is essential reading for every dog owner, especially if your dog isn't quite as well-behaved as you, your family or your friends would like him to be.

Signed by Peter Neville. . . only £11.50 inc UK p&p
(please send £14.50 for orders outside the UK)

Send orders with cheque (made out to BNP Publications) to:-
BNP Publications, 4 Quarry Cottages, Chicksgrove, Tisbury,
Salisbury, Wiltshire SP3 6LZ, England

DO CATS NEED SHRINKS?

The internationally best-selling book on feline behaviour and problem treatment

By leading
pet behaviourist

Peter Neville

173 pages

In this book, Peter Neville examines the relationship between cats and people and explains what cats and their owners need to enjoy a harmonious relationship. Using case histories from his files he describes the problems that can occur – ranging from the commonplace to the incredible, from the messy to the hilarious – and then outlines the reasons behind them and develops plans for treatment. Packed with practical information and insights into our our cats' behaviour, this book is essential reading for every cat owner, especially if your cat isn't quite as well-behaved as you would like him to be.

Signed by Peter Neville . . . only £8.50 inc UK p&p
(please send £11. 00 for orders outside the UK)

Send orders with cheque (made out to BNP Publications) to:-
BNP Publications, 4 Quarry Cottages, Chicksgrove, Tisbury,
Salisbury, Wiltshire SP3 6LZ, England

COOL FOR CATS

is a revolutionary new 60 minute video filmed especially for the modern cat to keep him amused and occupied in the comfort of his own living room while his owners are away. They need never feel guilty about leaving him alone again...he'll be having a whale of a time with his own mental work- out programme with the Cool for Cats video!

COOL FOR CATS is good feline therapy...it's official!

But there are serious positive benefits for your cat as he watches Cool for Cats, especially if he is one of the many in our towns and cities who are never allowed outdoors because of the risks of being run over on the road. Cool for Cats can be vital therapy for indoor cats or those left at home who pine for their owners.
'Cats need mental exercise and tend to focus this on activities with their owners. When left at home alone regularly they can become inactive and unstimulated. Cool for Cats offers a myriad of exciting views, sights and sounds to exercise a cat's mind and awaken dormant hunting instincts, bringing him a new medium of enormous pleasure. After all, the cat evolved as a predator, not a pet and even the best of owners can forget about their cat's mental wellbeing. Cool for Cats can make all the difference to any cat's quality of life in the modern world...and hopefully result in fewer cats seeking treatment on my psychiatrist's couch for the symptoms of living with modern man!'

Peter Neville
Feline Behaviour Therapist

PRICE: £12.99 + 2.50 P+P
OUTSIDE U.K. + EXTRA £2.50 FOR P+P

Send Cheque to:

PET VIDEO ENTERTAINMENTS

Crofton House, 1 New Cavendish Street
London W1M 7RP, England

Allow 28 Days for Delivery

Help For Pets with Behaviour Problems

The Association of Pet Behaviour Counsellors

My practice is one of the founder members of the Association of Pet Behaviour Counsellors (APBC). The APBC comprises many professional members throughout the United Kingdom and overseas who treat behaviour problems in pets exclusively on referral from veterinary surgeons. So if your pet has a behaviour problem, a member of the APBC may be able to help you with a detailed personal consultation. Please ask your veterinary surgeon for details of the nearest APBC member's practice or write to the Honorary Secretary, APBC, 257 Royal College St, London NW1 9LU England.